THIS IS POLITICAL PHILOSOPHY

THIS IS PHILOSOPHY
Series editor: Steven D. Hales

Reading philosophy can be like trying to ride a bucking bronco—you hold on for dear life while "transcendental deduction" twists you to one side, "causa sui" throws you to the other, and a 300-word, 300-year-old sentence comes down on you like an iron-shod hoof the size of a dinner plate. *This Is Philosophy* is the riding academy that solves these problems. Each book in the series is written by an expert who knows how to gently guide students into the subject regardless of the reader's ability or previous level of knowledge. Their reader-friendly prose is designed to help students find their way into the fascinating, challenging ideas that compose philosophy without simply sticking the hapless novice on the back of the bronco, as so many texts do. All the books in the series provide ample pedagogical aids, including links to free online primary sources. When students are ready to take the next step in their philosophical education, *This Is Philosophy* is right there with them to help them along the way.

This Is Philosophy: An Introduction
Steven D. Hales

This Is Philosophy of Mind: An Introduction
Pete Mandik

This Is Ethics: An Introduction
Jussi Suikkanen

This Is Political Philosophy: An Introduction
Alex Tuckness and Clark Wolf

Forthcoming:

This Is Metaphysics: An Introduction
Kristopher McDaniel

This Is Epistemology: An Introduction
Clayton Littlejohn

This Is Philosophy of Religion: An Introduction
Neil Manson

This Is Modern Philosophy: An Introduction
Kurt Smith

This Is Bioethics: An Introduction
Udo Schuklenk

THIS IS POLITICAL PHILOSOPHY

AN INTRODUCTION

ALEX TUCKNESS AND CLARK WOLF

WILEY Blackwell

This edition first published 2017
© 2017 John Wiley & Sons, Inc.

Registered Office
John Wiley & Sons, Ltd, The Atrium, Southern Gate, Chichester, West Sussex,
PO19 8SQ, UK

Editorial Offices
350 Main Street, Malden, MA 02148-5020, USA
9600 Garsington Road, Oxford, OX4 2DQ, UK
The Atrium, Southern Gate, Chichester, West Sussex, PO19 8SQ, UK

For details of our global editorial offices, for customer services, and for information
about how to apply for permission to reuse the copyright material in this book please
see our website at www.wiley.com/wiley-blackwell.

Library of Congress Cataloging-in-Publication Data

Names: Tuckness, Alex Scott, 1971– author. | Wolf, Clark, 1962– author.
Title: This is political philosophy : an introduction / Alex Tuckness and Clark Wolf.
Description: Chichester, UK ; Malden, MA : John Wiley & Sons, 2016. |
   Series: This is philosophy | Includes bibliographical references and index.
Identifiers: LCCN 2016013762 (print) | LCCN 2016015926 (ebook) |
   ISBN 9781118765951 (cloth) | ISBN 9781118765975 (pbk.) |
   ISBN 9781118766040 (pdf) | ISBN 9781118766002 (epub)
Subjects: LCSH: Political science–Philosophy.
Classification: LCC JA71 .T83 2016 (print) | LCC JA71 (ebook) | DDC 320.01–dc23
LC record available at https://lccn.loc.gov/2016013762

A catalogue record for this book is available from the British Library.

Set in 10.5/13pt Minion by SPi Global, Pondicherry, India
Printed and bound in Malaysia by Vivar Printing Sdn Bhd

10 9 8 7 6 5 4 3 2 1

BRIEF CONTENTS

How to Use this Book   xii
Preface   xiii

Part I   Core Values in Political Philosophy   1

1 Happiness   3
2 Freedom   31
3 Equality   54
4 Justice   81

Part II   Problems of Authority and Legitimacy   103

5 Democracy   105
6 The Obligation to Obey the Law   132
7 Political Violence: War, Torture, and Punishment   155

Part III   Specific Topics   183

8 Who Counts?   185
9 Religion and Politics   210
10 Money, Lies, and Political Corruption   236

Index   258

CONTENTS

How to Use this Book   xii

Preface   xiii

Part I   Core Values in Political Philosophy   1

1   **Happiness**   3
    Doing Political Philosophy   4
    Happiness, Welfare, and the Aims of Government   5
    If You're Happy Do You Know It?   5
    The Pursuit of Happiness   6
        Whose happiness?   7
        Can you measure pleasure?   8
        Future happiness   10
        Pleasure and pain   11
        Is happiness fulfilling your desires?   12
        Do the ends justify the means?   14
        Nozick's experience machine   14
        Happiness and virtue   15
        The case of John Stuart Mill   17
        Capabilities   18
        Conflicts between liberty and happiness   22
        Conflicts between equality and happiness   22
    Happiness and Government   23
    Happiness and Public Goods   24
    Free Riding and Small Contributions   25
        Philosophical objections   26
    Should We Evaluate Political Institutions According
    to their Ability to Make People Happy?   27
    References and Further Reading   28
    Online Resources   30

2 Freedom **31**

The Meaning of Freedom 34

The Fundamental Question 34

What Is Freedom? And Who Is Free? 35

    Subjective and objective freedom 36

    What counts as restraining freedom? 37

    Freedom and consent 38

    Republican liberty 39

    Private freedom and public freedom 40

    Negative and positive liberty 41

Paternalism, the Harm Principle, and Moralism 42

    Paternalism 42

    The harm principle 44

    Moralism 48

    Can (and should) we avoid moralism? 50

Conclusion 51

References and Further Reading 52

Online Resources 53

3 Equality **54**

Introduction 55

How Unequal Are People in the United States? 56

Against Equality: A Politics of Procrustes? 57

Unequal Treatment and Discrimination 59

Equality as a Baseline? 61

Equality of Resources and Luck Egalitarianism 62

    First objection: Disabilities 62

    Second objection: Slavery of the talented 63

    Third objection: Expensive tastes 63

Equality of Opportunity 64

    Should we level down? 66

    What does equality of opportunity require? 67

Inequalities in the Real World 68

Inequality or Deprivation? 71

Is Sufficiency Enough? 73

Complex Equality 73

Race, Gender, and the Social Construction of Inequalities 75

Affirmative Action 76

Conclusion 78

References and Further Reading 78

Online Resources 80

Contents

4　Justice　　**81**

Justice: A Brief Introduction　　82

Rawls's Theory of Justice　　83

　The original principle and the veil of ignorance　　84

　Rawls's two principles of justice　　85

The Libertarian Critique: Individual Liberty
Restricts Redistribution　　87

Utilitarian Critique: An Alternative Rationale for Redistribution　　91

Feminist Critique: The Public–Private Distinction
and Power Relations　　93

Communitarian Critique: Alternatives to Individualism　　96

Cosmopolitan Critique: The Demands of Global Justice　　97

Conclusion　　99

References and Further Reading　　99

Online Resources　　101

Part II　Problems of Authority and Legitimacy　　**103**

5　Democracy　　**105**

Democracy and Political Self-Governance　　107

What Is Democracy?　　108

Who Gets to Participate?　　108

Constitutional Democracy and Rights　　110

　Sources of rights　　111

　Claim and liberty rights　　113

　Interest and choice theories of rights　　114

Benefits of Democracy: The Instrumental Case　　115

　Would a kind dictator be a bad thing?　　115

　Do the people know best?　　116

　Can representation help?　　117

Is Democratic Self-Governance Intrinsically Valuable?　　118

Is There a Right to Democratic Self-Governance?　　119

What Are the Implications of a Right to Democratic
Self-Governance?　　120

Voting and Representation: Interests or Ideals?　　122

Does Democracy Rest on a Paradox?　　123

Deliberative Democracy as a Solution?　　125

Distorting Democracy: Persistent Minorities
and Electoral Inequalities　　126

　Persistent minorities　　126

　Electoral inequalities　　126

Do Democracies Decline and Fall? 128
References and Further Reading 130
Online Resources 131

6 The Obligation to Obey the Law 132
Breaking the Law 135
  Motives for breaking the law 135
  Ways of breaking the law 136
  Unjust laws 137
  Are we obligated just because it is a law? 137
  How strong are our legal obligations? 139
Breaking the Law: A "How to" Guide 140
  Civil disobedience 140
  Violence 141
  What should be on the menu? 143
  What should we choose from the menu? 143
  Principles for ideal and nonideal agents 144
Do We Have an Obligation at All? 147
  Consent 147
  Gratitude 150
  Fairness 150
  Duty 151
  Membership 152
Conclusion 152
References and Further Reading 153
Online Resources 154

7 Political Violence: War, Torture, and Punishment 155
Umkhonto we Sizwe 157
What Is Violence? 159
When (If Ever) Is Violence Justified? 161
Pacifism 162
  Gandhi's pacifism 163
  Russell's "relative pacifism" 163
Ius ad bellum: "Just War" and the Justification of
Large-Scale Violence 164
Testing Just War Theory 166
  Vagueness 167
  Manipulability 167
Ius in bello: Justice in the Conduct of War 168
Cultural Conflicts and the Laws of War 170

Pushing the Limits, I: Preemptive War   171
Pushing the Limits, II: When Are Captured
Combatants "Prisoners of War?"   172
Pushing the Limits, III: Torture, "Enhanced
Interrogation," and Ticking Bombs   173
Punishment   175
    Rationales for punishment   176
        Positive future consequences   176
        Desert   177
        Sending a message   178
War, Torture, and Punishment in Political Context   179
References and Further Reading   180
Online Resources   182

Part III   Specific Topics   **183**

8 Who Counts?   **185**
Who Gets Justice?   187
The Guano Ring   188
Animals   189
Moral Standing and Moral Personhood   191
Degrees of Moral Standing? The Constitutive View   195
Comparative Moral Standing: The Constitutive View   195
Comparing Characteristics and Abilities   196
Objections to the Constitutive View   197
Hard Case I: Fertilized Ova and Fetuses   198
Hard Case II: Childhood and Disability   201
Hard Case III: Distant Peoples and Future Generations   204
Hard Case IV: Posthumans?   205
Hard Case V: Ecosystems and the Natural World   205
Upshot   208
References and Further Reading   208
Online Resources   209

9 Religion and Politics   **210**
Religion and Politics   213
Is Religion Special?   214
    The limits of toleration   216
    Neutrality and religion   218
    Neutrality of intent   219
    Exemptions for nonreligious reasons   221

Multiculturalism 222
  Justifications for multiculturalism 223
  Which policies would multiculturalism recommend? 224
  Criticisms of multiculturalism 225
  Freedom of religion, freedom of conscience,
  or freedom of culture? 226
Is Religion Suspect in Politics? 227
  Four sample views on the environment 228
  Reasons everyone can accept 229
  Overlapping consensus 230
  Should religion and philosophy be treated the same? 230
  Arguing fairly 232
Conclusion 233
References and Further Reading 233
Online Resources 234

10 Money, Lies, and Political Corruption 236
Lying Politicians 238
  What is a lie? 238
  Why do people lie? 240
  Utility 240
  Intentions 241
  Hugo Grotius and the rights approach 241
  Virtue 242
  A license to lie? 242
  Sneaky ways to win an election 243
  When is lying justified? 245
  Dirty hands 246
Bribery and Corruption 247
  Is Blagojevich that different? 250
  Individual versus institutional corruption 250
  Campaign finance 251
  Ethics and institutions 252
  Just following orders 252
  Who is responsible? 253
  Compromise 254
Conclusion 254
References and Further Reading 255
Online Resources 257

Index 258

HOW TO USE THIS BOOK

There is no consensus in political philosophy about the order in which to introduce topics; and we realize that the order we have chosen may diverge from the order that some instructors will prefer. For this reason, the chapters in our book are designed to be substantially independent and can be used in any order. Although we occasionally refer to arguments from previous chapters to help students see connections, these references are not necessary in order to understand the material. Our goal is to create a flexible tool that can be used in a variety of different ways. Some may teach straight through. Others may want to pair this book with classic texts or case studies.

There is, however, a logic to the order of the chapters. Part I (Chapters 1–4) examines four core values that represent goals, or potential goals, of government: happiness, freedom, equality, and justice. In Part II we look at topics related to the nature of political authority: democracy and the conditions for legitimate government , the obligation to obey the law, and the legitimacy of political violence (including the topics of war and punishment). Part III (Chapters 8–10) looks at more specific questions: Who counts (Chapter 8) explores questions regarding who deserves justice, for example questions about animal rights, environmental ethics, and abortion. Chapter 9 looks at the relationship between religion and politics, including a discussion of multiculturalism. Chapter 10 addresses problems in political ethics.

Our overall approach is to try to move from examples and cases to philosophical investigation of the questions those examples and cases raise. Our hope is that the book will prepare students to have more thoughtful responses when the issues are discussed in class. Our goal is to introduce the central issues in political philosophy in ways that students will find both engaging and challenging.

PREFACE

Politics and philosophy initially seem a strange pairing. Philosophy is logical, rational, and abstract. Politics is often thought to be about power, connections, and persuading people however you can, regardless of whether the arguments are logical (or even true) or not. But this doesn't tell the whole story. Imagine the following conversation:

JUSTIN: You should support affirmative action policies.
SOPHIE: Why?
JUSTIN: Because I want you to.
SOPHIE: Why is that a reason for me?

Political arguments don't normally proceed like this, because merely asserting your wants is not a very persuasive way to explain your political views. In the real world, Justin is more likely to say something like: "Because affirmative action promotes justice and equality." When he merely says what he wants, there is not much to argue about. When he makes a claim about justice and equality, there is plenty to argue about. He must persuade us that justice and equality are good things and that affirmative action does in fact support them.

Political philosophy is about taking seriously the reasons people give for claiming that political positions are good, right, or true and asking whether the reasons they give are good ones. Are they better than the reasons for thinking the opposite? Perhaps we are all sometimes persuaded by bad arguments. But most of us like to think that we know the difference between a bad political argument and a good one. We don't like to think that people are manipulating us successfully with bad arguments. In this sense, studying political philosophy is like studying self-defense. People often throw around terms like "justice" and "equality" without defining clearly what they mean by them, without explaining why we should value them, and without considering their implications. By arming yourself with philosophical understanding, you can avoid being misled.

We think that the best way to introduce political philosophy is to begin with real political debates and to show how philosophy sheds light on those debates. For this reason we begin each chapter with a political discussion between Justin and Sophie. We picked these names because Sophie is related to the ancient Greek word for wisdom (*sophia*) in the word "philosophy," which means "love of wisdom." The name Justin comes from the Latin word for justice (*iustitia*), arguably the most important term in political philosophy. As you watch them argue, you will see political philosophy in action. In the book as a whole we will try to use examples and illustrations to make the ideas clear and interesting.

Part I

CORE VALUES IN POLITICAL PHILOSOPHY

1

HAPPINESS

SOPHIE	What are you reading about?
JUSTIN	Lying, cruelty, murder, and betrayal.
SOPHIE	About why these are bad things, I assume.
JUSTIN	That's what is interesting about the book: I think the author is saying that in politics these aren't necessarily bad.
SOPHIE	That sounds crazy. Give me an example where cruelty and betrayal are good.
JUSTIN	Here's one from the book. Back during the Italian Renaissance there was a man named Cesare Borgia. He became powerful because he was the illegitimate son of the pope. A territory he controlled was in chaos and turmoil. So first he sent in one of his men to restore order, using as much cruelty as was necessary to get the job done. The man restored order, but was hated by the people because of his cruelty. Then Borgia himself came to town and pretended to have had no idea about the cruelty his officer had used and had that very officer cut into two and his body left in the town square for all to see. Borgia both restored order and avoided a reputation for being cruel.
SOPHIE	What are you reading? That sounds like a show on cable.
JUSTIN	The book is Machiavelli's *The Prince*.
SOPHIE	So you think being "Machiavellian" is a good thing?
JUSTIN	I didn't at first, but the more I have thought about it, the more I agree. In politics you don't do anyone any good

This Is Political Philosophy: An Introduction, First Edition. Alex Tuckness and Clark Wolf.
© 2017 John Wiley & Sons, Inc. Published 2017 by John Wiley & Sons, Inc.

	unless you get results. Sometimes getting results means you have to lie or even kill.
SOPHIE	I disagree. People who say they are going to do evil to bring about good are just rationalizing. If you do evil it changes you; you become more evil. You'll keep going further and further.
JUSTIN	What else should Borgia have done? The region was in lawless chaos, and lawless chaos would have killed far more people in the long run. Politicians who go around trying to be merciful actually end up being cruel. The pain that these measures prevent outweighs the pain that they cause.
SOPHIE	I don't think one person's pleasure cancels out another person's pain. And besides, what about the rights of the people who were brutalized? If you intentionally inflict pain on an innocent person you are violating her rights, end of story.
JUSTIN	Nothing in politics really benefits everyone equally. We don't have any choice but to make tradeoffs. We have to pass laws asking whether the costs to some outweigh the benefits to others. Everyone's happiness is relevant.
SOPHIE	There has to be more to the public good than that. Some people find pleasure in humiliating others, but I don't think that should count as a reason for letting them do it.
JUSTIN	But the pain of the person being humiliated would be greater than the pleasure of the one doing the humiliating.
SOPHIE	Maybe, maybe not. You can't know that for sure. Anyway, the desire to humiliate others is wrong no matter how happy it makes the person who's doing the humiliation. We should protect people's rights no matter what.

Doing Political Philosophy

1.1 In this dialogue Justin and Sophie are discussing an issue in political philosophy. One of the most important questions is what values governments should promote. Is the point of government to increase happiness? What if promoting happiness conflicts with promoting freedom? In Aldous Huxley's book *Brave New World* people are happy and content, but the contentment comes from a society where people are genetically modified and brainwashed so that they will happily accept a life with very little liberty. Bouts of boredom or anxiety are remedied through easy access to psychedelic drugs. People live lives of comfortable, meaningless amusement. There is more happiness and less pain in a world like that than in ours, but would we really say that such a world is better? In this chapter we will explore debates about whether the purpose of government is to increase happiness.

Happiness, Welfare, and the Aims of Government

Political philosophers look for ways to evaluate political institutions and the 1.2 behavior of the people who shape those institutions. Are presidents better than kings? Is it better when governments leave people free to organize their own lives, or should governments constrain people's freedom, so as to prevent them from making mistakes?

Whether it is institutions or actions that we evaluate, it is natural to 1.3 consider whether they make people happy or unhappy. It is hard to conceive that a government could be good if it caused widespread suffering and misery. In the same spirit, it seems that any nation in which citizens are all happy and content must be doing something right. This chapter will examine the view that the goal of government is to make people happy. We will also consider the closely related view that the goal of *politicians* should be to promote the happiness of people who are affected by their choices.

To some philosophers, the view that government should promote peo- 1.4 ple's happiness has appeared to be so obviously true that it hardly seemed necessary to provide reasons for it. But happiness is more complicated than it might initially seem: what is it for people to be happy? Can we be wrong about our own happiness? Is it possible to know in advance which institutions will promote happiness? How should happiness be measured? If we can't gauge happiness directly, are there other standards we should use to measure well-being?

If You're Happy Do You Know It?

If political institutions are better when they make people happy, then we 1.5 need some way of judging whether people are happy. But we are often bad judges of other people's happiness. Worse, we may not even be reliable judges of *our own* happiness. If you think you're happy, could you be wrong? Those who advocate a *subjective view of happiness* say that you can't possibly be wrong about your own state of happiness. If we define happiness in terms of experiences like pleasure or satisfaction, a person who is experiencing these things knows it. Suppose a person's body were wasting away because of a terrible disease, but the pain medications were so good that she reported feeling happy. (Perhaps the medicines also keep her from realizing what is happening to her.) On the subjective view, she is happy.

1.6   Those who advocate an objective *view of happiness*, by contrast, would claim that people are sometimes wrong about whether they are truly happy. Suppose that a person is content to live a life devoted to video games. When asked, he honestly and sincerely says he is happy. Then he leaves virtual reality for actual reality and decides that having friends he sees with his own eyes is far better than his life before. He then looks back on his previous life and no longer sees it as a time of happiness. In principle, the same judgment could be made by someone else, that he is not happy even though he thinks he is. If a slave claims to be happy, should we believe her?

The Pursuit of Happiness

1.7 Philosophers often distinguish between things that are valued *intrinsically* and things that are valued *instrumentally*. A thing is valued *intrinsically* just in case it is something we want for its own sake. If you want something *instrumentally*, you want it because you can use it in order to get something else you want—perhaps something you want for its own sake. For example, suppose Sophie wants to be rich. If she wants money *for its own sake*, then she values it intrinsically. If she values money because she can use it to get things she wants, then she values it *instrumentally*. We might also ask whether money *has* intrinsic value—that is, whether it *should* be valued for its own sake—or whether its value is essentially instrumental.

1.8   Happiness, one could argue, is something that everyone wants. Even people who like depressing movies may go to them because they enjoy the sadness. An important school of thought in political philosophy, *utilitarianism*, takes the claim that happiness is the highest good as its starting point. In fact utilitarians would claim that nothing is good unless it is part of a person's happiness, or unless it contributes to a person's happiness. According to utilitarianism, happiness is the only thing we should value intrinsically. Everything else has only instrumental value.

UTILITARIANISM: Actions and policies should be judged according to the aggregate amount of happiness or well-being they produce. Actions are morally better the more happiness they produce.

According to utilitarianism, we should seek to *maximize* happiness. It is a popular theory: most economic theories of policy choice *assume* that the goal of policy is to promote the happiness or well-being of the people who are governed by them.

The view that we *should* promote happiness is sometimes associated with 1.9 a very different view: the view that people *do* pursue happiness, but their own happiness, not the happiness of everyone. This view is often called

PSYCHOLOGICAL EGOISM: People exclusively pursue their own happiness in all their voluntary actions.

Psychological egoism claims that each person acts on the basis of what she thinks will bring her the most happiness. She may be wrong, but even foolish things are done for the sake of what we think will bring us happiness. Notice that this is a claim about human psychology and motivation, while utilitarianism is a normative theory—a theory about what people *should* do. Some philosophers have tried to put these two views together. The nineteenth-century British philosopher Jeremy Bentham defended them both. But if psychological egoism were true, then utilitarianism would seem to be irrelevant. Why would we develop theories about what people should do if these people are already determined to act in a certain way anyway?

Whose happiness?

Subsequent philosophers have noted other problems that arise if one tries 1.10 to combine utilitarianism and psychological egoism. What I think will bring the most happiness to me is different from what will bring the most happiness to everyone. If I can steal something and get away with it, I might admit that the happiness I get is smaller than the pain others will feel but still think that stealing will maximize *my* happiness. If promoting my own happiness and promoting the happiness of everyone conflict, then the psychological claim and the normative claim are also in conflict.

There are different strategies for reconciling these claims. One is to note 1.11 that human beings have not only self-interest but also sympathy. Sympathy (or empathy; for present purposes we use them interchangeably) causes us to feel pain at the pain of others or pleasure when others feel pleasure. Through education and other forms of socialization we can encourage people to develop this sympathetic faculty. So pursuing your own happiness will often involve doing things that are good for other people too. While this strategy can reduce the gap between what is good for me and what is good for the world, it does not bridge it completely.

1.12   Scientists who study human motivation reject psychological egoism: human motivation is much more complicated than this simplistic theory would imply. Utilitarians reject it too: many contemporary utilitarians say that, while people generally do pursue their own happiness (including the happiness of those they are sympathetic to), this is not an iron-clad rule. What is central to utilitarianism is the normative claim about what people *should* do, not the psychological claim about what people's motives are.

1.13   Utilitarianism gets its name from the word "utility," which comes from the Latin word for "usefulness": *utilitas*. This seemed to be an apt name, because utilitarians say that we should choose things because they are useful for bringing about happiness. According to utilitarians, happiness is the only intrinsic good. Everything else is only instrumentally valuable.

Can you measure pleasure?

1.14   **Jeremy Bentham**, one of the first utilitarian philosophers, thought that utility is happiness and that they both can be reduced to *pleasure*. According to Bentham, pleasure is the only thing that is good *in itself*. Other things may be *instrumentally* good, but only if they bring pleasure. This view is sometimes called *hedonism*, a word based on the Greek word for "pleasure": *hēdonē*. Hedonism is one answer to the question of what human **well-being** consists in. Utilitarianism can be described as maximizing utility, maximizing happiness, or maximizing pleasure (and minimizing pain). Bentham sees all of these as meaning the same thing.

1.15   In **Bentham's** version of utilitarianism, there is a clear sense in which the ends always justify the means. I can't know if lying or stealing are wrong until I first figure out whether, in a given case, lying or stealing will increase or decrease overall pleasure. One potentially confusing aspect of Bentham's terminology is that, instead of only talking about utility as that which is useful for bringing about pleasure (or happiness), he also used "utility" and "happiness" as synonyms. So for Bentham maximizing utility and maximizing happiness are the same thing.

By identifying happiness with pleasure, Bentham meant something fairly 1.16
specific. He was targeting the sensible experience of pleasure. He also
included, as part of utility, the avoidance of pain, by which he meant, again,
an internal subjective experience. His idea was that we could add up the
pleasures, subtract the pains, and then arrive at an estimate of the total
amount of utility that a decision would likely produce.

This may sound odd. It is obvious how you add up numbers, but how do 1.17
you add up pleasures? Bentham's strategy was to quantify them, or at least
treat them in a way similar to the way we treat numbers. For any given
pleasure or pain we can, at least roughly, assess its intensity.

Imagine someone asking: "On a scale of 1 to 10, how much does *this*
hurt? OK, now how much does *this* hurt? OK, 58 more of these and
we will have the scale calibrated."

We can also measure its duration. We can add or multiply these together to
get an estimate of how much pleasure or pain something would bring.

There are many assumptions implicit in Bentham's view: not only does 1.18
he assume that we can assign numbers to pleasures and pains, so that the
numbers reflect the value or disvalue of these experiences, he also assumes
that one person's pain or pleasure is the same as another's and that it makes
sense to add up or multiply different people's numbers in a grand total. As
later utilitarians have insisted, these are controversial assumptions.

Other difficulties with this view are associated with uncertainty: we're 1.19
never certain what the consequences of our choices will be. But if we're not
certain, how can we know which of our actions will maximize utility or
happiness? A common strategy is to say that we should maximize *expected
utility*. That is, for any action, we should qualify the value of that action by
the probability that it will bring about the good results we hope for and
by the corresponding probability of bad results.

To get an idea how expected utility works, consider what happens when 1.20
I buy a lottery ticket. I might win, but I am much more likely to lose. If
I want to determine the expected utility (or expected value) of buying the
ticket, I should figure out the pain of buying a losing ticket times the high
probability that I won't win, added to the pleasure of winning multiplied by
the (very low) probability that I will win. If the expected utility of buying a
ticket is positive (perhaps this is unlikely?) then I should buy the ticket.

Focusing on expected utility means that, just because something pro- 1.21
duced good effects, it does not follow that I acted rightly. I might have done

something foolish and just gotten lucky. Similarly, things might turn out badly even though I did the right thing, perhaps I was just unlucky. If you chose the action with the highest expected utility, there is at least a case for the view that you did the right thing.

Future happiness

1.22 Bentham also thought that pleasures or pains that are in the future should count less than ones that are more immediate. Suppose that there are two pleasures that are equal in certainty, duration, and intensity but that one will happen tomorrow and the other will happen in three years. Most people would choose the present pleasure over the future one. This is sometimes called *discounting*. You might think that we value now over later because there is some chance (even if it is very small) that the delayed pleasure will not happen (perhaps we will die unexpectedly before then!). But this is not what Bentham means. We might discount for the *uncertainty* of future events, but that is separate from discounting for the very fact that they are *future*. Bentham's view is that, when we have done the math, even after discounting for the fact that things in the future are often more uncertain, we should also discount them simply because they are future.

1.23 Critics of discounting worry that it leads to undervaluing the lives of future generations, which can be important in calculations in areas such as environmental policy. Why should the welfare of future people matter less, merely because their suffering will take place in the future? Proponents note that there are many possible future generations. They worry that their happiness will always outweigh ours unless we discount, and that we might make ourselves miserable in the present while trying to improve the lives of people who don't yet exist. Critics of discounting note that we might be indifferent to future disasters if we discount future costs and benefits. Can it be just to take trivial present benefits for ourselves, at great cost to future generations? If we discount, such a choice might make sense; but perhaps that shows why discounting is a problem. These considerations are important for discussions of global climate change and for policies designed to mitigate change. Should we adopt climate policies that may involve present costs, when those who will benefit from them are our distant descendants—people we can never even meet?

1.24 Utilitarians also have to consider how to sum up pleasures and pains across future events. Pains and pleasures are often part of a chain of events. To assess them, you have to look at the whole chain. The exercise and healthier eating necessary to get in better shape may bring you less pleasure in the short run than lounging on the couch watching TV and eating chips, but it may well bring more pleasure and less pain in the long run. Some things produce pain in the short run and even more pain in the long run. Some pleasures do the same. In other cases pain now may bring pleasure later, or pleasure now may bring pain later. For example, utilitarians would say that you have to look at more than just the pleasure that casual sex brings, you have to look at all of the long-term effects. **The Center for Disease control estimates that half of sexually active young people in the United States will have a** sexually transmitted disease **(STD) by the age of 25.** That is part of the utilitarian calculation.

Pleasure and pain

Utilitarians often recommend that we both maximize happiness and minimize misery or unhappiness. Are these different goals? Are there contexts where the *positive utilitarian* requirement to "maximize happiness" will come into conflict with the negative requirement to "minimize misery"? If some people are badly off, we might maximize happiness by improving their situation. Or we might instead provide benefits for other people who are already quite well off. If the well-off people are more efficient at creating happiness and the badly off people would only be made a little less miserable with our help, we might maximize happiness by devoting ourselves to those who are better off instead of those who are worse off. But many people think that this would be just the wrong thing to do: we should work to improve the situation of those who are badly off before we add extra benefits for people who already are well off. Some people take this to be a decisive objection to positive utilitarianism.

While most utilitarians assume that you can cancel out pains with pleasures and vice versa, *negative utilitarians* argue that we should minimize misery instead of maximizing happiness. This view has the advantage of focusing our attention on the elimination of suffering, about which there is arguably more consensus than there is about what is pleasant. It has the unfortunate implication that destroying the entire planet instantaneously would be commendable since it would ensure that there is no more pain in the world. Some people regard this as a decisive reason against negative utilitarianism. Others, including **Karl Popper** and **Judith Shklar**, have argued that the elimination of pain, suffering, and humiliation should be the first goal of politics. Still others argue that the negative consequences of our choices should be given *more weight* than the positive consequences. Few philosophers defend negative utilitarianism as a complete theory of morality or political choice.

1.27   But perhaps the negative utilitarian view becomes more plausible if it is qualified by other principles. For example, we might consider a mixed view that requires (1) that people's rights must be respected; and (2) that, with that constraint, we should minimize misery. But if we add rights to the mix, have we left utilitarianism behind?

Is happiness fulfilling your desires?

1.28 A different approach is to identify happiness with desire satisfaction: on this view, happiness consists in satisfying your desires. People who define happiness this way point out that human beings often do desire things that don't seem to be connected to pleasure. Human beings are complex and have a wide range of desires. Sometimes they seek beauty, at other times friendship, at other times knowledge. It is overly simplistic to say that we only want these things as a means to pleasure. Sometimes we want things for their own sakes:

> Suppose that Erica and Allie are friends. Erica asks Allie why she chose to be her friend and Allie replies: "I find your sense of humor entertaining." Erica responds: "So if I quit being funny you would quit being my friend?" Allie says, coldly and without sarcasm: "Definitely."

Allie thinks of herself as a seeker of pleasure. Her commitment to the friendship is only as deep as the pleasure it brings her. This seems to be a shallow view of friendship. Friends value each other and value their friendship for its own sake.

1.29   Desire fulfillment, like hedonism, starts with the subjective perspective of each person. Both are nonjudgmental in that, if a person wants something or finds pleasure in something, then, all else being equal, all of us have a reason to help them get it even if we think it is a bad idea. Just as hedonists must find a way to compare pleasures, so desire fulfillment theorists need a way to compare the fulfillment of desires. Many of the same considerations apply: a person's well-being may depend more on the satisfaction of one big desire than on satisfying many small desires.

There are a number of objections to the desire satisfaction approach as 1.30
well. The hedonist will respond that what people desire will often bring
them great pain. Perhaps it is better to give people what they don't want, if
that will spare them pain or bring them pleasure in the long run. A child
may desire the chance to play in the busy street, but satisfying that desire is
a bad idea. Desire theorists respond by noting that a child who is killed by
a car will give up a whole lifetime of desire fulfillment opportunities, and
that desire theory justifies thwarting some desires so that even more desires
can be fulfilled over the long term.

A different version of the desire satisfaction theory says that we want to 1.31
satisfy people's informed desires, not their actual desires. By informed desires
we mean that people understand the basic facts of what will happen if they
go down a particular path. Suppose I prefer eating the steak to eating the
chicken, but, unbeknownst to me, the steak contains food poisoning. In that
case my informed preference would be different from my current preference.
Perhaps, in that case, the best way to promote my happiness would be to give
me what I believe to be my second choice. But is it right to prevent people
from getting what they want, because we know or think we know better what
would be good for them? Such a line of thinking might work best if we could
be confident that a person's preferences would change with new information.
Can we ever be confident about such a change in judgment?

Some versions of utilitarianism talk about satisfying the preferences of as 1.32
many people as possible as an alternative to talking about pleasure and
pain. This allows them to talk more easily about the fact that sometimes
people have a preference for sacrificing their own pleasure for the good of
others.

Virtue theorists hold that people should act in accordance with good 1.33
qualities of character (virtues) like courage, compassion, justice, and others.
Virtue theorists would point out that preference satisfaction approaches
have the same problem that pleasure theories do: if people are of poor character, then it might not be good to satisfy their preferences. Some people
cultivate a love of dog fighting and prefer to watch animals inflict pain on
each other. Aren't we justified to prevent the satisfaction of bad preferences
like this one?

Lastly, critics of desire satisfaction theory argue that it gets things back- 1.34
ward. We desire things because we already think they are good in some way.
Desire theory puts it the other way around. It claims that things only
become good because we desire them. This makes it mysterious or arbitrary
why we desire some things and not others.

Do the ends justify the means?

1.35 Utilitarianism's claim that one should maximize happiness (or well-being, etc.) implies that the means of achieving happiness are not intrinsically important, only the outcomes are. Critics claim that that there are some cases where the end—the goal pursued—doesn't justify the means used to achieve it. In Dostoyevsky's classic novel *The Brothers Karamazov*, one of the characters says:

> Tell me yourself, I challenge you—answer. Imagine that you are creating a fabric of human destiny with the object of making men happy in the end, giving them peace and rest at last. Imagine that you are doing this but that it is essential and inevitable to torture to death only one tiny creature—that child beating its breast with its fist, for instance—in order to found that edifice on its unavenged tears. Would you consent to be the architect on those conditions? (Dostoyevsky, 1958 [1880], p. 226)

What would you say? Those who emphasize the public good often argue that the good of the whole outweighs the good of the few. Utilitarianism in particular would say that in this case the happiness of a whole society outweighs the happiness of a single child. Perhaps the knowledge that a child is suffering would make it impossible for people to enjoy their utopia, but human beings are often quite accomplished at ignoring the suffering of others when they are having a good time.

1.36   In Dostoyevsky's case, the tradeoff is between the welfare of one child and the welfare of the rest of the society. In other situations, the conflict is between welfare (the public good) and some other value. Let's take a moment to examine potential conflicts between the public good and some of the other values.

Nozick's experience machine

1.37 Robert Nozick, in his book *Anarchy, State, and Utopia*, came up with a famous example designed to test whether what we value is the subjective experience of desire satisfaction or something more objective. It can be paraphrased thus (cf. Nozick, 1974, p. 42):

> Suppose that you had the opportunity to hook up your brain to an *experience machine* that would cause you to experience an entire life-time of incredibly pleasurable sensations. You would spend the rest of

your life hooked up to the machine, but you would think you were living a great life with lots of pleasures, minimal frustrations, and satisfied desires. Whatever life you desire or value most, the experience machine would make it seem to you that you were living it: If it you wanted a rich life that includes some poignant longings, the machine could include them. If you value a life of creative achievement, that's the life the machine would *seem to* provide for you. You might experience writing a great novel, followed by public acclaim. You might experience the pain of training for an Olympic gold medal followed by the pleasure of winning the gold! Of course, you would not actually *do* any of these things, but it would seem to you that you were doing them.

Would you plug yourself in if you were sure that it would work as advertised? If Bentham were right about our psychology, it would be irrational not to do so. If the best life is a life of satisfied desires, then the person in the experience machine would be living the best life. Many people, however, think that there would be something very wrong about hooking ourselves up to such a machine.

If you would not enter the machine, why not? Is the problem that you would be living a lie? You wouldn't know it, so the fact that none of the experiences is actually happening would not detract from your pleasure. Nozick suggests that we shouldn't enter the experience machine because it matters to us that we actually achieve things, not that we seem—even to ourselves—to achieve them. A parent who entered the machine might enjoy the experience of watching her children flourish and grow. But good parents don't want it to *seem* that their children are flourishing. They want their actual children to flourish! Where others' happiness is concerned, we want to actually bring happiness to others, not just to think that we are doing so. That question brings us back to the tension in utilitarianism between maximizing one's own happiness and maximizing *everyone's* happiness. If you would not enter the experience machine, perhaps this is because of something objective that matters to you, something beyond the subjective experiences you suffer or enjoy. 1.38

Happiness and virtue

Perhaps happiness is not really about adding up pleasures and pains. Perhaps it is about something the ancient Greeks called *eudaimonia*. This word is sometimes translated "happiness," which can give the impression 1.39

that Aristotle, who wrote much about it, was a utilitarian. Many philosophers prefer the translation "flourishing." A flourishing plant is an excellent example of its kind. Human flourishing requires action, not just experiences.

1.40   According to Aristotle, the virtues are whatever properties make an excellent person excellent. A flourishing human being is an excellent example of a human being. Aristotle's idea is that we find our happiness not in seeking pleasure but in becoming the sort of person who acts virtuously. And our greatest happiness, he recommends, is living a life that involves the exercise of these virtues. Part of virtue consists in becoming the sort of person who takes pleasure in things that are objectively good. Another part is developing character such that you act in virtuous ways because you value the good for its own sake.

1.41   Aristotle agrees that we all want happiness. But some objectives are difficult to achieve directly, when we are expressly aiming at them. Consider an insomniac, so intent on trying to fall asleep that she keeps herself awake. Or imagine two people who both go to an art museum. The first person is constantly thinking, "Which painting will bring me the most pleasure?" The second person is just looking for quality art because he loves good art. The second person, paradoxically, may end up having a better time. It may be better to think of pleasure, like Aristotle, as a byproduct or side effect of pursuing the right things in the right way instead of thinking about it as the actual goal of our lives.

1.42   Aristotle argues that people want to have flourishing lives and that the best way to flourish as a human being is to cultivate a virtuous character. The virtues, according to Aristotle, are qualities of character that are necessary to support our ability to make good choices. In order to flourish, we need to make good choices, but we also need to make them for the right reasons.

1.43   One way to test this theory is to ask yourself: "What is most essential to human flourishing?" Certainly there are some kinds of external things that we need: water, clothing, food, and shelter. If we can't live, it is hard to flourish. But some people manage to live flourishing lives with relatively little, while others, who have great wealth, don't flourish at all. Virtue theorists hold that people's character is more important than their circumstances.

1.44   Aristotle offered a specific list of virtues—characteristics that make good people good, and without which (he thought) people could not be truly happy. Some utilitarians are reluctant to provide such a list, since it involves taking a stand on what virtue actually consists in, something about which reasonable people disagree. Instead utilitarians often focus on political questions about how to change the circumstances of life: provide more money, better jobs, better healthcare, and so on. Virtue theorists will argue that all of this is insufficient. Without good character people who have all of these things will not flourish. Not only that, but utilitarianism, given its overemphasis on pleasure, may actually make it harder to become the sort of person who has the right sort of character.

A few years ago, **New York City tried to ban extra large sodas** on the 1.45 grounds that they're not healthy. The rationale was straightforwardly utilitarian: smaller sodas lead to less obesity, which saves on healthcare costs. Aristotle might suggest a different rationale for the same policy: the law will help people learn to be more self-controlled. What starts out as merely complying with the law might over time become a new way of living, which the person consciously and consistently embraces. As we will see, still others might regard such laws as an inappropriate intrusion on liberty.

The case of John Stuart Mill

John Stuart Mill, born in 1806, was raised by his father, James Mill, to be a 1.46 utilitarian. His father was a friend of Bentham's and an accomplished scholar in his own right. John Stuart Mill was homeschooled by his father and learned an enormous amount, but then had a mental breakdown in his twenties. In part, he felt that the utilitarian philosophy he had been taught to believe in couldn't make sense of the real world. For example, he denied that all pleasures have the same value. According to the earlier theory, the pleasure you get from watching a trashy TV show is similar in quality to the pleasure you get from reading a great novel or spending the week with your best friends on the beach. The pleasures might differ in quantity because they differ in intensity or duration, but pleasure is pleasure. This means that a certain number of TV shows would eventually be equal in value to a certain number of great novels or to a certain amount of time spent with friends.

Mill thought this was wrong. Pleasures differ in quality as well as 1.47 quantity.

> It is better to be a human being dissatisfied than a pig satisfied; better to be Socrates dissatisfied than a fool satisfied. And if the fool, or the pig, are [of] a different opinion, it is because they only know their own side of the question. The other party to the comparison knows both sides. (Mill, 1979 [1861], p. 12)

Perhaps human beings are often less satisfied than happy pigs. (This is not to imply that most pigs are happy!) Our ability to desire things routinely exceeds our ability to satisfy them. But Mill thinks that none of us would want to be a pig, no matter how good the slop or how comfortable the mud. There is no amount of merely animal pleasures that are equal to the distinctively human pleasures of rational thought and creativity.

1.48 Mill used this line of thinking in his political philosophy. He was a staunch defender of freedom of speech and argued that people should be able to live their lives as they desire so long as they do not harm others (see Chapter 2). The problem is that people can use freedom of speech in ways that cause unhappiness to others. People can make choices that will destroy their lives. It is not clear that utilitarianism will always favor liberty in these cases. Mill wrote: "I regard utility as the ultimate appeal on all ethical questions; but it must be utility in the largest sense, grounded on the permanent interests of man as a progressive being" (Mill, 1978 [1859], p. 12).

1.49 Mill's vision of a truly happy person is of someone who grows and develops in using his capacities for creativity, thought, and originality. It is someone becoming more like Socrates and less like a fool. Because the freedom to think and to criticize is so important to a person's ultimate happiness, the law must protect those freedoms: in the end we will be happier.

1.50 But when Mill argues for this view, has he left utilitarianism behind? Some readers interpret Mill as having become a virtue theorist in spite of himself. The virtue theorist has a particular version of what a flourishing human life looks like and wants laws and policies that help people become that sort of person. Mill is doing something very similar: his particular version of human flourishing emphasizes individual autonomy—but it is a vision of human flourishing nonetheless. He is willing to accept a world where there is more pain and more unsatisfied preferences, if it is populated by people who are creative and original and are autonomously in control of their own lives.

Capabilities

1.51 Another alternative to utilitarianism is the capabilities approach. We can think of it as a goal to be maximized, like utilitarianism. Also like utilitarianism, it arises from a concern for whether people's lives go well. Nonetheless, there are important differences. This approach owes much to the work of **Amartya Sen**. Sen developed the Human Development Index, which provides a rough measure of the quality of people's lives.

1.52 Suppose we want to ask ourselves how well a country is doing. We could start by asking how many people have most of their preferences satisfied. The capabilities approach would instead ask specific questions: how many people can read? At what level? How many people are able to work? How many people are in good health? How many people have enough access to transportation to move around easily? Rather than taking a poll of utility, the Human Development Index looks at factors such as literacy rates, infant mortality, and nutrition in order to determine the quality of life.

Martha Nussbaum has developed Sen's suggestion with a list of basic 1.53 human functional capabilities that can, she believes, serve both as a target for development and poverty reduction and as a way to compare the relative positions of different people in a given society. Here is Nussbaum's list:

Nussbaum's list of basic human functional capabilities

1. LIFE. Being able to live to the end of a human life of normal length, not dying prematurely, or before one's life is so reduced as to be not worth living.
2. BODILY HEALTH. Being able to have good health, including reproductive health; to be adequately nourished; to have adequate shelter.
3. BODILY INTEGRITY. Being able to move freely from place to place, to be free from violent assault, including sexual assault and domestic violence; having opportunities for sexual satisfaction and for choice in matters of reproduction.
4. SENSES, IMAGINATION, AND THOUGHT. Being able to use the senses, to imagine, think, and reason—and to do these things in … a way informed and cultivated by an adequate education including, but by no means limited to, literacy and basic mathematical and scientific training. Being able to use imagination and thought in connection with experiencing and producing works and events of one's own choice, religious, literary, musical, and so forth. Being able to use one's mind in ways protected by guarantees of freedom of expression with respect to both political and artistic speech, and freedom of religious exercise. Being able to have pleasurable experiences and to avoid nonbeneficial pain.
5. EMOTIONS. Being able to have attachments to things and persons outside ourselves; to love those who love and care for us, to grieve at their absence; in general to love, to grieve, to experience longing, gratitude, and justified anger. Not having one's emotional development blighted by fear and anxiety. …

6. PRACTICAL REASON. Being able to form a conception of the good and to engage in critical reflection about planning one's own life. ...

7. AFFILIATION. (A) Being able to live for and to others, to recognize and show concern for other human beings, to engage in various forms of social interaction; to be able to imagine the situation of another. ... (B) Having the social bases of self-respect and nonhumiliation; being able to be treated as a dignified being whose worth is equal to that of others. This includes provisions of nondiscrimination on the basis of race, sex, sexual orientation, ethnicity, caste, religion, national origin.

8. OTHER SPECIES. Being able to live with concern for and in relation to animal, plants, and the world of nature.

9. PLAY. Being able to laugh, to play, to enjoy recreational activities.

10. CONTROL OVER ONE'S ENVIRONMENT (A) *Political*: Being able to participate effectively in political choices that govern one's life; having the right of political participation, protections of free speech and association. (B) *Material*: Being able to hold property, and having property rights on an equal basis with others; having the right to seek employment on an equal basis with others; having freedom from unwanted search and seizure. In work, being able to work as a human being, exercising practical reason and entering into meaningful relationships of mutual recognition. (Nussbaum, 2011, pp. 33–34)

Nussbaum writes:

> My claim is that a life that lacks any one of these capabilities, no matter what else it has, will fall short of being a good human life. So it would be reasonable to take these things as a focus for concern, in assessing the quality of life in a country and asking about the role of public policy in meeting human needs. (Nussbaum, 1995, p. 85)

Utilitarians argue that we should maximize happiness or well-being. But Nussbaum argues that, rather than maximizing people's capabilities, justice requires that we bring everyone across a *threshold* of capability. The first priority is to bring people across the threshold beneath which, as she says, people's lives cannot properly be *human* lives at all. According to Nussbaum, people who are severely deprived, unable to exercise any of these fundamental capabilities, are living a life that is so impoverished and constrained that no human being should ever have to endure it. The second priority is to bring people over the threshold that enables their lives to be *good* human lives—once again, as measured by their ability to exercise basic functional capabilities. She writes:

> A commitment to bringing all human beings across a certain threshold of capability to choose represents a certain sort of commitment to equality: for the view treats all persons as equal bearers of human claims, no matter where they are starting from in terms of circumstances, special talents, wealth, gender, or race. (Nussbaum, 1995, p. 86)

There are several important advantages to a capabilities approach:

1. Oppressed people often lower their preferences to fit their available opportunities. A woman in the developing world who has never had an education may not express a preference for having an education because she simply accepts her lot in life, yet if she were educated her capabilities would increase.

2. Focusing on capabilities does not force people to use their capacities in a particular way. Suppose an educated woman decides she wants to stay at home and raise children rather than working outside the home. So long as she has the capability to work outside the home, it is not necessary that she chooses to exercise that capacity. Theories that focus on human flourishing are sometimes criticized for restricting our freedom, since they hold up a particular view of a flourishing life. The capabilities approach focuses on making sure that people have real options of how to live their life without telling them which option to pick. In a sense, the capabilities approach focuses on the opportunities to flourish rather than on the actual flourishing.

3. Different people have different degrees of need. If we want to make sure that people are nourished so that their bodies function properly, we should give different amounts of food to different people. Bigger people need more food. Pregnant women need more food. Handicapped people need more funding and support to attain the same level of capabilities as others. Proponents of the capabilities approach see it as a better and fairer way of thinking about equality.

Critics question whether this is really a different approach. It may just be a form of the virtue approach that happens to place more emphasis on capabilities. Moreover, like the virtue approach, one still has to make controversial decisions about which capabilities are important. Both approaches come up with some list of factors, character traits, or capabilities that are crucial to human well-being. There is, however, no agreement on what those lists should include.

Conflicts between liberty and happiness

1.54 When **Oliver Wendell Holmes, Jr** noted that **freedom of speech does not include the right to shout "Fire!" in a crowded theater** (see *Schenck v. United States*, 249 US 47 [1919]), he was claiming that the public good rightly limits freedoms. People will sometimes justify torturing suspected terrorists on the basis of this same concept of the public good, a topic we will turn to in Chapter 7. One explanation for his position is that the pain people experience in a fire far exceeds the pleasure people gain from shouting fire in a crowded theater. There is no serious damage to political deliberation from such a restriction, so on utilitarian grounds it makes sense.

1.55 Very few people are really "absolutists" when it comes to things like freedom of speech. Here are just a few examples of speech acts that are frequently against the law: incitement to riot, threatening the president, slander, libel, and commercial fraud. In all of these cases there are substantial numbers of people who believe that unrestricted freedom of speech would pose a risk to other people or harm them in some way.

1.56 On the other hand, it is easy to overstate the tension between the two. It takes many people working together "to secure the blessings of liberty." In other words, for many people having liberty or freedom is a crucial component of what it means to have a good life. One of the main "public goods" that governments provide is a general environment where people's freedoms are respected and protected.

Conflicts between equality and happiness

1.57 Suppose that you really could measure happiness the way Bentham suggested. Suppose there were two policies we could pursue that would lead to two different distributions of happiness in Table 1.1:

1.58 If you sum up the total amount of happiness for each policy, policy 1 (189 to 163) wins. If you are more interested in equality, policy 2 is much better. Policy 1 lets one person have seven times more happiness than another, while in policy 2 the gap is less than 20 percent.

1.59 In economic policies these sorts of tradeoffs can happen. Sometimes the policy that generates the largest amount of total wealth will cause the gap between the richest and the poorest to get much bigger. Take, for example,

Table 1.1   Distribution of happiness.

	Allison	Brent	Carlie
Policy 1	85	92	12
Policy 2	55	58	50

taxes on wealthy estates when people die. Critics will say that these taxes discourage people from being as productive as they could possibly be—with the result that overall productivity and wealth go down. Proponents will say that allowing inequalities to continue increasing from generation to generation makes a mockery of equality of opportunity.

Here, too, what looks at first glance like a simple conflict between the 1.60 public good and another value can be described in a different way. If we ask why people want equality so much, we find that it is often because they think of equality as a prerequisite for a certain kind of flourishing life. If democratic participation is central to a human life well lived, inequalities of wealth that put some people in a position of relative powerlessness are a barrier to flourishing. If poverty keeps some people from being able to participate in the key cultural activities of their state, that may also make their lives less fulfilled. If only those with money have access to education and jobs that will help them fully utilize their abilities and talents, that is also a barrier to their living a fulfilled life. In other words, arguments for equality are often in large parts arguments about what a good society would look like.

Happiness and Government

One explanation of the purpose of government is that it exists in order to 1.61 allow us to live happier, more contented lives than we otherwise would. Certainly governments that prevent crime and mayhem contribute much to our happiness. In countries where there are failed states and the rule of law breaks down, the consequences for people's lives can be devastating. Modern governments do far more to promote happiness than just restrain crime. They build roads, provide libraries and schools, regulate pharmaceuticals, fund academic research, facilitate access to healthcare, and much more. One way to analyze all of these policies is simply to ask whether the costs outweigh the benefits. Do the policies have a net positive impact on human happiness or not?

1.62   But this is not the whole story. Many people would question the premise that the purpose of government is to maximize happiness. That, after all, really could end in something like *Brave New World*. We must also consider arguments that other values, such as freedom or equality, rightly constrain the government in its pursuit of happiness.

Happiness and Public Goods

1.63   Bentham argued that the phrase "public good" just means the sum of the pleasures and pains of the individuals who compose the public. For him, utility and the public good were interchangeable concepts. The discipline of economics is heavily influenced by utilitarian philosophy. Economists often analyze policies by adding up the costs and benefits, in terms of utility, to each individual affected. They also frequently assume that people will choose the option that maximizes their personal utility.

1.64   One example is the classic "prisoner's dilemma" scenario:

> Suppose that two people are arrested and charged with armed robbery and a misdemeanor. The police have enough evidence to convict on the misdemeanor but need more evidence to convict on the felony. The culprits are questioned separately and both of them are made the same offer. "If you implicate your friend and your friend does not implicate you, we will give your friend a 10-year sentence and will give you probation. If you don't implicate your friend and your friend implicates you, the sentences will be reversed. If you both implicate each other, you both get a five-year sentence. If neither of you implicates the other, we will not be able to convict either of you on the main charge, so you both get a three-month sentence."

> What should you do? The rational thing, the economists say, is to implicate your friend. No matter what your friend does, you get a lighter sentence that way. If your friend confesses, five years is better than 10. If your friend does not confess, probation is better than three months in jail.

1.65   What is interesting about this case is that, if both people act "rationally," they end up serving a five-year sentence, whereas if they both acted irrationally they would only have had to serve three months. It is possible for the rational pursuit of self-interest to lead to very suboptimal outcomes.

A similar kind of logic is important in politics. Consider the following 1.66
example:

The city of New Orleans needs levees to protect it from flooding.
The levees will cost billions of dollars. One solution is to ask everyone
in the city (and those outside the city who would benefit from it) to
make a voluntary contribution to pay for the levees. Not enough people make pledges, and so nothing happens. Someone else proposes a
tax on everyone who would benefit to pay for the levees, claiming that
the levees will promote the public good. Would they?

Economists use the term "public good" for cases like this, but they mean
something specific by it. On balance, the city will be better off with the levees.
Many people would benefit. The problem is that, if you rely on voluntary contributions or user fees, the levees will probably not be built. This is because
there is no way to exclude from enjoying the benefit the people who don't pay
for it. If you build a levee and it keeps the city from flooding, people will benefit
whether they helped pay for it or not. A public good (in the economist's sense)
is something that would benefit the public but that will not occur (in the
absence of policy intervention) because there are not enough individuals who
will think that the benefit justifies the contribution. A mandatory tax is one
policy intervention that might overcome this sort of public good problem.

Free Riding and Small Contributions

Economists often assume a version of the psychological hedonism of Jeremy 1.67
Bentham. They assume that everyone acts so as to satisfy her own preferences,
which are normally about her own pleasures or pains. From the standpoint
of a self-interested individual, one of two things will happen. Either enough
other people will contribute to building the levees and you can enjoy the
benefits without paying the costs (since for a large project your individual
contribution will not be decisive) or there will not be enough people contributing to build the levees and you are better off keeping your money.

In this example there are actually two different problems. One is that 1.68
there is no way to exclude those who benefit but don't pay. The other is that,
because there is a large number of potential contributors, one person's
contribution will not make a difference to whether the project is completed.
Both reasons lead a self-interested person to not contribute.

1.69 This is a paradox, because you may actually think that you would happily pay your share of the cost if you could be assured that the levees will be built and that other people will pay their part as well. This is why economists like government intervention for these sorts of public goods. The government can use taxation to make sure that everyone contributes. Without government intervention, the levees will not be built. With government intervention, levees that, on balance, make people better off will exist.

1.70 Climate change is a policy area where these issues become very important. If there are environmental benefits from reducing CO_2 emissions, the whole earth will experience them. People in one country would benefit from the policies of other countries without contributing. Moreover, no one country could make a substantial difference to the long-term outcome without cooperation from other countries. A self-interested country might therefore conclude that it is better to keep emitting large amounts of CO_2.

1.71 Not everything a government does promotes a public good in this strict sense. A highway is not a public good in the same way as a levee, because it is relatively easy to charge people who benefit: set up a toll road. Economists tend to support taxation in cases where there is something that would benefit many people and where you can't exclude people from enjoying the benefit after you provide it. There are lots of things that fall in to this category. Once we have an army to provide national defense, everyone benefits from that defense. There is no way to defend only some of the people.

1.72 There are also many things that are mixed. It is possible to charge admission to a park, but people who live nearby can enjoy looking at it from the outside whether they pay for it or not. If your high-rise apartment looks out over Central Park, that is worth a lot of money. It is possible to charge tuition for elementary education rather than providing it for free, but it is also the case that all of us benefit from having a more educated workforce. In these cases, economists would say that, if we only pay for the good by individual purchases, there will be too little of the good provided. If people can enjoy without paying they will not pay, but that means that often the thing they would enjoy never happens.

Philosophical objections

1.73 Some philosophers think that economists have the wrong definition of "public good." First, economists tend to focus only on what people actually want (as many versions of utilitarianism do). They normally do not ask the question: is what people want actually good? People may want a levee to protect the town from flooding, but the levee may destroy wetlands that provide a home for endangered species.

Second, the economists assume that, as long as the benefits, on balance, 1.74 outweigh the costs, this is enough to make something "good." This ignores questions about the distribution of the good. Not everyone benefits equally from the levee. Those who own property in the flood zones benefit much more than those who do not. Why should the guy on the hill pay as much for it as the guy in the valley, when they will not benefit to the same extent? Suppose that those who will benefit the most from the policy are those who already are the most affluent. Just looking at net costs and benefits doesn't show you the distribution of those costs and benefits. What people are willing to pay depends a lot on what they are able to pay.

Third, there is an assumption built into the economists' argument. The 1.75 assumption is that the default is for the market to provide things. If people want something, they will pay for it themselves and the market will supply it. Government intervention is only necessary when there is a "market failure." This whole way of thinking privileges people's acting as consumers over people's acting as citizens.

Fourth, many philosophers question the definition of rationality. Kant, for 1.76 example, would have said that free riding on the goodwill of others is actually an example of acting irrationally. The rational action is to act on the principle that you would want others to act on, whether they act on it or not. A Kantian would contribute to a public good even if she could free ride and still enjoy that public good. Interestingly, a utilitarian who believed that people are motivated to act on the principle of utility directly would also disagree. If my goal is the happiness of everyone, I should contribute even if I don't have to. A virtue theorist might consider public-spirited generosity a mark of virtue.

Should We Evaluate Political Institutions According to their Ability to Make People Happy?

Almost everyone agrees that happiness is good and that, other things being 1.77 equal, institutions are better when they make people happy. But happiness turns out to be a difficult objective: it is difficult to measure, even in ourselves. Different theorists have different accounts of what happiness is and of how we might measure it: are people well off when their desires are satisfied, or, as Nussbaum suggests, when they are able to be and do a wide range of different things? Some people conclude from Nozick's experience machine thought experiment that happiness is neither our only goal nor our most important goal. And, as we have seen, the goal of making people happy may come into conflict with other important political goals, like protecting people's rights.

1.78 Utilitarians, who believe that actions and institutions are better when they more effectively promote happiness, will regard these problems as difficulties to be resolved. Others regard them as objections that constitute reasons not to advocate a utilitarian view. Some people urge that political institutions can't promote happiness, because different people need and want different things in order to be happy. They might urge that what people need is liberty—the freedom to pursue their *own* happiness. On one version of this view, political institutions should be judged according to their ability to protect people's freedom, not according to their ability to make people happy. The following chapter will consider the value of freedom and the idea that political institutions should focus on liberty instead of on well-being.

References and Further Reading

Bentham, Jeremy. 1988 [1948]. *Principles of Morals and Legislation*. New York: Prometheus Books. Bentham's defense of utilitarianism as a theory of government, law, and morals is one of the first full-borne defenses of the view (especially chapters 1–4).

Crisp, Roger. 2013 [2001]. "Well-Being." In *Stanford Encyclopedia of Philosophy*. http://plato.stanford.edu/entries/well-being (accessed February 12, 2016). Crisp offers a very helpful and detailed account of various theories of human well-being.

Dostoyevsky, Fyodor. 1958 [1880]. *The Brothers Karamazov*. New York: Signet Classics. Dostoyevsky's deeply philosophical novel addresses, among many other things, the question whether it is permissible to inflict suffering on some innocent people if the overall effect will be to make others happy.

Galston, William. 1991. *Liberal Purposes*. New York: Cambridge University Press. Galston argues that politics should promote not only happiness, but also virtue as a component of well-being.

Goodin, Robert. 1995. *Utilitarianism as a Public Philosophy*. New York: Cambridge University Press. Goodin's book is a collection of essays that, together, constitute a powerful defense of utilitarianism as a theory of politics and government. It is one of the very best contemporary defenses of utilitarianism as a public philosophy.

Haybron, Daniel. 2008. *The Pursuit of Unhappiness*. New York: Oxford University Press. Haybron argues that we are not good judges of our own happiness. He develops a sophisticated view about what happiness is and how it might be promoted.

Machiavelli, Niccolò. 1988 [1513]. *The Prince*. New York: Cambridge University Press. Machiavelli argues that the ends are more important for political leaders than the means. See especially chapters 8 and 15–18.

Mill, John Stuart. 1978 [1859]. *On Liberty*. Indianapolis: Hackett. *On Liberty* was co-written by Mill and Harriet Taylor. Mill said she wrote most of it, but there is good reason to think that it was truly a joint effort and that the view expressed is one they carefully discussed. *On Liberty* defends a liberal theory of law, arguing that the only legitimate reason to limit people's liberty is to prevent harm to other people.

Mill, John Stuart. 1979 [1861]. *Utilitarianism*. Indianapolis: Hackett. Mill wrote this as a pamphlet, and may not have regarded it among his best works. However, it is the most famous and most widely read defense of utilitarianism in the history of philosophy.

Nozick, Robert. 1974. *Anarchy, State, and Utopia*. New York: Basic Books. Nozick's book is the most famous twentieth-century defense of libertarianism as a political theory but also includes spectacular examples (like the experience machine) that challenge traditional moral and political views.

Nussbaum, Martha. 1995. "Human Capabilities, Female Human Beings." In *Women, Culture, and Development: A Study of Human Capabilities*, edited by Martha Nussbaum and Jonathan Glover. Oxford: Clarendon, pp. 61–115. This article goes in greater depth into her view of the capabilities approach and its implications for women.

Nussbaum, Martha. 2011. *Creating Capabilities*. Cambridge, MA: Harvard University Press. This brief book is a popular presentation of Nussbaum's version of the so-called capabilities approach.

Sen, Amartya. 1979. "Equality of What?" Tanner Lecture on Human Values, Stanford University. Lecture delivered at Stanford University, May 22. http://tannerlectures.utah.edu/_documents/a-to-z/s/sen80.pdf (accessed February 12, 2016). This paper develops Sen's capabilities approach.

Sidgwick, Henry. 1981 [1874]. *Methods of Ethics*. Indianapolis: Hackett. Sidgwick provides a more systematic and "modern" defense of utilitarianism than either Bentham or Mill. Sidgwick's complex version of utilitarianism urges that *institutions* should be set in place to maximize utility but that individual actions people undertake might not appear to be justifiable on utilitarian terms.

Sher, George. 1997. *Beyond Neutrality: Perfectionism in Politics*. New York: Cambridge University Press. Sher argues that a good state will not only protect people's liberties or promote their happiness, but should also make them better people.

Online Resources

1   http://plato.stanford.edu/entries/bentham/
2   http://plato.stanford.edu/entries/well-being/
3   http://www.utilitarianism.net/bentham/
4   http://www.cdc.gov/std/stats/STI-Estimates-Fact-Sheet-Feb-2013.pdf
5   http://plato.stanford.edu/entries/popper/
6   https://en.wikipedia.org/wiki/Judith_N._Shklar
7   http://www.nytimes.com/2014/06/27/nyregion/city-loses-final-appeal-on-limiting-sales-of-large-sodas.html
8   https://en.wikipedia.org/wiki/Amartya_Sen
9   https://en.wikipedia.org/wiki/Oliver_Wendell_Holmes,_Jr.
10 https://www.law.cornell.edu/supremecourt/text/249/47
11 http://www.nola.com/hurricane/index.ssf/2013/08/upgrated_metro_new_orleans_lev.html

2

FREEDOM

SOPHIE   I can't believe that the government is going to force me to buy health insurance—that is an insane violation of my freedom. If I want to take the financial risk of not having insurance, that's my business.

JUSTIN   So do you think all laws take away your freedom? Speed limit laws take away your freedom to go fast on the highway and you don't think they are unjust. You generally may not obey them, but you don't question the right of the government to set speed limits. Why is this so different?

SOPHIE   It's different because the government is actually making me do something. The speed limit law just keeps me from putting other people at risk. Forcing me to perform a specific act is a different kind of infringement on my liberty from forbidding an action that risks harm to others. Forbidding particular actions still leaves me lots of choices about other things I can do.

JUSTIN   So the amount of freedom you have is measured by the number of the things you are actually able to do by comparison to those you would like to do?

SOPHIE   Not exactly. There are some things I'm unable to do just because I lack the ability. I can't fly, but that doesn't restrict my freedom. What I don't like about having to buy health insurance is that the government is actively stopping me from doing what I want to do. Freedom is taken away when

This Is Political Philosophy: An Introduction, First Edition. Alex Tuckness and Clark Wolf.
© 2017 John Wiley & Sons, Inc. Published 2017 by John Wiley & Sons, Inc.

others prevent you from doing something that you otherwise would have been able to do.

JUSTIN   So you would say that, if someone breaks my legs so that I
can't walk, that person is taking away some of my freedom?
Not being able to fly is a natural characteristic of human
beings and so that inability doesn't affect my freedom. If
people are the cause of my inability, that's different from a
case where my inability is natural.

SOPHIE   Right.

JUSTIN   Suppose I get an illness that's easy to treat but will leave me
paralyzed if it's not treated. Paralysis takes away my opportunity to do many things. Right?

SOPHIE   Yes, but paralysis is caused by an illness, not by people. I
don't think your decreased opportunities count as a
decrease of your freedom.

JUSTIN   If our political and economic system is set up so that I can't
afford the treatment and I end up paralyzed, I think I can fairly
say that people caused my paralysis. It wasn't any one particular person, but the system of laws took away my freedom. I
think this is important because without health a person can't
really enjoy freedom. Freedom is about being able to do things,
and poor health limits our ability to do what we choose.

SOPHIE   You're confusing promotion of liberty with infringement of
liberty. If you are in jail and I could bail you out but I don't do
it, I didn't take away your freedom. I simply decided not to
increase your freedom. On the other hand, if I were to kidnap
you and lock you in my basement, I would be actively taking
away your freedom. Wouldn't you agree that there is a big
difference between kidnapping you and not bailing you out?

JUSTIN   Yes.

SOPHIE   Okay. Then you should agree that my failure to buy you
medicine doesn't take away your freedom. If I break your
legs, I do. In the case we started from, the government is
actively taking away my freedom to do without health
insurance, and it's doing so as part of a plan to make me pay
for other people's health insurance.

JUSTIN   Suppose that the government actively takes away some of
your freedom by making you buy health insurance and
that the health law also improves access to healthcare for

someone else, so that the other person avoids paralysis. So, if we have to choose between forcing one person to buy health insurance and allowing someone else to end up needlessly paralyzed, we are obligated to choose the latter?

SOPHIE If we decide on the basis of freedom, I think so.

JUSTIN I think that's wrong. While the difference between taking away freedom and not enlarging freedom is sometimes important, it isn't everything. I think it is also important to think about how valuable the freedoms are. Forcing you to buy health insurance will only make a tiny difference to what you are free to do with the rest of your life. The only people who will be forced to pay for it are people who make enough money for it not to represent a significant percentage of their income. Compare that to how devastating a serious illness can be for a person's freedom. Your having less money to spend on beer is trivial by comparison to the potential benefit to someone's health.

SOPHIE Maybe I was going to spend the money helping orphans and widows, but that is not the point. According to your way of thinking, what makes a person free and what makes a person happy are two things getting all blurred together. Being healthy or sick may affect my happiness, but freedom has to do with whether other people intentionally keep me from doing what I want to do.

JUSTIN What if what you want to do is punch people in the nose? Does a law that prevents you from punching people take away your freedom too?

SOPHIE Actually it does, but in that case it is justifiable. If I punch someone I'm taking away that person's liberty. You know the saying: "My freedom to swing my fist stops at the end of your nose."

JUSTIN I think you're being inconsistent. A swollen nose decreases my happiness, but it doesn't really change my freedom to do what I want to do. There are lots of times when we keep people from doing whatever they want just because it will harm other people in some way, not because it might take away freedom. If you don't get health insurance and then you are in a car accident, the emergency room will treat you even if you can't afford it, and then other people—either

the taxpayers or other patients at the hospital—will have
to pay for it.

SOPHIE   But look where your argument leads. If I eat too many
French fries and don't exercise, I might have health problems that would make me less able to contribute to the
economy. Does that mean that the government has the
right to force me to eat healthy food and exercise?

The Meaning of Freedom

2.1 Freedom may be the most widely celebrated political ideal of them all.
People praise nations "conceived in liberty," and many are willing to fight to
protect freedom as the most cherished value. But what does it mean to be
free, or to say that a nation protects people's freedom? Is a person free if no
one else can tell her what to do, even if her life leaves her few reasonable
choices? If a person suffers under crippling debt, is he free? Do laws that
regulate guns, or abortion, or drugs make people less free? This chapter will
discuss several of the different things people mean when they use the term
"freedom." But before doing that, we must ask…

The Fundamental Question

2.2 When do other people have the right to tell you what to do? Ordinarily, they
do not. If you are a competent adult, you are able to take charge of your own
life and your own decisions. When you were a child, your parents had the
right (and a *duty*) to tell you to go to school, to be polite to other people, to
do your homework, and perhaps to finish your oboe practice before going
out to play. But, once you are an adult, they no longer have that right as a
matter of course.

2.3   If your parents are paying your college tuition, of course, you have obligations to them. In extreme circumstances, even good parents might use
the fact that you still depend on them as leverage, in order to get you to do
what they think you ought to do. But do you have to do what they tell you
to do, or are you *free* to do as you wish?

2.4   One face of this question is the face of *authority*: when do people have
the *authority* to tell you what to do, and when (if ever) is it appropriate to
disobey? This question will be taken up later, in Chapter 6. But the other

side of authority is freedom: under what circumstances are we free to do as we like, without other people organizing our choices for us? Is our freedom circumscribed simply by the "silence of the laws," so that we are free only to the extent that no law constrains our choice? Or is freedom something more substantial? Can our freedom be limited by own choices and our own desires? What is freedom anyway? If "freedom" is an ambiguous word—a word that is used to refer to very different things—then we need to distinguish the different *senses* of the word before we can discuss it sensibly.

What Is Freedom? And Who Is Free?

Let's start with drug laws: would a law that legalized heroin increase or 2.5 decrease freedom? Some might say that it would increase freedom, because there are people who want to use **heroin** but the law prohibits them from doing so. If **the law were changed**, they would be free to do what they now can't do. People who don't want to use heroin would still be free to abstain. Is this a clear win for freedom? If more people are free to use heroin, does this mean that more people are more free?

Some addicts don't feel that their choice to use heroin is truly free: they 2.6 suffer horrible symptoms of withdrawal if they stop. Perhaps these addicts are enslaved by the drug: they'd like to kick the habit, but it is just too hard. If legalizing heroin results in more addicts, then maybe legalization would *reduce* freedom instead of increasing it.

What does it mean to say that an addict's choices are not free, or that they 2.7 are not fully free? One way to understand this the language of **first- and second-order desires**: a *first-order desire* is, simply, a direct want, like the desire for heroin or the desire to go shopping. A *second-order desire* is a desire about what kind of desires you want to have. We might say that the addict has a second-order desire to be rid of the strong first-order desires he cannot control. In cases of addiction, we might even say that the addict is unfree, because the addiction makes some choices impossible.

Second-order desires are often based on reasons—perhaps it is inappro- 2.8 priate to call them desires at all, since many of them may instead be *judgments*. Some philosophers have argued that we should associate a person's second-order desires with her "true self." On one conception, freedom is acting according to what your true self wants, not according to your momentary impulses.

2.9   If we want to pass laws that will promote people's freedom, we have a dilemma. Do we pass laws that leave people free to choose, even if their choices make them enslaved to addiction? Or do we pass laws that constrain people's choices, so that they reflect these people's "true selves" instead of their addictive desires? Does legislation increase freedom when it protects people from their own bad choices or when it removes the barriers that prevent people from doing as they wish?

2.10   We might imagine what would happen if the government tried to regulate behavior in order to ensure that people act on the second-order desires of their "true selves." Whenever people seem to be acting on motives they might prefer not to have, legislators constrain their behavior, so as to ensure that they don't do what they want to do (first-order desires) but are instead compelled to do what they *should* want to do (second-order desires). Would the result be a free society? If people can be legally constrained whenever the majority thinks they are acting on inappropriate desires, they might come to be constrained quite a lot.

Subjective and objective freedom

2.11   Do people who are free *know* that they are free? Or can we be unfree, but still believe that we are free? The view that people who believe themselves to be free can't be wrong about this is sometimes called

> THE SUBJECTIVE CONCEPT OF FREEDOM: A person is free if she believes herself to be free.

This view sets aside questions of free will, as well as the question whether I can unknowingly be enslaved to my own desires. A person in the grip of an uncontrollable addiction may be free in the subjective sense. The German poet Goethe did not agree. Goethe is quoted as having said, in Book 2, chapter 3 of *Elective Affinities*: "No one is more enslaved than those who falsely believe themselves to be free" (*Niemand ist mehr Sklave, als der sich für frei hält, ohne es zu sein*). On Goethe's view, we can't always *know* when we are free. Worse yet, we are at risk of being in the deepest kind of slavery only when we *believe falsely that we are free*.

2.12   How can you be enslaved without your knowledge? Try a sci-fi example first:

> Suppose an evil (but brilliant) neuroscientist attaches a device to your brain that allows him to control your desires. When he presses one button, you experience a strong desire to eat burritos. When he

presses another, you want to go dancing. And when he presses a third, you are possessed by an overpowering desire to study philosophy.

If you are always doing what you want to do, when you want to do it, you may be "free" in the subjective sense. But are you *really* free?

> JUSTIN   No way! If I'm only doing what I'm caused to want to do, then someone else is controlling all my actions. I might feel free, in that case, but I wouldn't be free at all!

To make sense of Justin's response, we need

> THE OBJECTIVE CONCEPT OF FREEDOM: Whether a person is free depends on his situation, not on the way he feels.

We don't need to resort to science fiction to see the sense of an objective conception of freedom. If drug addicts are not fully free, some of them might still claim to be and believe that they are free. Or people might be bamboozled by a powerful dictator or trickster into believing that they are free, even when the circumstances of their lives are tightly controlled. Physical chains constrain people's bodies, but, on Goethe's view, the most violent form of slavery involves chains that bind people's minds.

Marxists might argue that capitalism itself rests on a form of slavery in which the very wealthy substantially control the actions of those who labor for them. The fact that many capitalist laborers think they are free shows, on this account, that they have only subjective freedom, not true freedom. Similarly, some feminist scholars would argue that women who have embraced a patriarchal system think they are free but are not. People who are exploited may not realize it. 2.13

What counts as restraining freedom?

Citizens of North Korea are taught to fear the outside world. They are not allowed to travel, but, because of what they have been taught, many of them might be afraid to travel even if they were at liberty to do so. In order to understand the different ways in which these people are not free, we need to think not only of the physical constraints, but also of the *mental constraints* that keep them where they are. 2.14

Some chains are easier to see than others: the fence around North Korea is a visible, physical barrier that keeps most of them where they are. Such 2.15

physical restraints are the clearest case of a constraint that limits freedom. But people in North Korea who don't want to leave might not regard the physical barrier as an impediment: it doesn't prevent them from doing what they want to do. We might even consider the laws of physics to be a kind of physical constraint: if I want to fly, the laws of physics will usually bring me back to the ground.

2.16   Even when you are not physically constrained, other people's actions can reduce your freedom. One way to do this is through fear. If a bully with a baseball bat threatens to beat you if you try to leave the room, you might reasonably decide to stay inside. We can call this *restraint by threat of violence*. For a threat to work, it needs to be credible and serious. A threat to flick you on the arm with a finger is not the same as a threat to beat or kill you. Perhaps a threat of only minor harm doesn't count as a restraint on freedom at all.

2.17   Even *social pressure* might affect your freedom. Most likely, you are legally allowed to change your religion. But suppose the change would alienate you from your family and friends? What if you were to become a social outcast, because everyone in your community were strongly opposed to the religion you'd be "free" to adopt? Sometimes social pressure can be even more daunting than a physical threat.

2.18   Even our own *needs* may be a constraint that prevents us from doing what we would freely choose. Some people are not free, in an important sense, because they lack the means to do what they would like to do, or because they suffer under crushing debts. In such cases, *financial pressure* might make it impossible for them to pursue the life they would have chosen. Political cartoons often represent debt as a chain and the debtor as a slave. There is a sense in which you are less free if you are poor, or if you are financially dependent on others. If other people can use your dependence as leverage to get you to do what they want you to do, then your choices are not entirely your own.

Freedom and consent

2.19 But what if people have this leverage over you only because of your own choices? You have the right to accept a job, to undertake a debt to someone else, and a right to quit. By signing up for a class, you *gave* the teacher the power to grade your work—a power she would not have unless you had given it. Perhaps constraints that are freely undertaken in this way should not be considered an impediment to freedom. On the *consent view*, we should not regard restrictions as limitations of our liberty if the limitations were freely undertaken.

THE CONSENT VIEW: When people's choices are limited by their own free action, the limitations cannot count as a restriction of their liberty.

If your life and your opportunities are constrained because of the choices you yourself have made, advocates of this view would say that the result is not truly a restriction of your freedom. Others would urge that your freedom really is restricted, but that the restrictions are not unjust *if* they were freely undertaken.

Are there some conditions of life that can't be free, even if people consent 2.20 to them? If slaves were to consent to their slavery, would they become free slaves? People periodically try to sell themselves as **slaves on Ebay**, only to be told that this is against the rules. On the consent view, if a person wants to give up some of her freedoms, she can do so and she is no less free for it. Opponents argue that this is contradictory. If that one free act of entering slavery is effective, then it is irrevocable and for the rest of the person's life she will be unfree. Thus those who take this position would say that limiting the freedom to consent to slavery means more freedom in the long run. According to some philosophers, people can sometimes be oppressed by their own choices.

Republican liberty

Can you be oppressed even if you never experience an unjust limitation of 2.21 your liberty? Suppose the government has the power to throw you in prison for any reason it deems sufficient and you have no way to challenge its decision. Are you free? Some would say that this depends on whether the government actually uses that arbitrary power.

Imagine a benevolent absolute monarch who rules justly even though 2.22 there are no checks on his power. As a citizen in his state, you might feel free, since your liberty to do as you wish is never unjustly constrained. But proponents of what is sometimes called called **republican liberty** would say that the mere threat of being treated arbitrarily without recourse is enough to take away liberty, even if that threat is never carried out.

REPUBLICAN LIBERTY: People are free just in case no one has the power to dominate or unjustly restrict their liberty.

The term "republican" here refers to a tradition in political philosophy, not to any contemporary political party. American Democrats and Republicans might both accept a republican conception of liberty in this sense.

2.23   On the republican conception of liberty, a slave lacks freedom just because there *is* someone who is a master: someone who has the power to constrain. On this view, even a slave who is never given an order is still a slave, and therefore unfree. Advocates of republican liberty argue that arbitrary power degrades your status and puts you in a situation where you may have to flatter the master (or ruler) in order to avoid arbitrary mistreatment.

2.24   Consider debates over **immigration**. Some businesses want to expand the number of people who enter the United States under special work visas—the sort of visas that only admit people who will be working for a particular company. A foreign worker on such a visa has very limited power, since the employer can typically fire the worker at will, and that would result in that worker's deportation. On a republican understanding of freedom, such foreign workers are not truly free because of the subordinate status they have. This is true even if their employer happens to treat them well during their stay, and even if their decision to come and work under such terms was voluntary.

Private freedom and public freedom

2.25 So far we have been talking about freedom in individualistic terms. A person is free if she freely consents to the rules or laws that apply to her, if she is not subjected to arbitrary power, threats, or social pressures, or if she can act according to her true desires. A final perspective on freedom challenges this view and says that freedom is collective: I am free if I have a meaningful opportunity to participate with others in shaping the laws that govern me. People who are denied the right to vote in a democracy are not free. Can a person really be free if she has no say in the governance of the country?

2.26   The main objection to this view is that the majority might decide to restrict a person's choices greatly. If the majority takes away my freedom of religion, am I free just because I got to vote on it? **Benjamin Constant referred** to the right to participate in making public decisions as the "liberty of the ancients" and to the right to particular individual freedoms as the "modern liberty." According to Constant, in ancient Rome people viewed themselves as "free" if they were citizens who had the right to participate in collective public decision making. But they viewed this freedom as entirely compatible with the complete subjection of the individual to the authority of the group. We don't think this way any more, urged Constant: what we mean when we say that people are free is that they have rights against imprisonment and arrest—along with the rights to free expression, free movement, and freedom of association and along with a right to influence and make demands on public institutions.

Negative and positive liberty

In the dialogue that begins this chapter, Sophie and Justin's disagreement reflects yet another ambiguity in the term "freedom." On Sophie's view, your freedom is not impaired unless there is someone actively *forcing* or *coercing* you. Because of this, Sophie says that illness and poverty don't limit freedom, but a law forcing her to purchase health insurance does. Justin is using a different conception of liberty: according to him, your liberty depends in part on what you are able to do. If illness or poverty restrict your choices, then you are less free than you would be if you weren't sick and poor.   2.27

The philosopher Isaiah Berlin would say that Sophie is referring to **negative liberty**—freedom from others' interference. Negative liberty is the kind of liberty you enjoy if other people just *leave you alone*. Justin, on the other hand, sees freedom as **positive liberty**—the freedom to act on a wide range of available choices. In order to enjoy positive liberty, a person may need resources, or help from other people. A person who is poor or sick lacks positive liberty if her condition leaves her with meager alternatives.   2.28

Consider Tom Hanks in the film *Cast Away*, stranded on a remote island in the middle of the ocean. In such a situation his negative liberty would be complete, since there is no one around to prevent him from doing whatever he chooses. But he is still not free, because there are very few things he can do.   2.29

One of the important debates in political philosophy has *focused* on this distinction between negative and positive liberties. Some people (like Sophie) argue that the government should only promote *negative* liberty—freedom from others' interference. They argue that the government oversteps its rightful authority if it tries to ensure that people have the resources they need in order to be able to make choices. Others (like Justin) point out that negative liberty is useless for a person who is poor or disabled. On this view, the government needs to ensure that people who are poor have a way out of poverty; it needs to provide accommodation for people who are not   2.30

able to provide for themselves. The idea that the government should provide basic minimal healthcare for people who need it fits naturally into a conception of freedom as *positive liberty*. But people like Sophie, who believe that only *negative* liberties can be legitimately supported by the government, will not approve of the idea that the government should support healthcare or other basic services.

Paternalism, the Harm Principle, and Moralism

2.31 As we have seen, there are many different theories about what freedom is. In political philosophy, we are interested in how freedom shapes the laws and rules that regulate life and the policies that governments pursue. For that reason, this can't just be a debate where we all agree to disagree. However we organize our legal system, laws will fit better with some understandings of freedom than with others. We therefore need to look at the way different conceptions of freedom shape different laws and policies. In this section we look at three different arguments that help shape contemporary political debates on the topic.

Paternalism

2.32 The first debate is about **paternalism**. Laws are *paternalist* if they limit your freedom in order to prevent you from doing things that aren't good for you … or things someone *else* thinks are not good for you!

> PRINCIPLE OF PATERNALISM: Laws may appropriately limit people's liberties in order to prevent these people from doing things that would be bad for them, even when such things would be harmless to others.

Paternalism interferes with a person's freedom for her or his own good. For example, if the government forces a person to enroll in drug rehabilitation in order to help that person get better, this is an example of paternalism. Normally calling someone "paternalistic" is a criticism. But, historically, that was not always true. The word comes from *pater*, the Latin word for "father," and its derivative, the adjective *paternus*—"fatherly." Being paternalistic means, etymologically, treating someone the way a father would treat a child. Many people today reject the idea that the government should be able to act as if it were a parent. While parents have the right to make many life-shaping decisions on behalf of a minor child, it would be obnoxious for the state to take over this role vis-à-vis adult citizens.

Perhaps some forms of paternalism are easier to justify than others. If a 2.33 person checks herself into a drug rehabilitation program and surrenders the right to leave until the program is completed, the program has a form of paternalistic power. The drug user may later want to leave before the program is completed but the employees may prevent her from doing so, because they believe that being prevented is in her best interests. Perhaps this is easier to justify because the drug user expressly consented to paternalistic treatment. Likewise, some forms of paternalism are "soft" in that they make it more likely for people to choose something beneficial while still allowing them to opt out and make a different choice if they desire. For example, the law might require all employers to enroll all employees in a forced contribution retirement plan but might allow people to opt out if they declare in writing that they do not wish to participate. Since many people go with the default option, this is a way to alter behavior while respecting people's right to make the final decision for themselves.

Now consider an example: a father might require his children to wear 2.34 seatbelts or sit in car seats even if the law did not require it, because he believes it is in their interest. The government might require the father himself to wear a seatbelt for the same reason. The father might object that this is unjust: the children lack the capability to weigh the risks, but he is a mature adult. He might object to governmental paternalism because it interferes with his liberty to choose his own path of life, even if this means that his life may turn out worse. Opposition to paternalism is one of the characteristics of liberalism and **libertarianism**. Libertarians and liberals both emphasize that people have the right to live their lives as they please, so long as they do not harm others (though they disagree about what counts as "harm").

If we think the father's argument about seatbelts is persuasive, we should 2.35 note that it applies to many other circumstances, where the government uses a logic similar to his logic on seatbelts. Social security forces people to save at least a minimal amount for retirement. The underlying assumption is that many people wouldn't save enough on their own. Some libertarians argue that they should be able to opt out of social security, invest money for themselves, and live with the consequences. In a similar vein, the US Food and Drug Administration (FDA) tests drugs before they can be sold, even to people who have a doctor's prescription. But some libertarians argue that they should be able to research medications for themselves and to take them if they think that the benefits outweigh the risk. The FDA could still make recommendations, but the final decision about whether to take a proposed medicine would be with the individual. Is it appropriate for the government to step in to require prescriptions for potentially harmful drugs, or to prevent people from making bad decisions about retirement savings? Or are these policies an inappropriate restriction of individual liberty? The same questions arise in the debate over whether the government can rightfully require people to have health insurance.

The harm principle

2.36 How far should we go with this logic? One popular answer is what is called the *harm principle*. This is our second major topic in this section. The harm principle is often linked to the philosopher **John Stuart Mill**, who wrote in *On Liberty*: "The only purpose for which power can be rightfully exercised over any member of a civilized community, against his will, is to prevent harm to others" (Mill, 1978 [1859], p. 9). This principle is a centerpiece of some theories of political liberty.

> HARM PRINCIPLE: The only legitimate reason for limiting a person's freedom is to prevent harm to others.

Mill denies that it is legitimate for the government to take away your freedom in order to keep you from harming yourself. He would probably oppose seatbelt and prescription drug laws for that reason. The **legalization of marijuana** is often justified by claiming that responsible use does not harm anyone. In fact some claim that criminalizing marijuana actually creates more harm than it prevents, which is another way to run afoul of the harm principle (failing to actually prevent harm). On the other hand, the government may restrict freedom if our freedom would harm other people. The word "may" is important, because there might be some instances where an action that harms others should not be prohibited. For many students of political philosophy, this principle will seem an obvious solution to the problem of how much liberty we should have.

2.37   The problem with this principle is that, while it is easy to state in generalities, when we start actually trying to apply it, it becomes complicated and contentious. First, what counts as harm? Suppose that I make fun of your political views in front of many people and the result is that you are humiliated. Have I harmed you? It depends in part on whether we accept a subjective or objective understanding of harm. On the *subjective view of harm*, you are harmed if you think you are harmed. If you think you are worse off, we assume that you know better than anyone else. The great strength of this position is that it keeps us from having to pass judgment as to who is right and who is wrong about what counts as a harm. Each person can be the judge for him or herself. The problem with the subjective view is that it would greatly restrict liberty to prevent people from doing things that impose subjective harm on others. Some people are *very* sensitive and easily offended. Jay might feel harmed by Kay's annoying habits, but it would be inappropriate to restrict Kay just because Jay is sensitive. In addition, the subjective view of harm leads to inconsistencies: Jay might regard Kay's outspoken political activism as a harm, but Kay might find Jay's puritanical and censorious attitude harmful. It would be an excessive restriction of liberty to restrain actors every time other people are offended or claim to be harmed. The political speech, the religious speech, and the artistic speech that need to be protected most are precisely those that some people are likely to find hurtful or offensive.

2.38   That concern was certainly on the minds of the framers of the US constitution when they put in place provisions to prevent the majority from restricting the liberties of minority groups and to protect freedom of conscience for people with different religious convictions. It was on Thomas Jefferson's mind as well when he wrote, in Query 17 of his **Notes on the State of Virginia** (Jefferson, 2008 [1782]): "The legitimate powers of government extend to such acts only as are injurious to others. But it does me no injury for my neighbor to say there are twenty gods, or no god. It neither picks my pocket nor breaks my leg." Here Jefferson, like Mill, affirms the harm principle and denies that the subjective view of harm is correct. On Jefferson's view, a person who claims to be harmed by someone else's religious beliefs is simply wrong.

2.39   Another way to address the problem of harm is to say that people are not harmed if they consent to what happens to them. A boxer may not view being punched in the face as a harm, just as part of a job he consented to take on. Even some seriously harmful actions might not be "harms" that justify the limitation of liberties, if the person who is disadvantaged has given consent. But we might ask whether there are harms to which we *cannot* rightfully consent. Can a person consent to being killed or maimed? Different theorists disagree about this question.

2.40   On the *objective view of harm*, some things are harmful whether they are regarded as harms or not. While one might decide that "merely being offended" is not a harm because one has no right to live life without being offended, an objectivist might urge that it is always harmful for a person to be treated with disrespect, even if that person is unconcerned about others' disrespectful treatment. The advantage of this view is that we may be able to define harm in a way that better protects freedom. The disadvantage is that we may find ourselves right back in the same thicket of problems we started with: people may disagree about which things are objectively harmful.

2.41   A second distinction has to do with intentions. Sometimes we classify an act as right or wrong on the basis of whether a person *intended harm*, and hence the harm was *intentional*, or whether it was an *accidental harm*. Smokers rarely intend to harm others, but second-hand smoke can nonetheless cause harm to nonconsenting third parties. A person who accidentally caused harm but has not been reckless or negligent may be legally responsible for compensating those who have been harmed. But such a person will not be punished as a criminal. On the other hand, we are sometimes responsible for unintentional harms, if we should have taken steps to protect other people from the unintended results of our choices yet failed to do so. Thus a driver whose brakes fail does not intend the harm that may result; but if he was responsible for keeping his brakes in working order, then he is responsible for the unintentional harm he caused when he failed to do this.

2.42   Sometimes people who *intend* to harm others may wind up benefiting them instead. Suppose Alice wants to harm Beth and releases embarrassing video footage. Beth might not care about the release of the video, except that it later goes viral, making her a famous celebrity—a life she enjoys. Beth might look back on the release of the video as a benefit. The fact that Beth liked how the story ended doesn't really change our view of Alice: she intended harm. But we might not think that Alice's wrongful action should be classified as a harm.

2.43   A third distinction is between *direct harms* and *indirect harms*. In principle the distinction seems clear: if George hits Jim, he directly harms Jim. On the other hand, if George hits Jim and Jim's injury causes him to be unable to provide for his children, the children are harmed indirectly. In practice this distinction is difficult to apply. Suppose the whole reason why George hit Jim was that he wanted to harm Jim's children. The fact that the action is indirect doesn't seem terribly important for determining whether George's action harms the children. The intention is to harm in either case, and the fact that the harm is indirect doesn't necessarily mean that it is any less likely to happen. As we saw in the previous case, attempts at direct harm sometimes fail. If the intention to harm is the same and the probability that the action would result in harm is the same, it is not obvious why the difference between direct and indirect harm should matter very much.

The reason why the direct harm–indirect harm distinction is popular is 2.44 that it is normally used to make a narrower point related to intention. Remember the law proposed in New York City in 2013, which would have outlawed **extra-large fountain drinks** because legislators urged that it's not good for people to drink so much sugary soda? Some people objected to the law as paternalistic. The government responded that, while the law will improve the health of people who will drink less soda, the policy is not paternalistic because it also prevents harm to others. People will be healthier if they drink less soda, which will avoid lost productivity due to poor health. Lost productivity would make *others* worse off. If unhealthy soda guzzlers consume healthcare supported by taxes, they impose costs (harms?) on those who pay the taxes! Almost everything we do affects other people indirectly in some way, and so people who claim that indirect harms do not justify restricting liberty often just mean that we shouldn't use indirect harms to justify policies that are primarily paternalistic in their goals.

Suppose Carrie refuses to carry liability insurance and then causes an accident that leads to Donald's being hospitalized. If Carrie has no money or other assets to pay for Donald's bills, Donald might claim that Carrie's refusal to carry liability insurance harmed him. In this case, the primary purpose of the law is not Carrie's well-being. Rather it is Donald's well-being. It might indirectly help Carrie too. If she had $20,000 in assets and Donald has $100,000 in medical bills, the insurance the government forced her to purchase will protect much of her wealth.

Thus, again, our judgment turns in part on what is taken to be the primary intent of the legislation.

Different people have different views on harm. Is Prude harmed by the 2.45 fact that racy books are available in the local bookstore? Is Lewd harmed if these books are not available for purchase? As we have seen, subjective conceptions of harm immediately give rise to contradictions. For this reason, philosophers who have developed and defended versions of the harm principle do not leave the question of whether one has been harmed to the subjective judgment of people who believe themselves to be victims. According to Joel Feinberg, to show that Lewd harmed Prude, it is *at least* necessary to show (1) that some action of Lewd set back prude's interests; and (2) that Lewd's action violated Prude's rights.

2.46   If Prude's rights are not violated when Lewd has access to racy books, then the harm principle, on Feinberg's interpretation, will not support censorship. But to fill this view out, we need a theory of rights, and we need to be able to judge which "setbacks of interests" violate others' rights. And, one might ask, if we have good reason to believe that some actions are objectively wrong, even though they don't cause harm, shouldn't we prohibit those actions *just because they are wrong*?

Moralism

2.47 Some people argue that all wrong actions are harmful to others in some way. But can behavior that is immoral count as a harm, even if it is not possible to show that any specific person is worse off? Consider government regulation of pornography: some people try to justify these regulations by showing that pornography causes direct or indirect harms. One claim is that many of the people who work in the pornography industry are exploited, a direct harm. Another claim is that watching pornography increases the probability of violence against women, an indirect harm. But there is a third type of objection, which claims that viewing other people as mere objects of sexual fantasy is morally wrong in and of itself, even when no one is harmed by it. Some forms of pornography highlight domination and humiliation of other people. One might argue that such pornography encourages us to view people as mere objects and thus is intrinsically demeaning. Even if there is no harm to any particular person, it is morally wrong to do things that will lead you to objectify and dehumanize other human beings. When people's liberty is constrained for the sake of preventing people from doing things that are morally wrong even though these things do not cause harm to anyone, this is called *moralism*. Moralism, like paternalism, is normally a term of criticism. But, like paternalism, it may be difficult to dismiss when we look at the position more closely.

> PRINCIPLE OF MORALISM: It is legitimate to limit people's liberty in order to prevent them from doing things that are morally wrong, even when their actions are harmless.

Are there any harmless immoralities? Some people argue that the only thing that makes an action morally wrong is its propensity to cause harm. Can you think of any actions that are immoral even though they cause no harm? (For example, is it wrong to say mean things about other people behind their backs, as long as they never find out about it?) Some critics of moralism argue that the principle itself is morally wrong: they hold that it is wrong to force other people to conform to moral values they do not accept, unless it is necessary to do so in order to prevent harm.

2.48 Many states impose moralistic restrictions. There was a time when interracial marriage—miscegenation—was prohibited by law in many US states. Racist legislators, who regarded miscegenation to be immoral, passed laws that imposed their conception of morality on everyone, whether others accepted the same principles or not.

2.49 Moralistic laws often impose restrictions on sex and sexuality: until recently, the state of Georgia had laws that prohibited oral and anal intercourse, whether performed by gay or straight couples. Some US states used to prohibit gay marriage because some legislators regarded homosexuality to be morally wrong.

2.50 These laws exemplify one of the main objections people raise against moralistic legislation: in a pluralistic society, different people have different moral views. If we were to accept the principle of moralism, which morality should we enforce? But while some of our moral values are parochial, there is a sense in which harm is universal: when people suffer objective harm, they are disadvantaged. This disadvantage does not depend on their convictions—harm is a disadvantage to *everyone*. So, when we protect people from such harms, we are not adhering to the morality of one group or another, but protecting everyone from what we all recognize to be disadvantage. One principle underlying this thought might be the plural values principle.

> PLURAL VALUES PRINCIPLE: In a society that protects freedom of conscience and whose citizens do not all share the same moral values, it is oppressive and unjust for some people to use the force of law to impose their parochial moral values on other people, whose values are different.

While this view is popular right now, a critic might question the use of the word "parochial." Many people think that their moral values are *true* and that they only appear "parochial" insofar as other people are wrong about what morality requires. When we say that someone's values are "parochial," is this just a way of saying that their values are different from our own? Suppose I regard my own moral values to be universal, not parochial: can I impose them on other people *then*?

Can (and should) we avoid moralism?

2.51 To oppose moralism does not mean that we should try to eliminate *all* moral values from law and policy. The harm principle itself promotes moral values, since it claims that harming others is morally wrong. Does the harm principle also run afoul of the plural values principle? After all, not everyone agrees that the harm principle should set the boundaries for political liberty. People who support the harm principle generally claim that there are good moral arguments to support it and that those arguments justify enacting laws that will bind even those who disagree with it. The question of the sorts of goals that the government can pursue is itself a controversial one, where people bring moral arguments to bear on both sides.

2.52 Freedom is an important value, but it is not the only value. In order to defend the harm principle, one has to show that the value of freedom and the other values that freedom might promote (we might think that freedom increases happiness, for example) have a different status from other values, such as cultivating virtue or the importance of majority rule. In fact the harm principle normally requires the cultivation of virtues—such as toleration—that prevent us from interfering with other people even when we disapprove of what they are doing.

2.53 Second, we have already noted that it is not easy to decide what counts as a harm. Objective theories of harm say that some interests should be protected from interference whereas others need not be. But to say this is to make a moral judgment.

> Suppose Ed likes living in a society where people dress modestly and where the law prevents public nudity; he likes it because he thinks public nudity is morally wrong. The law is then changed to allow public nudity on the grounds that people should be able to dress—or not—as they please. Those who support the new rule say that how a person dresses or doesn't dress does not harm other people. Ed thinks that he is harmed when he sees people walking about town naked. Is he wrong? We might accuse him of moralism: he is imposing his moral views about public nudity on other people. He has no right to dictate how other people must dress, even if some ways they might dress could offend him. As long as other people don't harm him, he must let them do as they choose.

The same reasons why freedom, as we often say, protects offensive speech might also be used to protect the right to go naked in public.

Some liberal theories include a special category of things that are *offensive* 2.54
and argue that offense is not a harm. We find some things offensive because
we believe they are morally wrong, but we may find other things offensive
without making a moral claim. Some people may think that there is nothing
morally wrong with public nudity, but that it is still offensive. They might
feel similarly about extreme body odor. They might describe their negative
reaction as visceral rather than moral. Even some liberals, such as Joel
Feinberg, admit that offense is sometimes a sufficient reason to limit
liberty.

Interestingly, most societies that have strong protections for freedom of 2.55
speech still have laws (moralistic laws?) against public nudity. The law often
defends a person's right to criticize, or in some cases even burn, the sacred
scriptures of another religion as well as the right to say false things about
members of the opposing political party while denying the right to public
nudity, even though the former actions might seem to cause an even greater
harm to those offended. One explanation is that what is really going on in
these cases is an implicit value judgment is being made about the importance of particular forms of expression. Because religious and political
expression are particularly valuable, the threshold for limiting them is very
high. Because public nudity does not seem to be as valuable a form of
expression, it is more easily regulated. If that is true, however, then all of us,
not just the "moralist," are making laws on the basis of judgments about the
relative value of different sorts of activities.

Suppose someone has lived in, and deeply values living in, a society 2.56
where certain moral norms govern behavior and where the law helps support those norms. If, in the name of liberty, the law is changed so as to allow
people to act differently, the person who valued the old way of life might
well perceive this as a harm. Suppose he is told about the new law: "It is not
a harm just because you are not able to live in the sort of society you would
like!" It is not at all clear that this argument follows from anything intrinsic
to the word "harm." Perhaps it expresses, instead, a commitment to the
value of freedom.

Conclusion

Most people agree that freedom is a key political value. Many people 2.57
regarded it to be the most important value of all. In this chapter we have
seen that freedom is complicated: different people have different views

about what "freedom" means, and there are cases where people's different conceptions of freedom come into conflict. Part of the attraction of freedom is that it appears to require tolerance and to prevent people from imposing their moral values on others. But, when people invoke different views about freedom, this usually involves reference to deep moral values, about which people disagree. And what should we do when the goal of freedom conflicts with other important political values, like democracy or equality?

References and Further Reading

Berlin, Isaiah. 1969. "Two Concepts of Liberty." In Isaiah Berlin, *Four Essays on Liberty*. Oxford: Oxford University Press, pp. 118–172. Berlin's essay developed the idea of positive and negative liberty and applied that distinction to philosophers from previous centuries.

Constant, Benjamin. 1819. "The Liberty of the Ancients Compared with that of the Moderns." Early Modern Texts. http://www.earlymoderntexts.com/assets/pdfs/constant1819.pdf (accessed February 12, 2016). Constant contrasts the ancient liberty to participate in governing one's political community with the modern liberty of being able to live one's life as one wishes without interference from the public.

Cudd, Ann. 1994. "Oppression by Choice." *Journal of Social Philosophy*, 25: 22–44. Cudd argues that we can be oppressed by our own choices.

Feinberg, Joel. 1984–1988. *The Moral Limits of the Criminal Law*. Oxford: Oxford University Press. Feinberg's four-volume set is the most thorough reworking of Mill's basic idea in contemporary philosophy and political and legal theory. His books explore harm, offense, paternalism, and moralism in great detail.

George, Robert. 1993. *Making Men Moral*. Oxford: Clarendon Press. This book is a defense of moralism in politics and law.

Hobbes, Thomas. 1994. *Leviathan*. New York: Hackett. Hobbes develops here a political philosophy in which liberty is primarily the absence of constraint. Originally published in English in 1651, then in a revised Latin translation in 1668, this is one of the most important books in the history of political philosophy; it repays the effort to read Hobbes's seventeenth-century prose. Part II is of special importance for politics.

Jefferson, Thomas. 2008 [1782]. *Notes on the State of Virginia*. New Haven, CT: Lillian Goldman Goldman Law Library, Yale Law School. http://avalon.law.yale.edu/18th_century/jeffvir.asp (accessed February 12, 2016). Jefferson's remarks included an early statement of one variant of the harm principle.

Kateb, George. 1989. "The Freedom of Worthless and Harmful Speech." In *Liberalism without Illusions: Essays on Liberal Theory and the Political Vision of Judith N. Shklar*, edited by Bernard Yack. Chicago: University of Chicago

Press, pp. 220–240. Kateb polemically argues that religious speech is frequently worthless or harmful yet nonetheless worthy of protection and that other forms of worthless and harmful speech should be protected as well.

MacCallum, Gerald C., Jr. 1967. "Negative and Positive Freedom." *The Philosophical Review*, 76(3): 312–334. MacCallum argues that there are *three* dimensions of liberty, not two, as Berlin had claimed.

Mill, John Stuart. 1978 [1859]. *On Liberty*. Indianapolis: Hackett. Mill's classic work ***On Liberty*** argues for the harm principle. Mills wants to abolish paternalistic laws and also paternalistic social pressure.

Smith, Steven D. 2010. *The Disenchantment of Secular Discourse*. Cambridge, MA: Harvard University Press. In chapter 3 ("Trafficking in Harm") of this book, Smith criticizes Mill and Feinberg, arguing that that our definitions of harm involve contested moral judgments.

Waldron, Jeremy. 2012. *The Harm in Hate Speech*. Cambridge, MA: Harvard University Press. Waldron argues that restrictions on hate speech are justifiable.

Online Resources

1   http://www.nytimes.com/1998/04/12/nyregion/heroin-in-your-backyard. html?pagewanted=all&src=pm
2   http://www.vice.com/read/legalize-heroin
3   http://plato.stanford.edu/entries/desire/
4   http://www.ndtv.com/world-news/man-puts-himself-up-for-sale-on- ebay-489607
5   http://plato.stanford.edu/entries/republicanism/
6   http://plato.stanford.edu/entries/immigration/
7   http://www.uark.edu/depts/comminfo/cambridge/ancients.html
8   http://www.earlymoderntexts.com/assets/pdfs/constant1819.pdf
9   http://plato.stanford.edu/entries/liberty-positive-negative/
10 http://plato.stanford.edu/entries/liberty-positive-negative/
11 http://plato.stanford.edu/entries/paternalism/
12 http://plato.stanford.edu/entries/libertarianism/
13 http://plato.stanford.edu/entries/mill/
14 http://www.constitution.org/jsm/liberty.htm
15 http://www.cnn.com/2013/12/28/us/10-things-colorado-recreational- marijuana/
16 http://avalon.law.yale.edu/18th_century/jeffvir.asp
17 http://www.nytimes.com/2013/03/12/nyregion/judge-invalidates-bloomb ergs-soda-ban.html?pagewanted=all&_r=1

3

EQUALITY

JUSTIN Hey Sophie! I got a job!

SOPHIE Great, where are you working?

JUSTIN It's just sorting files in the admissions office—not much. But hey, it means I've got a little extra cash!

SOPHIE The admissions office, eh? So you get to see who is applying to study here?

JUSTIN I do.

SOPHIE You know, I think the admission standards we use at this university are just wrong. They're unjust!

JUSTIN Wow, you feel strongly about this! What's so wrong?

SOPHIE It's the policy of preference for people who fit into some arbitrary minority category, regardless of their need. If the university bases admissions on the color of a candidate's skin, it's just racism!

JUSTIN Now wait a minute here…

SOPHIE No way: if equally qualified candidates apply for admission, it's simply discrimination to admit one and reject the other just because one of them is black, or because one of them is a woman. These are arbitrary and irrelevant characteristics! We shouldn't treat people differently because of arbitrary differences like race or gender! People should be treated as *equals*.

This Is Political Philosophy: An Introduction, First Edition. Alex Tuckness and Clark Wolf.
© 2017 John Wiley & Sons, Inc. Published 2017 by John Wiley & Sons, Inc.

JUSTIN   Look, the *world* treats people differently because of race and gender. The policy of affirmative action favors people who face barriers in other areas of life. It creates equal treatment, it doesn't undermine it.

SOPHIE   Maybe those policies were justified in the 1950s and 1960s, when people were really treated horribly. But we've moved beyond those times! Discrimination is a thing of the past now.

JUSTIN   Are you telling me that you think racism and discrimination are *over*? There's so much evidence proving that you're wrong, I can't even begin.

SOPHIE   No, I don't think racism is a thing of the past. I think we have racist policies *now*, and I think the policy of the university admissions office is a great example: the school policy uses the color of a person's skin—something no one has any control over—to determine whether to accept or reject that person. It's just unfair. And you! You're helping to promote these twisted values! I hope you're proud of yourself!

JUSTIN   I *am* proud of myself, and I think you completely misunderstand the policy and its function. We haven't yet eliminated the older forms of racial discrimination: it's *still* a significant disadvantage to be black in this country. There is still discrimination against people who are disabled, and against women. And it's a good thing—it's only fair and just—that we make an effort to compensate for those disadvantages and to give people an equal chance. If we didn't have these policies, the people who discriminate would get the last word, and people's opportunities would be unfair and unequal.

Introduction

In the Declaration of Independence, Thomas Jefferson wrote: "We hold these truths to be self-evident that all men are created equal." But what does it mean to say that people are equal? In obvious ways, people are very different from one another—physically unequal in strength, speed, and height; mentally different in their interests and talents and acquired abilities. Perhaps the words express an *ideal* of equality, then: people *should* be equal. But what would we need to do to make unequal people equal? If one person 3.1

has less ability than another in some area, one way to "make them equal" would be to raise up the person with less. Perhaps this could be done through training and education, or through other kinds of help. But another way to make people equal would be to pull back or hold down the person who is *more* able. In the short story "Harrison Bergeron," Kurt Vonnegut describes a world where people who are more able or talented have to wear handicaps designed to bring them down to the level of everyone else. This can't be what the framers of the Declaration of Independence had in mind! But what *did* they have in mind? Many people are concerned about the extent of inequality in the United States and in the world. Does concern about inequality commit them to the view that everyone should be made equal, even if this means constraining people who are talented, so as to make sure that they don't have advantages that other people lack?

How Unequal Are People in the United States?

3.2   Let's start close to home: how much inequality is there in the United States? In the world? The simplest way to compare people is in terms of their wealth. We might begin by considering how unequal we are, and how unequal (if unequal at all) we would like to be.

3.3   One way to get an idea how wealth is distributed in a society is to consider what proportion of the total wealth belongs to different sectors of society: how much is held by the top 20 percent? How much by the next richest 20 percent? And so on. If the distribution of wealth were exactly equal, then each group would have the same amount. Obviously the United States' population isn't equal in this sense—we have wealthier and poorer people. Take a moment to consider how unequal *you believe* the United States population is: in Table 3.1, on the line at the left, write in your estimate

Table 3.1   Percentage of the total wealth owned by US citizens.

How unequal do you believe we are?		Ideally, how unequal (if at all) should we be?
_____%	Richest 20%	_____%
_____%	Second richest 20%	_____%
_____%	Middle 20%	_____%
_____%	Second poorest 20%	_____%
_____%	Poorest 20%	_____%

of the percentage of total wealth owned by each of the groups listed. For example, if you think that the middle 20 percent of the population holds 20 percent of the total wealth owned by US citizens, you should write that number in the box on the left.

Now, on the line to the right, write numbers that represent the distribu- 3.4 tion you would favor, other things being equal, if you didn't know which position you occupied: would a more equal distribution of wealth be better, if it could be accomplished without violating people's rights? Is there some distribution of wealth that would be best of all? One we would achieve if we lived in an ideal society? Perhaps the ideal distribution would not be an equal distribution: inequalities provide incentives, after all, and different people spend their time differently. For example, maybe it's a good thing that people earn more if they're willing to spend years of study to become a surgeon or an engineer. You might think about different things that might justify and explain why even a good society would include an unequal distribution.

Remember, this chart contains only your *perception* of existing US inequality 3.5 and your view, before reading this chapter, of what the ideal might be. We will come back to these considerations later in the chapter.

Against Equality: A Politics of Procrustes?

Political ideals that recommend human equality are called "egalitarian." 3.6 In Greek mythology, there is a famous egalitarian: **Procrustes**, we are told, was a giant who lived at a crossroads. When travelers passed by, Procrustes made them lie in a special bed he maintained just for his guests. But instead of letting people rest in his bed, he measured them against it. If people were longer than the bed, he cut off pieces of them until they were the right size. If they were shorter than the bed, he would stretch them to make them longer. Whether they needed to be cut or stretched, when Procrustes was done with them people were *equal.*

Some critics of equality as a political ideal worry that egalitarian ideals 3.7 are a Procrustean bed (Flew, 1981). We might imagine a conception of equality that would consider pluralism and human difference to be something that should be eliminated, so that people would be more equal. We could enforce equality by forcing people to be the same: wear the same clothes, live in similar houses, work similar jobs, and be paid the same wages. But when we think of equality in this way it hardly looks like an ideal: this kind of enforced equality is the stuff of nightmare dystopian fiction, not a political ideal to celebrate.

3.8   Others have criticized equality as an empty ideal: we can treat people equally, but still treat them all *badly*. The American comedian W. C. Fields is reported to have said that he was free of all prejudices because he hated everyone equally. It hardly seems ideal to treat people equally by treating them all badly, or by working to ensure that everyone is equally poor or equally miserable, or to ensure that all are suffering equal agony and distress.

3.9   Yet other critics point out that restrictions can apply equally to everyone, but still be cruelly unequal in their effects. The French novelist **Anatole France** has this in mind when he notes, with bitter irony, that "the majestic equality of laws prohibits the wealthy as well as the poor from begging in the streets, and from stealing bread" (France, 1894, Chapter 7). He has a point: a law forbidding people to sleep under bridges (or in public parks) imposes no disadvantage at all on people who have a home and a bed. But enforcing such a law may severely disadvantage homeless people who have no other place to sleep. Laws that apply "equally" to everyone may not be equal in their effects.

3.10   Another concern is that equality and liberty may be at odds with each other: suppose we value liberty and we do what we can to make sure that people in our society are free. Then different people will be free to pursue different goals and will shape their lives around different ideals. Suppose these people start out equally well-off and are left free to shape their lives as they wish. Some of them might spend their time pursuing education or doing research, or building houses or roads, or building a business. Others might spend as much time as possible in leisure—perhaps they work just enough to meet their basic needs, then spend the rest of their time surfing, or mountain climbing, or playing the guitar. After a while, different people who pursued different goals will be in different circumstances: people who worked to build a business, or who saved resources, or who developed special, valuable talents and abilities may be wealthier than those who spent all their free time surfing. But now they are unequal. By pursuing different goals, they have altered the equality they had at the start. Would it be appropriate to readjust everyone's holdings so that they can be equal again?

3.11   It seems reasonable to respond that to do this would be terribly *unfair*. If the people who are wealthier *worked* for what they have—earned it—and the other people chose not to do this, then justice isn't served by transferring goods from those who have to those who don't. In fact the surfers—people with less wealth—might not really be "worse off" than the wealthy entrepreneurs. They chose the thrill of the perfect wave over the thrill of a big bank account. Who are we to tell them that their choice was a bad one?

Any admirable egalitarian ideal would need to respond to these impor- 3.12 tant objections: if egalitarianism is a politics of Procrustes requiring that everyone fit the same cookie-cutter mold, then it is not a desirable ideal. And if equality can be achieved only if we sacrifice liberty, perhaps we should leave it in the box: it's just too expensive.

Unequal Treatment and Discrimination

On the other hand, some kinds of inequality are outrageous and unjust. 3.13 It's one thing to say that people who *start out equal* may get different things as they make different choices. But what about people who *start out unequal?* Is it a problem if some American children are able to get the best education and to attend excellent schools, while others attend schools that are dangerous, filthy, and education-free? Maybe the surfer in the example above made her own choices and must live with them. But it's not a child's fault if the circumstances of her life simply offer inadequate opportunities, and it's unfair if her life prospects are diminished because of something that is so entirely beyond her control. Some inequalities are just unfair.

One of the most pernicious forms of inequality is racial discrimination. 3.14 In 1955 in Montgomery, Alabama, black passengers were expected to sit in the back of the bus, leaving the more desirable front seats for Montgomery's white citizens. Black and white children attended different schools, and schools for black children were terribly inadequate. When they went to the polls to vote, African Americans were asked to prove their education by taking a "literacy test," while white voters didn't have to take a test. Here are some examples of the questions black voters were asked to answer. They are taken from **a literacy test given in Louisiana in the 1960s** (Box 3.1):

Box 3.1   Could you pass Louisiana's "literacy test" and vote?

Question 15: In the space below, write the word "noise" backwards and place a dot over what would be its second letter should it have been written forward.

Question 23: Draw a figure that is square in shape. Divide it in half by drawing a straight line from its northeast corner to its southwest corner, and then divide it once more by drawing a broken line from the middle of its western side to the middle of its eastern side.

Question 28: Divide a vertical line in two equal parts by bisecting it with a curved horizontal line that is only straight at its spot bisection of the vertical.

Question 29: Write every other word in this first line and print every third word in same line (original type smaller and first line ended at comma), but capitalize the fifth word that you write.

These questions weren't intended to *test* voters; they were intended to humiliate people and to provide a pretext to prevent them from voting. The humiliation and rage caused by this horrible treatment give us one reason to regard these tests as evil. But, even aside from that, the main purpose of these tests was to give white people in Louisiana an opportunity to express their disrespect for black voters and to prevent the latter from exercising their equal right to vote. They were an expression of the racist idea that black Americans weren't as good as white Americans. They provided a way to enforce social inequalities that would already have been frustratingly obvious to every black citizen in the state.

3.15   This kind of discrimination is a *paradigm* of unjust inequality. Perhaps the phrase "all men are created equal" should mean that discrimination of this kind is wrong: people have a right to equal treatment, and should not suffer disadvantages because of characteristics of themselves that don't matter and are beyond their control.

3.16   The idea that it is wrong to treat people differently unless they are different in some relevant way has a long history: more than two thousand years ago, in **Book 5** of Plato's *Republic*—where Socrates and his interlocutors are drawing an ideal or hypothetical city—Socrates proposed that men and women who are equally capable should receive the same education and training and the same public benefits and respect. He argues that the physical differences between women and men are irrelevant and do not justify treating them differently. Plato's Socrates compares the differences between men and women with the differences between bald men and hairy men. It would be silly, he writes, to treat men differently because they have different haircuts. For the same reason, it is silly to treat people differently because they are different genders. In an ideal city, he says, people would be treated the same way, unless there were some relevant respect in which they were different.

Which differences are relevant? It is easy to think of contexts where it seems 3.17 *right* to treat people differently. If one person gets the answers right on a math test while another person doesn't, they should not get the same grade. Whether one got the answers right is a relevant difference, so "discrimination" on this basis is not wrong. But if people receive different grades because of the color of their skin, because of their gender, or because of some other *irrelevant* characteristic, then they have a legitimate complaint. One way to make sense of this is to say that differences between people are irrelevant unless there are good reasons to regard them as relevant. If we think of discrimination in this way, we can make judgments about individual cases by considering whether people's reasons for treating people differently are good reasons.

Equality as a Baseline?

This idea that people should be equal unless there is some reason that justifies 3.18 and explains why they should be unequal can be generalized into a principle. **Aristotle** proposed something like this—what we may call a "principle of proportional equality":

> ARISTOTLE'S PRINCIPLE OF PROPORTIONAL EQUALITY: Treat equals equally, and treat unequals unequally.

According to Aristotle, equality is inappropriate when people are differently deserving. But this principle is quite abstract and formal. Before we can use it, we need some account of which inequalities justify unequal treatment. An even more general principle might look like this:

> FORMAL PRINCIPLE OF EQUALITY: People should be treated as equals unless there are good reasons justifying unequal treatment.

Aristotle believed that it is wrong to treat people the same when one of them is more deserving than the other. So he regards this difference in deservingness as a good reason to justify different treatment. But we shouldn't assume from the start that it is the *only* reason.

Like Aristotle's principle, the formal principle of equality takes equal treat- 3.19 ment as a *baseline* distribution. It's like the default setting on a computer: unless you take a step to change the default setting, the default is what you get. In the same way, under the formal principle of equality, unless you take a step to justify treating people unequally, equality is what you get.

3.20   This principle is *merely* formal, since it doesn't specify which reasons are good reasons, or what differences between people count as inequalities. We have already seen some bad reasons in the sections above: it's not appropriate to treat people differently merely because of race or gender. To find other reasons that might justify unequal treatment, we may consider some more substantive—that is, not merely formal—principles of equality.

Equality of Resources and Luck Egalitarianism

3.21 One widely discussed egalitarian theory recommends that people should have equal resources. What they do with their resources is up to them, but if everyone starts with the same basic set of stuff, maybe the inequalities that arise over time aren't a problem.

> RESOURCE EGALITARIANISM: Everyone should start with the same share of resources.

It's easy to see why this principle might seem appropriate: it is one version of "starting-gate equality." Just as a race is *fair* if all the runners start at the same place, life is fair if everyone starts with the same basket of resources. Consider what egalitarianism implies in different circumstances.

First objection: Disabilities

3.22 First, consider what this view implies for people who, through no fault of their own, suffer a disability of one kind or another. Even if they start with equal resources, these people will need to use their resources to meet basic needs, while others will be able to use them for whatever they might want. We might argue: it's not the *fault* of people who are disabled that they have special needs, and it's wrong if people are worse off than others *through no fault of their own*. Since possession of a disability isn't a good reason for the inequalities that *follow* from an initially equal distribution of resources, it follows that equality of resources is not an appropriate conception of political equality.

3.23   Is this argument persuasive? Notice that the argument relies on an additional principle, which is sometimes called the principle of *luck egalitarianism*:

> LUCK EGALITARIANISM: It's wrong if some people are worse off than others because of something that is not their fault or because of something for which they are not responsible.

The central idea behind luck egalitarianism is that differences in people's situation should not be the result of simple bad luck. It's not *fair* if some people suffer for something that isn't their fault. As much as possible, people's circumstances should reflect their own autonomous choices, not differences in circumstance over which they have no control. As expressed here, luck egalitarianism does not assume that the *only* thing that makes distributions wrong is that they aren't the consequence of people's autonomous choices. So a luck egalitarian might hold that some of the inequalities that *are* the result of voluntary choice are still problematic from the moral point of view.

Second objection: Slavery of the talented

Another objection to resource egalitarianism is the charge that the theory 3.24 will lead to the *slavery of the talented*. Just as disabilities present a problem for resource egalitarianism, special talents can present another kind of problem. People aren't responsible for their basic talents, though they can be responsible for developing or neglecting to develop them. But, like the possession of a disability, possession of a talent or special ability is, to a significant extent, a matter of good luck. Some lucky people seem to be born with intellectual gifts, or with other kinds of special abilities that give them a significant advantage. Two violinists who practice with the same diligence may not play equally well after many years of work; two mathematicians or engineers who both work just as hard to hone and develop their native abilities may not be equally brilliant after years of labor and education. If we provide differently talented people with the same basic resources, what are we to make of inequalities that result from different basic abilities?

We might seek to equalize the end result by treating the advantages enjoyed 3.25 by people with extra talents as a public good. We could require that people who have special talents share some of the benefits associated with their talents with other people, who weren't so lucky. But it seems unfair to force those who are talented to labor on others' behalf. It might be thought to violate their autonomy, or to make them slaves to the people they're working to benefit.

Third objection: Expensive tastes

A third objection to resource egalitarianism also begins with underlying 3.26 differences between people: people have different tastes. Because of this, some are fully satisfied with less, or with relatively cheap goods. Others won't be nearly as satisfied, unless they are able to consume more expensive goods. So, when people start with the same resources, those with expensive tastes will be worse off than those with simple tastes.

3.27   Is this really a problem? Perhaps we should tell the people with expensive tastes: "Hey, tough luck! We'd all be better off if we could drink expensive champagne instead of cheap beer. Your expensive tastes don't entitle you to anything extra!" For tastes that are trivial, like a taste for expensive champagne, this response might be enough. But people aren't always responsible for acquiring expensive tastes, and not all tastes are like the trivial taste for fancy foods. Some tastes and preferences may be *cultivated*. So, when people make a point of becoming expert gourmets, we might properly hold them responsible if their tastes are hard to satisfy. But most of our tastes aren't like this: most of the time we don't chose them at all, we simply find that we have them, perhaps as a result of our biological makeup, or because of the way we're socialized as we grow up. If people are worse off because of tastes for which they are not responsible, they can't be at fault for having those tastes. But if people are worse off because of something that's not their fault, this violates the principle of luck egalitarianism.

3.28   How serious are these objections to resource egalitarianism? Perhaps what matters about resources is what a person can *do* with them, not simply their equal distribution. Maybe it's a mistake to focus on equality of goods instead of somehow equalizing the things that access to resources enables us to do and the persons it enables us to become. One version of this position is

WELFARE EGALITARIANISM: Resources should be distributed such that each person's expected welfare is equal to another's.

The objections above show that providing people with equal resources won't leave them equally well off and that those who are worse off may be disadvantaged because of factors for which they are not responsible. Resource egalitarians need to abandon the principle of luck egalitarianism and to accept the various kinds of inequality of well-being that can exist even when everyone has the same resources. Is this price too high to pay? Perhaps there is another egalitarian view that can avoid these problems.

Equality of Opportunity

3.29 One possible alternative is to focus on equality of *opportunity* instead of equality of resources, wealth, or welfare.

EQUALITY OF OPPORTUNITY: Everyone should have the same opportunity as others to achieve her aims or to acquire goods and resources.

On this view, what people deserve is not equal possession of some good, but a fair and equal opportunity to acquire goods or achieve their objectives.

An opportunity is a chance to get something if you work for it, not a 3.30 guarantee. According to the principle of equal opportunity, what people deserve is not equal possession of some *good* or another, but a fair and equal chance to acquire goods or to achieve their life goals. People's opportunities are unequal if some people have more or better chances than others.

As an ideal, equality of opportunity incorporates some of the important 3.31 values we considered earlier: perhaps a guarantee of equal opportunity is the best we can do to ensure that people's circumstances will reflect their choices. If so, it may be the best way to ensure, as luck egalitarianism recommends, that the disadvantages people suffer won't be the result of circumstances beyond their control. We can't entirely eliminate the influence of bad luck (or good luck), but we can at least take steps to ensure that people have a fair and equal chance.

Adopting a principle of equal opportunity would commit us to 3.32 instituting policies that compensate when some people, through no fault of their own, suffer from discrimination or other disadvantages. For example, in a society marked by racial discrimination, a principle of equal opportunity might justify a policy of preference that offers special consideration to members of the disadvantaged group. Such a policy would treat people unequally in one sense, but, if it worked properly, it would not provide an unfair advantage to the people who benefit from it. Instead it would simply compensate for the disadvantage they suffer because of discrimination.

But a principle of equal opportunity needs to be made more specific: 3.33 opportunity for what? We could articulate a principle of equal opportunity *for resources*, for example, or equal opportunity for wealth, or equal opportunity for welfare. Such principles would need to be carefully evaluated, to ensure that they are not vulnerable to the objections we considered earlier. If physical disabilities constitute a problem for the principle of equality of resources, for example, won't they constitute a similar problem for a principle of equal opportunity for resources?

Should we level down?

3.34 But is it reasonable to expect that we can provide everyone with equal opportunities? Some people's opportunities are cruelly constrained by circumstances: consider the predicament of people who grow up in poor communities, or who live in places where schools are blighted with violence and drugs. The principle of equal opportunity recommends *changing* these circumstances: we should improve their schools and do what we can to mitigate school violence and crime.

3.35   There are other conditions, however, which restrict people's opportunities just as cruelly but are even more difficult to address: for example, some people are born with the most serious disabilities, and, even with the best accommodations we can provide, the opportunities they face may be seriously constrained. Certainly a principle of equal opportunity will recommend that we give these people the best accommodations we can give. In this respect, the principle recommends a policy similar to the one embodied in the Americans with Disabilities Act, which requires that we make "reasonable accommodation" so that people with disabilities can be full participants. But what if someone's opportunities are still unequal and constrained, even when the best available accommodations are in place?

3.36   In such cases the principle of equal opportunity will recommend that we continue to look for better and better accommodations, which seems appropriate. But there is another way to equalize opportunities: we could equalize by adding *disadvantages* designed to constrain people who would otherwise have more or better opportunities. Working to achieve equality by providing benefits for people who are worse off is sometimes called "leveling up." By contrast, working to achieve equality by clamping down on people who are better off is called "leveling down." Leveling up makes people better off; but, once we have provided all the benefits we can for people who are disadvantaged, is it worth pursuing equality by leveling down?

3.37   Leveling down imposes disadvantages on those who would otherwise be better off than equality would permit. Does it have any advantages? One might argue that inequality itself is a disadvantage for those who are worse off. If so, then maybe leveling provides an advantage to those who are worse off by ensuring that they are *equal*. On the other hand, leveling down seems like a Procrustean egalitarian policy. We may well have an egalitarian obligation to address the disadvantages of people who are poorly off, or who unfairly lack opportunities that could be made accessible to them. But it seems unfair and an unjustifiable imposition to constrain people *only* for the sake of making everyone equal.

What does equality of opportunity require?

Many people find equality of opportunity a more appealing principle than 3.38 equality of outcome. Equality of opportunity gives everyone an equal starting point but then subsequently allows inequalities on the basis of how people live their lives. Equalizing outcomes risks massive government intervention into every area of life and getting rid of some of the incentives that encourage people to work hard and develop their talents.

But what would equality of opportunity actually require? We have 3.39 already mentioned the problem that, even if we give people equal resources, we would not solve the problem of unequal talents. Now consider another source of inequality: parents. Parents differ widely in their parenting abilities, values, and practices. Someone from a middle-class family whose parents greatly value education, instill a strong work ethic, and provide a loving and stable home has significant advantages over someone from a family with similar economic resources where the children suffer emotional neglect and physical abuse and where the parents are poor role models. The same is true for the rich and the poor.

We don't get to choose our parents, yet they have a tremendous influence 3.40 on our set of opportunities and our chances of success. In the same way, whether we are born into money or whether we are born to good parents is a matter of good (or bad) luck. Would full equality of opportunity require raising children in state-run centers that provide everyone with the same basic experiences, training, and values? What if pursuing equality to this extent actually made the poor worse off, because they would have been better off raised by their parents than being raised in a state-run center? We will return to this question in the chapter on justice.

The distinction between equality of outcome and equality of opportunity, 3.41 so appealing in theory, runs into the following practical problem: **in the real world, outcomes create opportunities. If your parents have more resources, you have more opportunities**. Money buys homes in neighborhoods with better schools, or access to quality private schools. Money provides access to better healthcare. Money provides access to many educational and cultural opportunities outside of school that can give children additional advantages.

3.42   Wealthy parents are highly motivated to provide these opportunities for their children precisely because they don't want opportunity to be equal. Saying "I want my children to have the best opportunity to succeed" is normally another way of saying that you want your children to have better opportunities than other children. The only way to equalize the opportunities of children is to equalize their parents' resources, which means that, in practice, we may face many of the same dilemmas with equality of opportunity as with equality of outcome.

3.43   Even if we decide that the best goal is something short of full equality of opportunity, we shouldn't conclude that equality of opportunity is unimportant. As we will see later, some people opt to ensure that people have sufficient opportunities rather than equal opportunities. No matter how the goal is defined, the case for working toward greater equality of opportunity grows stronger if we consider the reality of inequality as it exists today.

Inequalities in the Real World

3.44   Of course, inequalities in the real world *are* of the kind that includes grinding poverty and misery and hideous disadvantages to those who are worst off. Perhaps some of these people are responsible for their poverty, in the sense that their disadvantage is the result of voluntary choices—choices that they made and for which they can legitimately be held to account. But is it plausible to think that this is true as a general rule? Before we can be in a position to answer such a question, we need to know more about the extent and the nature of actual inequalities.

3.45   We have already discussed overt discrimination as a striking form of unjust equal treatment. But surely, you might say, this is a thing of the past. Black voters no longer face humiliating tests when registering to vote. If we eliminate *overt* discrimination, have we solved the problem of unjust unequal treatment?

3.46   Unfortunately, we have not: even if we eliminate *explicit* forms of discrimination, serious injustice may still result from implicit associations and from the implicit bias that remains in our behavior and attitudes. One test that shows this is an implicit association test involving fire arms. In this test subjects are shown the image of a person and are asked to report whether the person shown is carrying a weapon. The results show that most people are more likely to mistake nonweapons for weapons when the person shown is black. When subjects do recognize that the person shown is not carrying a weapon, it takes them longer to do so when the person is black.

By the same token, **onlookers are more likely to call the police when** 3.47 **they see a black person involved in questionable behavior than when they see a white person involved in the same behavior.** Is it surprising, then, that black people are more likely to be arrested than white people? That black people are more likely to be shot than white people?

Sex discrimination can also result from implicit bias. Studies show that 3.48 equally qualified candidates are considered to be less qualified and are offered lower salaries when those who hire them believe them to be women than when the candidates are believed to be men. In one experiment, laboratory directors were presented with a candidate for a postdoctoral researcher. **The same letters and credentials received average offers of $30,283.10 when the candidate was believed to be a man, and $26,507.94 when the candidate was believed to be a woman.** It may be surprising that laboratory directors who were women discriminated against women candidates just as male laboratory directors did. It is clear that unjust discrimination based on race and gender are not a thing of the past.

Earlier in the chapter you were asked about your *perception* of existing 3.49 inequalities: how much of the wealth of the nation *do you think* is held by the top 20 percent of the population? By the top 40 percent? **Researchers Michael Norton and Dan Ariely posed these questions to more than five thousand Americans,** randomly drawn from a panel of more than one million. When asked how unequal they believed American society to be, they estimated that the top 20 percent held a bit less than 60 percent of the total wealth, that the next best-off 20 percent held about 20 percent, that the middle 20 percent held 10 percent, and the poorest groups combined held about 10 percent. When asked what distribution would be ideal if they found themselves randomly assigned to any of the possible wealth positions, they preferred a much more equal distribution. These results did not significantly differ across Democrats and Republicans, conservatives or liberals. It is interesting, however, that most people *radically* underestimated the actual extent of inequality in the United States. The results of this study are given in Figure 3.1.

The extent to which people underestimated the amount of actual 3.50 inequality is striking. In the bar representing the actual distribution, the percentage of total wealth held by the bottom 40 percent is so small (three-tenths of 1 percent) that it doesn't even appear on the chart. The middle

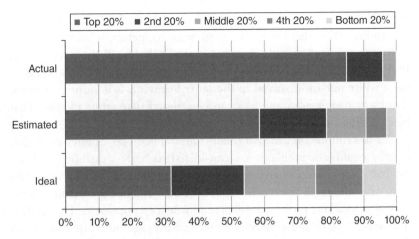

Figure 3.1 Actual, estimated, and preferred distributions of wealth in the United States (with related **video**). Source: Norton and Ariely, 2011.

group—the third quintile—holds 4 percent. The remaining wealth—about 96 percent of the total—is held by people in the top two quintiles; but even within this top 40 percent of the population the amount of inequality is striking: people in the top 20 percent hold about 85 percent of the total wealth, leaving 11 percent for the quite well off second best off quintile. Within the top 20 percent, those in the top 1 percent stratum hold about 42 percent of the wealth, which means that even within the top 20 percent the amount of inequality is striking. By most standard measures, this means that the United States is more *unequal* than any other developed country in the world. The authors also urge that their data mean that Americans don't *understand* the extent of US inequality.

3.51   But do the data from Norton and Ariely tell us what is *relevant* about US inequality? The information given is a static "time slice": it describes inequality as if it were a fixed feature of society. But is it relevant to compare people by their *wealth*? We might instead consider their *income*. Note that not all people who lack wealth are *poor people*. A lawyer who earns $150,000 a year but has significant debt and spending might have no accumulated wealth, but it would be a mistake to regard such a person as "poor." If she spends what she earns and takes out loans, such a person might even have *negative* wealth—more debts than assets. But if her income is predictably sufficient to cover these costs, she's *still* not poor.

3.52   Another consideration is the *mobility* of wealth: high school and college students don't typically have a lot of money in stocks or savings. Many students take out loans to pay for college, expecting that their education will enable them to get a better paying job so that they will be able to pay back their debts. Norton and Ariely include these students among those who have no wealth at all or have negative wealth. But are college students really a disadvantaged group? If their prospects for an adequate income are good, it is odd to count them among the poor. A society marked by lots of static inequality might not be *unjustly* unequal if the poor people were all *young* and if the young people had the same lifetime prospects for wealth as the older wealthier people.

These considerations do not imply that wealth inequality is not a prob- 3.53 lem. But they *do* mean that we need to know a lot more about the situation before we will be in a position to make a judgment about whether existing inequalities in wealth are bad or unjust.

Inequality or Deprivation?

We know, however, that there are people in the United States and in the world 3.54 who are truly poor—even destitute. Is it possible that the repugnance we may feel about inequality has more to do with the misery and deprivation suffered by people who are poor, and less with the inequality itself?

In his famous **Discourse on the Origin of Inequality**, the French 3.55 philosopher Jean-Jacques Rousseau considered the question whether the inequalities between people are *natural*—the result of natural law—or whether they are *unnatural*—by which Rousseau meant that they would be *contrary* to the law of nature. Rousseau concludes with the following observation:

> since inequality is practically non-existent in the state of nature, it derives its force and growth from the development of our faculties and the progress of the human mind, and eventually becomes stable and "legitimate" through the establishment of property and laws. Moreover, it follows that moral inequality, authorized by positive right alone, is contrary to natural right whenever it is not combined in the same proportion with physical inequality: a distinction that is sufficient to determine what one should think in this regard about the sort of inequality that reigns among all civilized people, for it is obviously contrary to the law of nature, however it may be defined, for a child to command an old man, for an imbecile to lead a wise man, and for a handful of people to gorge themselves on superfluities while the starving multitude lacks necessities. (Rousseau, 1987 [1755], p. 81)

Rousseau's conclusion is about inequality, but it is about a specific *kind* of inequality: inequality in which the poor are a destitute starving multitude, unable to provide themselves with basic necessities of life. Their predicament, according to Rousseau, is "contrary to the law of nature" (he means by this that it's unjustified and shameful), if there are also people who are super-rich. If the inequality, and not the poverty, is the source of our sense that this predicament is unjust, then we should feel the same repugnance for a society in which the inequality is just as wide, but in which the worst off members of society are quite well off indeed.

> Imagine a society marked by radical inequalities, so that some people have vastly more wealth, more welfare, more opportunity, or more resources than others. Suppose this society is vastly more unequal than the most unequal country in the world. But suppose that the worst off members of this society are all quite well off by contemporary standards. In this imaginary society, the worst off person enjoys a standard of living equal to that enjoyed by people whose yearly income is half-a-million dollars.

If inequality is a problem, this society is very unequal. But it's hard to get worked up over wealth inequalities if no one is suffering from them! Rousseau's sense that it is unjust when some people suffer from life-crushing poverty while other people are wealthy may derive, in part, from a sense that the wealthy people should do something to help—that their claim on the resources they control is less significant than the claim of the needy. Perhaps justice would require that we address the misery of the destitute by taxing the wealthy; this would provide for the needs of the worse off and would ensure that they have an adequate range of opportunities.

3.56   In a world where everyone had *enough*, inequality might be a less striking and disturbing problem. Perhaps we should consider, in place of an *egalitarian* theory, a *sufficientarian* theory that holds that people should not lack *adequate* opportunities, or *adequate* access to resources, or *adequate* welfare, or adequate < whatever egalitarian principles would equalize >.

> SUFFICIENTARIANISM: It doesn't matter whether or not people are *equally* provided with opportunities or wealth, what matters is that people should not lack *adequate* opportunities or wealth.

Sufficientarian views have the benefit that they do not recommend leveling *down*. The fact that someone has extra advantages does not give us an independent reason to impose constraints or to pull that person down, to the level of others. But do sufficientarian views provide adequate protection for legitimate egalitarian ideals?

Is Sufficiency Enough?

In some contexts it does seem that people should be equal: the ideal of 3.57 *equality under the law* means that no one should be arbitrarily favored by the legal system: the laws that constrain some of us should similarly constrain all of us. Laws forbidding discrimination may be thought to enforce—to the extent that such enforcement is possible—a guarantee of equal *respect*. Public expressions of disrespect, like the Louisiana "literacy" test mentioned earlier, are prohibited because everyone deserves *full* respect as a citizen and as a voter.

And even sufficientarians can recognize that inequalities create other 3.58 problems: it has sometimes been argued that vast inequalities in wealth make it difficult to guarantee equality in other crucial areas of life. It may be that democracies can't work properly when some people have vast independent resources that can be used to shape public opinion, or to provide independent funding for a political campaign. It may be difficult or impossible to ensure political equality, or even equality under the law, when some people have vast resources and others are relatively poor. If so, then perhaps inequalities are a problem because of their *effects*, and not because they are intrinsically repugnant or unjust.

Complex Equality

As we have seen, many political theorists don't regard inequalities *as such* as 3.59 a bad thing. Before we can know whether inequalities are bad or unjust, we need to know more: whether those who are worse off are *responsible for their own choices*, whether people faced *equal or adequate opportunities from the start*, whether the *conditions of competition were fair*. While poverty and suffering are bad, inequality isn't necessarily associated with poverty or suffering or deprivation.

People's concern about inequality often seems to stem from deeper 3.60 underlying concerns, and the sources may be diverse. Is there any reason to think that our interest in preventing arbitrary discrimination has the same source as our concern that some people shouldn't suffer grinding poverty while other people have much more than they need? Is there any reason to think that the same reasons that support a principle of equal treatment under the law will also support a principle of equal access to resources or goods or opportunities?

3.61   Michael Walzer thinks that we should strive for "complex equality." Under simple equality you find out what the dominant good in a society is and you strive to distribute it more equally. If those who have money can use it to buy everything else (political power, education, healthcare, etc.), then you redistribute the dominant good until it is equal. In another culture the dominant good might be birth status—say, in a caste society. In another culture religion might be the dominant good. Whatever the dominant good is, simple equality tells us to solve the problem by distributing it more equally. The problem, Walzer thinks, is that a new good will becomes the dominant good and the inequalities will reappear. In practice, attempts to realize communist ideals have often begun with redistribution of property. But, in notable cases where this was done, membership in the elite positions of the communist party became the new form of power, and the societies have remained very unequal.

3.62   Walzer's alternative is to imagine different spheres of life, each with its own logic, which makes sense for the particular culture. It is fine for some to have more money than others, as long as they can't translate that into advantages in all the other areas of life. Can we have a properly working democracy if elections are strongly influenced by political advertising, and if people who are wealthy can spend money to shape public opinion so that they can achieve their favored electoral outcomes? If not, then our concern for the value of democracy may be a centerpiece of our interest (if we have one) in preventing huge inequalities in wealth, or it might justify the imposition of barriers in order to ensure that the wealthy aren't able to use money to purchase unfair political leverage or to determine electoral outcomes.

3.63   In a similar way, inequalities in wealth present a challenge for the ideal of equality under the law. Is it possible for people to have the chance of a fair hearing and of equality in court when some can pay a legal team to make their case, while others must rely on the efforts of an overworked public defense lawyer? Perhaps it is a mistake to group these concerns under the single category "inequality," as if this were the characteristic that unites them and that explains the basis for our underlying discomfort and disapproval. Complex equality tries to keep advantages in one area (such as money) from translating into advantages in politics or before the law. In the real world, is it plausible to think that inequalities could be kept safe in their separate spheres of life?

Race, Gender, and the Social Construction of Inequalities

To this point in the chapter we have focused primarily on the inequalities 3.64 related to resources, but that is only one aspect of equality. There are substantial differences in wealth and income between men and women and between racial and ethnic groups. Redistribution of wealth and income would benefit those who are currently disadvantaged. But it might not solve the problem. Inequalities are also associated with stereotypes and attitudes that people within a given culture may have.

The idea of "social construction" refers, roughly, to the claim that our 3.65 concepts and presuppositions influence the way we perceive reality. A census form may ask people to designate a certain "race," but for many people it is difficult to know how to answer this question. Part of the reason is that there is no purely biological definition of race. People vary by skin color, but the variations are along a continuum, they don't occur in natural groupings. Where does white start and black stop? Sometimes what we call race really has more to do with perceived cultural differences than with biology. The designation "Hispanic" is technically not about skin color but about the language of one's culture of origin. In Rwanda there have been fierce battles between two ethnic groups, the Hutu and the Tutsis. Those designations were created by European colonists who divided people into two groups on the basis of characteristics such as height. Wars have been fought on the basis of an "identity" that didn't even exist a few centuries ago!

These constructions have important implications for equality. In the 3.66 case of gender, a brother and a sister growing up in the same home often have roughly similar resources. Both may attend the same school, participate in similar activities, and have the same parents. Many of the normal sources of inequality do not apply. Nonetheless, if there are widespread assumptions about what types of jobs are inappropriate for men and what types of jobs are inappropriate for women, the opportunities for men and the opportunities for women will be different. Similarly, if there are widespread differences in perceptions of how childcare and housework responsibilities ought to be distributed between men and women, this will also affect the opportunities that men and women have. Stereotypes about racial and ethnic groups can have a similar effect.

If the sources of inequality exist not just in laws or in the distribution of 3.67 resources but also in the very ideas and concepts that we use in thinking about reality, does the government have a role to play in trying to actively shape these concepts? While one argument for affirmative action is that it is just leveling the playing field by giving advantages to those who have suffered previous disadvantage, another popular argument is that affirmative action helps create role models. If you grew up and never saw a black doctor or a female lawyer, this would influence your view of the world. According to their advocates, affirmative action programs don't just aim to advance the opportunities of those who have been unjustly set back. They also aim, at least in part, to change the way we understand race.

Affirmative Action

3.68 Let's return to the topic of affirmative action, with which the chapter began. Starting from a baseline of formal equality means that there needs to be a relevant reason for unequal treatment. Critics of affirmative action say that race, gender, and ethnicity are never relevant qualifications for admission to a college or university. Thus including these criteria in admissions or in scholarship decisions creates inequality.

3.69 Proponents can respond in more than one way. One is to argue that affirmative action is just compensating for past barriers that some people face and others do not. It is just "leveling the playing field." This argument assumes either that equality of opportunity is required for justice or that members of historically disadvantaged groups will be denied adequate opportunity without affirmative action. One complication is that, in practice, past barriers do not track precisely with class, race, ethnicity, or gender, in part because these categories can pull in opposite directions. A black child with millionaire parents might have fewer barriers than a white child who has poor parents. This problem is partly remedied by taking the various characteristics as factors that increase or decrease an applicant's chances instead of applying a rigid quota system. Proponents can also argue that to expect perfection is too much. If the categories of people who benefit from affirmative action *normally* track with people who have faced obstacles, then the net effect is greater fairness.

3.70 Interestingly, this line of argument has not been the dominant one in the United States. In the famous 1978 case of *Regents of the University of California v. Bakke* (438 US 265), the US Supreme Court ruled that the justification presented above was insufficient. The case involved a white male who was denied admission to medical school when minority students with lower grades and exam scores had been admitted. It raised the question of what justifications, if any, are permissible or acceptable for affirmative action. The court argued that people have a right to be evaluated as individuals rather than as group members. Generalizations about group members' having been discriminated against in the past are set to the side because they are not true in all cases.

As a result, the US debate has often focused on the second type of argu- 3.71 ment, which is about relevant qualifications and the purpose of a university. The *Bakke* decision held that diversity is a legitimate goal in education because it contributes to the educational mission and that therefore race and gender are in a sense a relevant qualification, which can count as a plus on an application so long as a rigid quota system is not used. This justification is entirely distinct from the argument that affirmative action is appropriate in counteracting the present effects of racist and sexist discrimination. Critics of affirmative action think that nonacademic factors like race, gender, class, and ethnicity are irrelevant to your scholarly abilities and therefore should not be factored into admissions decisions. Yet most selective universities already include nonacademic factors in admission and scholarship decisions. Some schools intentionally try to keep a roughly equal male–female ratio, which sometimes results in affirmative action for men. Other schools strive for geographical balance, which means that it is easier to get into Harvard if you live in Iowa than if you live in New York. Many schools give preference (and scholarships) to athletes, even though athletic ability is unrelated to academic ability. Perhaps most interestingly, many elite private colleges and universities give preference to children of alumni.

What should we make of this? One solution would be to say that all of it 3.72 should stop. Academic merit is the only relevant qualification for college admission and for scholarships. But the dominant view has been that uni- versities have a variety of legitimate purposes, and that admission strategies that further those purposes are permissible. Legacy preferences increase donations and provide more resources for everyone, including those on financial aid. Participating in and attending athletic events is an important part of the college experience for many people. Students may learn more (or differently) in a diverse student body, hence preferences for groups that have been historically marginalized might help further that goal.

It is also important to recognize that discrimination is not just a thing of 3.73 the past. Implicit bias tests show that people are still disadvantaged in many social circumstances *just because they are African American*, or *just because they are women*. Recall that laboratory directors were prepared to offer thousands of dollars less to an applicant when they believed that applicant to be a woman than to what they believed to be a man with *the same résumé*.

Similar studies show that applicants with African American-sounding names need to submit many more résumés than equally qualified people whose names sound "white." In a world where racism and sexism persist in this way, there is reason to think that apparently equally qualified candidates who are members of a disadvantaged group may in fact be *more* qualified than their competitors: if two runners cross the finish line at the same time, isn't it reasonable to think that the one carrying a bag of cement is a better runner than the one who ran without a burden? Considerations of implicit bias might lead one to conclude that affirmative action policies compensate for *present* disadvantages, or that they may be justified as recognition that women and minority candidates carry a burden of discrimination. Because of this burden, it is reasonable to suppose that women and minority candidates may be more qualified than others who seem to have crossed the finish line at the same time.

3.74   In order to decide whether affirmative action policies are appropriate or just, we need to know whether there are relevant reasons for deviating from strict equality. In this and others contexts, debate about equality is not separable from debate about other political values. They are all interconnected.

Conclusion

3.75 Arguments based on equality are powerful. Every major approach to contemporary political philosophy emphasizes equality in some sense. Libertarians focus on the equal right of all people to contract. Utilitarians say that we cannot make arbitrary distinctions between the welfare of one person and that of another. When evaluating claims for equality, we need to know whether inequalities are justified by good reasons. But which reasons will serve such a purpose—of showing us which inequalities are just and which are unjust? To answer this question, we may need to situate problems of (in)equality within a broader theory of justice. It is to this topic that we turn in the next chapter.

References and Further Reading

Cohen, Gerald Allan. 1995. *Self-Ownership, Freedom, and Equality*. Cambridge: Cambridge University Press. Cohen argues that Rawls's difference principle is insufficiently egalitarian, and defends a more radically egalitarian alternative.

Dworkin, Ronald. 2000. *Sovereign Virtue*. Cambridge, MA: Harvard University Press. Dworkin defends a complicated version of resource egalitarianism.

Flew, Antony. 1981. *The Politics of Procrustes: Contradictions of Enforced Equality*. New York: Prometheus Books. A provocative and accessible philosophical treatment of egalitarianism.

France, Anatole. 1894. *The Red Lilly*. Project Gutenberg. http://www.gutenberg.org/files/3922/3922-h/3922-h.htm (accessed February 15, 2016). Anatole France's novel contains a famous, brief critique of formal equality that masks vast substantive inequalities.

Norton, Michael I. and Dan Ariely. 2011. "Building a Better America: One Wealth Quintile at a Time." *Perspectives on Psychological Science*, 6: 9–12. A fascinating study of the gap between how much inequality Americans think there is and how much more there actually it is. It also shows that in the abstract most Americans would prefer a more equal distribution of wealth. Critics might argue that people would adjust their ideal in light of more information about actual inequality.

Nozick, Robert. 1974. *Anarchy, State, and Utopia*. New York: Basic Books. Nozick presents a famous libertarian critique of egalitarian views.

Okin, Susan Moller. 1989. *Justice, Gender, and the Family*. New York: Basic Books. An excellent discussion of justice and gender inequality in contemporary political theory.

Rousseau, Jean-Jacques. 1987 [1755]. "Discourse on the Origin and Foundations of Inequality," translated by Donald A. Cress. In Jean-Jacques Rousseau, *The Basic Political Writings*. New York: Hackett, pp. 23–109. A classic critique of inequality. Rousseau argues that human beings are naturally equal and that the inequalities that exist are primarily the result of the corrupting influences of human society.

Sen, Amartya. 1997. *On Economic Inequality*. New York: Oxford University Press. Sen's somewhat technical book is a philosophical treatment of economic and mathematical models to represent and analyze inequalities. This book is not for the faint of heart, or for students who have not taken calculus or mathematical economics!

Temkin, Larry S. 1993. *Inequality*. New York: Oxford University Press. Temkin's book is a remarkable analysis of philosophical puzzles that arise when egalitarian ideals are made articulate and unambiguous. He demonstrates that the philosophical problems have very real implications for egalitarian political theories.

Rawls, John. 1971. *A Theory of Justice*. Cambridge, MA: Harvard University Press. Many regard Rawls's book as the most important twentieth-century work in political theory.

Walzer, Michael. 1983. *Spheres of Justice*. New York: Basic Books. Walzer's book is the source of the idea of "complex equality." It is a very accessible book with lots of interesting historical examples.

Williams, Bernard. 1973. "The Idea of Equality." In Bernard Williams, *Problems of the Self*. Cambridge: Cambridge University Press, pp. 230–249. Williams argues that inequality requires relevant reasons and that, for example, the relevant reason for distributing healthcare resources unequally should be unequal health: people in worse health need more medical care.

Online Resources

1   https://en.wikipedia.org/wiki/Procrustes
2   https://en.wikipedia.org/wiki/Anatole_France
3   http://www.slate.com/blogs/the_vault/2013/06/28/voting_rights_and_the_ supreme_court_the_impossible_literacy_test_louisiana.html
4   http://classics.mit.edu/Plato/republic.6.v.html
5   http://plato.stanford.edu/entries/aristotle/
6   https://www.washingtonpost.com/news/wonk/wp/2013/05/29/no-one- really-believes-in-equality-of-opportunity/
7   https://www.youtube.com/watch?v=8ABRlWybBqM
8   http://blogs.scientificamerican.com/unofficial-prognosis/study- shows-gender-bias-in-science-is-real-heres-why-it-matters/
9   http://www.theatlantic.com/business/archive/2012/08/americans-want- to-live-in-a-much-more-equal-country-they-just-dont-realize-it/260639/
10   https://www.youtube.com/watch?v=JTj9AcwkaKM
11   http://www.amazon.com/Basic-Political-Writings-Jean-Jacques-Rousseau/ dp/0872200477/ref=sr_1_1?ie=UTF8&qid=1379008539 &sr=8-1&keywords=rousseau+hackett

4

JUSTICE

JUSTIN	So. Pay your taxes yet?
SOPHIE	Yeah, they take their pound of flesh even from a poor college student like me. What gives?
JUSTIN	Well, you're making the big bucks working in a lab. At my job I hardly earn enough to owe anything at all.
SOPHIE	You know what really bugs me though? We pay this money to the government, and then they do *all sorts of things with it*, and a lot of them seem useless or wrong to me. I think we should be able to earmark our tax contribution—and that's how it should be seen: a contribution—so that our money is only used for purposes we approve.
JUSTIN	Yeah, riiiight. Like that would work great. So if not enough people earmark their tax money for public defense, we wouldn't have a military? If people don't understand the value of scientific research, we'll do away with the National Science Foundation? No way. Much better for our representatives to make budgeting decisions than to have them decided by individuals in the way you suggest.
SOPHIE	But we're supposed to have freedom of conscience! It violates my freedom of conscience to force me to contribute to things I don't like or approve.
JUSTIN	What do you have in mind?
SOPHIE [rolls eyes]	Too many things to list. But I'll give you two examples: first, there's health insurance. Why should I have to contribute to other people's healthcare? People should take care of

This Is Political Philosophy: An Introduction, First Edition. Alex Tuckness and Clark Wolf.
© 2017 John Wiley & Sons, Inc. Published 2017 by John Wiley & Sons, Inc.

themselves, should buy their own insurance. If they
don't, they're taking their own risk. And, second, there
are all these social welfare programs designed to aid people who are needy. Don't get me wrong: I think people
who are truly in need should be helped. You know I work
at the Food Pantry to provide food for people who can't
afford it, and I've also worked with Habitat for Humanity
helping to provide homes for people. But these should be
private decisions, not forced contributions. The government doesn't have the right to force us to be charitable—
charity is a *virtue*, not an obligation of justice. It can't be
enforced.

JUSTIN   I see your point, but I'm not convinced. *Everyone* needs
healthcare—at least a basic minimum of care. And *everyone*
needs food and shelter—and other things too, like education.
Private "charity" just isn't enough. Besides, should people
have to depend on charity for basic needs? Things like food,
shelter, and education are necessities. People should be able
to demand them as a right.

SOPHIE   Don't get me started on education again. Why should I be con-
scripted to pay for the education of *other people's children*?

JUSTIN   I'm just not convinced, Sophie. You didn't pay for *your* own
education before college—none of us could, we were
children. It's unfair if other children don't have the same
opportunity you had. In the same way, it's unfair if some
people can't afford health insurance and don't get medical
care, or if some people don't have enough to meet their basic
needs. If we're making money in this economy and doing
well enough, it's only *fair* for us to be taxed a little bit to support people who aren't as fortunate as we are.

Justice: A Brief Introduction

4.1   On a widely shared view, the requirements of justice are the most minimal
requirements that apply to us. Obligations of justice are based on the rights
of others: when people fail to meet these obligations, the people whose
rights have been violated become their victims or complainants. Because of

this, the obligations of justice include only those obligations that can be enforced by others, or by the state. We may well have unenforceable obligations: for example, we may have an obligation to be grateful to people who are kind to us, an obligation to be diligent, an obligation to be kind and compassionate toward others—people who are not grateful or compassionate may rightly be considered to lack good moral character or virtue. Such failures may be moral failings but are not violations of the requirements of justice, because it would be either impossible or morally wrong to force someone to be grateful or compassionate or virtuous. Physical actions can be forced, but the internal actions of conscience and passion and thought are beyond the reach of others.

Even before thinking about justice in a philosophical way, each of us 4.2 probably starts with something like a theory of justice of our own. Many people already have views about which obligations can appropriately be enforced by the state and which obligations should not be enforced. The goal of philosophical reflection, in this case, is to articulate and examine principles we may already partly accept and that may already influence our judgments. But, once we have done that, the next step is to consider our own views about justice in light of other, more thoroughly developed theories defended by philosophers and political theorists.

Rawls's Theory of Justice

The book that has to the greatest extent shaped debates about justice over 4.3 the past several decades is *A Theory of Justice* by John Rawls. Since it appeared in 1971, thousands of books and articles have been written in response. We will begin with Rawls's account of justice, then look at some important criticisms and at alternative approaches to justice.

The principles of justice, according to Rawls, are the principles people 4.4 would choose as the terms of a contract—or mutual agreement—about the basic structure of society. You might imagine a group of people gathering together to decide on rules for social cooperation and mutual protection and support.

But contracts are only valid if they are made in circumstances that are 4.5 fair. What if one person brought a machine gun to the negotiating table and said "OK let's make a social contract: I think we should do things *my* way. Does anyone disagree?" Unfair circumstances detract from the power of mutual agreement. While differences of wealth and power create one type of unfairness, another type stems from bias for or against certain groups. If most people in a society despise a particular ethnic group, they may either exclude it from political participation or use their superior numbers to force the minority to accept unfair terms.

The original position and the veil of ignorance

4.6 Rawls claims to have a solution to the problem of unfair agreements, but it is a solution that requires us to use some imagination. The goal is to create a procedure that will yield a fair outcome if we follow it.

4.7 Before we look at Rawls's solution, consider a simple problem: dividing up a cake between two people. One procedure is to let the first person cut the cake into two pieces and let the other person pick. The first person, not knowing which piece he will get, is likely to cut the pieces equally. Thus ignorance of an outcome (which piece you will get) leads to a fairer choice. Also, cutting equally is a way to make sure that the worst possible outcome is half the cake, whereas cutting unequally could mean getting less than half in case the other person picks the bigger piece.

4.8 What Rawls calls "the *original position*" is a variation on this idea. His goal is to describe imaginary circumstances for choosing principles of justice in such a way that we would have confidence that the principles chosen would be fair. The original position is supposed to describe circumstances for an ideally fair contract. Not only does Rawls prevent people from bringing a weapon to the negotiating table, he tries to describe circumstances that would remove all *possible* distorting factors that might make a contract unfair.

4.9 Even if agreements in the real world often occur under unfair circumstances, perhaps we can imagine conditions that would generate a fair agreement. Suppose you were asked to reach an agreement with other people about the basic principles of justice in governing society. Here are the rules:

1. No one knows the details of theirs or others' particular place in society (whether they are rich or poor, for example) or of the particular philosophy, religion, or concept of "the good life" that they hold.
2. Each person does know that there are certain things everyone typically wants, regardless of his religion or philosophy or conception of the good life: things such as economic resources and civil liberties that give you a greater ability to pursue your conception of the good life, whatever it is.

3. The people making the agreement think of themselves as representing others, whose identities are also hidden, who will live under the principles of justice so chosen.
4. The decision must be unanimous and must involve rules that people will be willing to follow even after they know more about themselves and those they represent.

The list above describes what Rawls calls the original position; its most distinctive feature is the *veil of ignorance*. According to Rawls, the veil of ignorance (if we had one) would deprive us of any knowledge we might use to make the social contract unfair: if you don't know *who you are* in society, then you can't rig the system to advantage yourself, your family, or your group. The veil of ignorance ensures that the original position is fair, but it also guarantees that agreement will be unanimous: unanimity would be impossible if each person insisted that justice should match her own particular religion, philosophy, or conception of the good life. Rawls then asks: what principles of social cooperation would people select in the original position, from behind this veil of ignorance?

Rawls's two principles of justice

According to Rawls, there are two main principles of justice, and the second 4.10 principle is complex (for a video explanation, click **here**):

a. Each person has the same indefeasible [undefeatable] claim to a fully adequate scheme of equal basic liberties, which scheme is compatible with a similar scheme of liberty for all.
b. Social and economic inequalities are to be arranged so that they satisfy two conditions: first they are to be attached to offices and positions open to all under conditions of fair equality of opportunity; and second, they are to be to the greatest benefit of the least-advantaged members of society (the difference principle). (Rawls, 2001, pp. 42–43)

Since the parties in the original position don't know the kind of life they want to live, they would place the highest priority on liberties that allow them to lead that life. Of course liberties can't be unlimited, since one person's actions can detract from the liberty of another person (see Chapter 1). The only solution that can yield unanimous agreement is maximal equal liberty for all.

4.11   Once each person has been guaranteed an adequate set of equal basic liberties, the second issue is the distribution of resources and opportunities. This part of Rawls's theory has been the most controversial one. What if, instead of cutting a cake for two people, you were cutting it for 12? You would probably still try to cut it into 12 equal pieces, since that guarantees you the biggest piece: if you cut unequal slices you could end up with less than 1/12 of the cake. Similarly, Rawls assume that each person will want a distribution of resources that guarantees the best possible *personal* outcome. But behind the veil of ignorance you can't tailor the rules to provide personal advantages. Rawls argues that the best you can do in this circumstances is to make the worst option as good as possible. The decision-making rule to maximize the worst (or "minimum") outcome is sometimes called "maximin." From behind the veil of ignorance, this means, according to Rawls, that you should consider the circumstance of the worst member of society under alternative rules that might be selected. Choose the rules that will leave the worst off person—whoever that might be—as well off as possible. According to Rawls, inequalities are *tolerable* (in the sense of being "not unfair") just in case they serve to maximize benefits to those who are worst off.

4.12   In the cake example, we end up with equal slices of cake, but Rawls does not think we would select exactly equal shares of resources. There is an important difference between slicing a cake and structuring an economy: in an economy inequalities sometimes promote greater total wealth. So, by analogy, a cake with unequal slices might be a much bigger cake than a cake with equal slices. According to Rawls, you want the smallest piece to be as big as possible, but that could mean having a smaller share of a bigger cake. By analogy, the worst off group might be better off if we permit some inequalities and live in a wealthier society overall.

4.13   Consider an example: **By some measures**, Afghanistan has a more equal distribution of wealth than Denmark, but most people would rather live in Denmark, since the poor in Denmark are much better off than the poor in Afghanistan.

One might reasonably think that Rawls's principles of justice imply that most (if not all) societies should go further and use progressive taxation so as to provide better opportunities for the poor and disadvantaged. This might include better public schools, designed to reduce the gap in educational opportunities, better public healthcare, designed to reduce the gap in life expectancies, and a much better social safety net. Rawls himself argues that such taxation is fair and that just institutions should provide all citizens with means and opportunities to pursue a decent and meaningful life.

But one need not think that this is so: some libertarian critics argue that 4.14 the best way to promote the welfare of the worst off members of society is to institute a minimal state that protects property rights and supports the operation of a free market.

The Libertarian Critique: Individual Liberty Restricts Redistribution

One of the first and most famous objections to Rawls came from his 4.15 Harvard colleague **Robert Nozick**. Nozick is the most famous proponent of *libertarianism*. He argued that Rawls's theory of justice requires excessive redistribution of property and that this would take away liberty and undermine justice. There are several parts to the libertarian critique. In this section we will look at them and consider how Rawlsians might respond.

Rawls assumes that we are born into a society and that we must find fair 4.16 terms of cooperation with the other members of society. But is this the right starting assumption? Nozick goes back to earlier versions of social contract theory, where we start instead with individuals who already have rights and must decide whether to join society or not. On Nozick's view, we cannot begin with the assumption that people are already cooperating members of a society; we need to begin with the assumption that people are autonomous individuals who can chose to contribute or not, depending on how they decide to use their liberty. Nozick argues that this way of thinking about justice is better, since Rawls assumes that people are already part of a cooperative community. Shouldn't a person be able to refuse to join?

On one view, society is a bad deal for those who join, so the most 4.17 reasonable course of action is to refuse. *Anarchists* deny that governments are justifiable at all. Some anarchists argue that government coercion is unjust tyranny unless people rationally consent, but it would be irrational to consent to others' force. Others urge that government could only coerce people if all people consented, but there has never been a time when people unanimously consented. An anarchist could claim that Rawls assumes without argument the core principle on which his theory rests: that I am obligated to agree to terms of fair cooperation. Why not think of people as individuals who are free to cooperate or not, as they see fit?

4.18   Nozick's position is less extreme than anarchism, because Nozick believes that a minimal state could be just. But, like the anarchist, he thinks we must assume that people have a choice about whether to join the state. Nozick asks us to imagine people who live without a government but have rights. Specifically, they have a right to life, to liberty, and to property they have acquired. Without a government, these rights are precarious: they can be taken away by others and one has little recourse other than fighting back and hoping one wins. Nozick assumes that, in such a situation, people would agree to join a protective association that would (for a fee) safeguard the rights that each person already has. The protective association would administer impartial justice and defend people from external enemies. People who chose not to join the protective association could do so, but they would be on their own and at a great disadvantage if they came into conflict with someone who had joined a protective association, since a person who has joined would have the combined strength of the association behind him.

4.19   Over time, more and more people would join. Eventually something like a state would emerge, because it is more efficient if one agency has a monopoly on the use of force. It would be a minimal state, one that restricts itself to enforcing contracts that people freely enter into, to protecting property rights, and to helping people who have been wronged get appropriate compensation. It would not, however, build schools and roads or run programs to support social welfare. Nozick urges that such a state is legitimate because we can imagine it arising out of the free choices of individuals who were not coerced to join.

4.20   Even more importantly, he argues that alternative states, which could *not* arise out of the free, voluntary choices of their participants, must involve unacceptable coercion. Like earlier social contractarians, Nozick argues that we need to consider existing institutions in light of the actions and choices that created them. If institutions could not have arisen without some people forcing others to cooperate against their will, then those institutions cannot be just.

4.21   In a second, closely related objection, Nozick argues that Rawls treats wealth like "manna from heaven" that is simply there to be distributed (or redistributed) in whatever way helps most the worst off. Nozick argues that this is a mistake, because people have prepolitical property rights that the government must respect. If I have spent the day fishing and caught several fish, the fish are my property (assuming I wasn't fishing in a pond that someone else owns). If the government takes half of my fish away, it violates my rights. Nozick thinks that rights trump considerations of the public good (he calls rights "side constraints" on the state). Even if torturing a person would save lives, it should not be done, because the right not to be tortured is a side constraint on what the government may do. Property rights limit the government's right to redistribute property.

One argument Nozick employs to support this position makes an analogy with **slavery**. Imagine the predicament of a slave with a master who can order her around at will. Suppose her situation gets progressively better: the master decides that she can work for him three days a week and for herself the other four. But the master reserves the right to change the number of days at any time. Is she still a slave? Now imagine he tells her that she can find whatever job she wants, but still owes him three-sevenths of whatever she makes. Is she still a slave? What if, instead of her giving three-sevenths to a specific person, there is a government where everyone except her gets to vote on how much taxation she must give to the rest of them? Is she still a slave? Now suppose she is given a vote, but her vote only matters if there is a tie, and ties never happen. Is she still a slave? Nozick thinks she is: after all, the majority can claim a right to three-sevenths (or more!) of her wealth. Is that so different from ordering her to work for the majority for a certain number of days? 4.22

According to Nozick, this slave's predicament precisely mirrors your situation if you live under a government that taxes you to support welfare programs that benefit others. When the government taxes you in this way, it is as if it takes from you—steals—the labor you undertook to earn the money the government takes as tax. While you may benefit from some of what your taxes buy, the benefits you get are not proportional to what you paid in. That, argues Nozick, is the essence of redistributive taxation. 4.23

A different argument urges that it is inappropriate to take away people's liberty in order to ensure a particular pattern of distribution. 4.24

Imagine that society has achieved a perfectly just distribution of wealth. What if one member of society—Sally—is a talented singer-songwriter. She offers people the chance to listen to concerts in her home, where she sings. Many people love this opportunity and happily pay $10 each for it. She then takes the money she makes and uses it to build a small auditorium in her backyard; and then she can sing to even more people. Then she buys a bigger property, and even more people pay to hear her sing. Now she is very wealthy and has upset the perfect distribution, but she achieved it through a series of voluntary transactions that people wanted to make. The only way to protect the pattern would be to take away liberty from both the singer and her audience.

If justice requires that people's holdings conform to some predetermined pattern, like equality, or even the difference principle, then even *gift* giving will upset the pattern. Suppose we start from an initially just distribution of goods that satisfies some pattern—whatever pattern distributive justice is supposed to achieve. If Rae gives Jon a gift, that will disturb the pattern, since Rae no longer possesses what she initially did. Any theory of justice that requires people's holdings to satisfy some prearranged distribution, Nozick argues, will require intervention to return the pattern to the one justice requires. If even gift giving is prohibited by patterned theories of justice, then patterned theories must require unreasonable interventions in people's lives.

4.25   Those sympathetic to Rawls can respond in several ways. Rawls denies that his theory is a patterned theory of the kind Nozick criticizes. He argues that the principles of justice apply to basic social institutions, not to individual holdings. So, they will not support invasive interventions like those Nozick ridicules.

4.26   In addition, Rawlsians argue that Nozick's libertarian approach looks only at formal liberty and undervalues substantive liberty. Nozick puts high value on prohibiting interference with a person's liberty. But does it make sense to say that a person who is starving or who lacks basic necessities is free to do as she wishes? If liberty includes the ability to make choices and shape one's own life, then liberty is increased when people are provided with the basic goods they need in order to act autonomously. The taxes paid by those who are better off may provide adequate opportunities for some people, without significantly diminishing the opportunities of others. Would that make such taxation just?

4.27   According to Rawls, people who are better off may have earned their income through their own efforts, but they would earn far less without the cooperation of all, and without the basic institutions, including protections for market transactions and the rule of law. These institutions are supported through taxation. It is not unjust, therefore, to ask people who have enjoyed these benefits of mutual cooperation to pay taxes that support others' opportunity to participate on equal terms.

4.28   Finally, Rawls can argue that the net effect of Nozick's system is radical inequality of opportunity, since those who are wealthy secure much better opportunities for their children than the poor are able to do. It is unfair, argues Rawls, that some people lack adequate opportunities just because of bad luck. When inequalities are extreme, they may even undermine fundamental institutions like democracy. Even if simple-minded egalitarian intervention that aims to give one person goods earned by another is unjust, as Nozick and Rawls would agree, intervention to ensure the survival of democracy may be *required* by justice.

Some libertarians meet this response head-on, by claiming that massive 4.29 inequality is in fact justified as a matter of principle. Property rights are simply nonnegotiable. Others take a different tack and argue that property rights are instrumentally valuable by stimulating economic growth and that the poor in a capitalist society will ultimately be better off than the poor in a more redistributive society. If this is true, over the long term capitalism might actually satisfy the difference principle. A third option, sometimes called "left libertarianism," argues that there should be initial redistribution, so that people have roughly equal (or initially adequate) opportunities, but no further government intervention after that. This view attempts to combine the concern for equal opportunity with a libertarian belief that people should live with the consequences of their subsequent decisions.

Utilitarian Critique: An Alternative Rationale for Redistribution

Rawls presented his original theory of justice as a direct attack on 4.30 utilitarianism, so it is not surprising that utilitarians have attempted to defend their position. Utilitarianism assumes that benefits to one person cancel out burdens on another. But Rawls argues that this is wrong: sometimes forcing some to bear burdens so that others can enjoy great benefits is *unfair*. By specifying that the worst-off group be as well off as possible, Rawls is rejecting the claim that the worst off must accept the justification "you must be worse off so that other can be better off."

Utilitarians think that Rawls's theory leads to some strange conclusions. 4.31 What if confiscating half of the wealth of 80 percent of the people made the worst-off 20 percent slightly better off? The difference principle seems to command this, but utilitarians would argue that it takes redistribution to excess. The unhappiness caused to the 80 percent would far exceed the happiness gained by the 20 percent.

Utilitarians are not opposed to redistribution in principle. In fact in 4.32 some cases they require it, because of the principle of diminishing marginal utility. The more wealth you already have, the less happiness you gain from a small increase. If you give a billionaire $100, how much additional happiness can it bring? If you give $100 to someone with nothing to eat, the gain may be immense. Utilitarianism thus has a rationale for redistribution but says that one should stop at the point where the gains to the person in receipt of the aid are equal to the net loss in utility for society as a whole.

4.33   Another way of putting it is to say that people in the original position seem excessively risk-averse. Only looking at the worst possible scenario keeps you from noticing instances where there are two choices such that both have acceptable worst case scenarios but one has much better outcomes in the other cases. Why not choose the distribution that has the highest average, since you probably will not be the worst off person? If the situation of the worst off position is not terrible, you might be even more willing to tolerate additional inequality for the sake of improving the average level of happiness.

4.34   Rawls claims that it is a mistake to think that the argument for the difference principle rests on the claim that rational people in the original position are risk-averse. Rather he stipulates that people in the original position have no access to probabilities, so they cannot judge on that basis. Moreover, argues Rawls, the worst outcomes will be very bad in societies that are unfair. People in the original position would not be willing to risk being the worst-off member of an unfair society just in order to gain greater benefits for those who are better off. As long as there is a situation where all the possibilities are acceptable—where everyone enjoys the opportunity for a good (or at least a decent) life— that is the one they should pick. Rawls thinks that it is important that people behind the veil choose principles that they will endorse as just once the veil is removed. He argues that the worst-off members of society could not endorse a system that imposed costs on them and made them even worse off than they might have been, only to provide additional benefits for others, who are better off.

4.35   Perhaps there is an intermediate position that gains some of the advantages of Rawls's view with less redistributive cost. Rawls states that in the original position we would insist on a minimal level of provision for everyone, such that everyone has an opportunity to lead a decent life. But some argue that, once this is obtained, additional inequalities are acceptable. Such positions are sometimes called *basic minimum views*, or *sufficientarianism*. Sufficientarians agree that some circumstances are unacceptable— no one should suffer extreme deprivation. But, once deprivation has been addressed, subsequent inequalities are not objectionable.

> SUFFICIENTARIANISM: As a first priority, justice must ensure that no one lacks the sufficient minimum of resources and opportunities necessary for a good (or decent) life.

The sufficient minimum need not be thought of as bare subsistence; it might involve sufficient resources for a good education, healthcare, and opportunities for meaningful political participation. But sufficientarians argue that distributive inequalities are tolerable as long as everyone has adequate welfare and opportunities.

Feminist Critique: The Public–Private Distinction and Power Relations

Up to this point we have considered injustice and inequality in the abstract. 4.36
But many *actual* inequalities are associated with discrimination or disadvantages that people suffer because of their race, gender, or other arbitrary characteristics. Feminist accounts of justice draw attention to the way in which people's gender can influence life prospects.

Some feminist critics have argued that Rawls inappropriately ignores 4.37
gender in the development of his theory of justice. This section will focus on two prominent feminist critics of Rawls: Susan Moller Okin and Iris Young.

Responding to Rawls's original version of his argument in *Theory of* 4.38
Justice, Okin points out that Rawls's principles of justice apply only to the basic structures of society, not to private associations or to the family. This, she argued, is a serious omission, and a recurring problem in liberal thought. Liberalism concerns itself only with that which is "public." The family, which is "private," is exempted from scrutiny, despite the fact that it is in the family that women experience widespread and serious injustice. For example, many studies show that women do a larger percentage of household tasks and child-rearing. **Even in families where men and women work equal hours outside the home, women tend to work more inside the home**. Worse, the idea that the home is "private" has sometimes made it difficult to protect women from domestic abuse. Okin suggested that, if one took Rawls's approach and asked what sort of laws and structures one would want for society not knowing in advance whether one was male or female, the result would be a series of reforms designed to increase opportunities for women and to treat them more justly.

In his later work, Rawls acknowledged and incorporated much of this 4.39
critique. His point was not, he says, to shield the family from reform or to perpetuate the current structures, in which women experience the results of unfair divisions of labor. His point was instead twofold: first, the principles of justice do not apply directly to families or other private associations.

For example, parents do not need to parent by the difference principle. Second, the laws of society, including family law, need to promote the fair opportunities of all citizens, including women. This places some constraints on private associations and would place some constraints on families as well. Rawls supported reforming family law to enact policies that create greater equality of opportunity for men and women.

4.40   Another feminist political theorist, Iris Young, argues that Rawls pays insufficient attention to the dynamics of power. There are forms of injustice, argues Iris Young, that cannot be adequately represented as problems of *distribution*. Young argues that standard theories of justice, including Rawls's theory, systematically overlook injustices that are essentially forms of oppression. Oppression, as she interprets it, has at least five different aspects or "faces": exploitation, marginalization, powerlessness, cultural imperialism, and violence.

Iris Young's five faces of oppression

1. EXPLOITATION. People are exploited when those for whom they work treat them as if they were things, in a way that harms them. Exploitation takes place when one person gains an advantage at cost to another.
2. MARGINALIZATION. People who are *marginalized* are effectively "expelled from useful participation in social life and thus potentially subjected to severe material deprivation and even extermination."
3. POWERLESSNESS. Social power is sometimes measured as the ability to accomplish what one wants to do. When people lack social power, they are at the mercy of others. The powerless "lack the authority, status, and sense of self" that more powerful people tend to have.
4. CULTURAL IMPERIALISM. "To experience cultural imperialism means to experience how the dominant meanings of a society render the particular perspective of one's own group invisible at the same time as they stereotype one's group and mark it out as the Other."
5. VIOLENCE. Members of some groups must "live with the knowledge that they must fear random, unprovoked attacks on their persons or property, which have no motive but to damage, humiliate, or destroy the person." (Young, 1990, pp. 48–63)

According to Young, inappropriate focus on contract and distribution has led people to overlook injustices created by differences in social and economic power and their associated tendency to create opportunities for some people to oppress others. But, on Young's account, oppression is not simply something bad that some people do to others; it is a structural feature of social institutions. **Her argument is an example of a feminist critique of power relations**. As an example, consider sexism and racism and the way they operate in most modern societies. One "face" of discrimination is embodied in overt actions where people self-consciously impose disadvantages on others, who are members of the disfavored group. The rules that prohibited women from voting and the rules that forced black Americans to sit at the back of the bus involved this kind of overt discrimination. But even well-meaning people can inadvertently discriminate against others—not because they are willfully racist or sexist, but simply because they employ language and concepts that express and reinforce disadvantageous stereotypes. An overt racist might avoid hiring an applicant expressly because she is a woman, or because she is black. But another person might simply systematically perceive women or African Americans to be less competent or less able, even when there is ample evidence of competence and ability.

The view that political theorists should focus on oppression and power relations and on the influence of social power on the lives of people who are disadvantaged has indeed a different orientation from the contractarian views considered above. But there is a long history of theorists who make similar recommendations and from whose work Young is able to draw. Young draws on the work of Karl Marx and Max Weber. More recent work on oppression and exploitation, by Ann Cudd and Ruth Sample, shows that this is a productive path for future work in political theory. 4.41

How might Rawls respond to his feminist critics? Perhaps he should simply acknowledge their critique and work to incorporate their insights. But he might also argue that the redistribution of resources required by the difference principle would have enormous implications for power relations. Rawls's commitment to fair equality of opportunity means that society should take measures to deal with the more subtle ways in which power relations take away opportunities. In practice, Rawls said little in response to his feminist critics, though he does mention that he accepts features of Okin's critique. It is worthwhile to consider whether theories like those of Rawls and Nozick need to pay more attention to issues of race, gender, and power. How would libertarian and liberal views change if their proponents were more attuned to discrimination and to nonmaterial sources of inequality? 4.42

Communitarian Critique: Alternatives to Individualism

4.43 A different critique of Rawls focuses on its individualism. The *communitarian* critics of liberalism argue that it is inappropriate to begin developing a theory of justice by trying to imagine what people would be like if they didn't live in society—if they were isolated social atoms or society-less individuals. The things that are important about people, argue some communitarian critics, are just the things that are "imagined away" in theories like those of Rawls and Nozick.

4.44   For example, what are we really doing when we try to imagine people in Rawls's original position? In some ways, the "people" in the original position are hardly people at all. Michael Sandel argued that they have been stripped of everything that makes them recognizably human: their conceptions of the good, their nationality, family membership, their religious views, their friendships, and their past histories. In fact Rawls himself admits that the idea of "unanimity" in the original position is misleading since all the people are, by definition, identical. Instead of imagining a group, we could achieve the same result by thinking of an original position with only a single person.

4.45   Sandel argues that this stems from a tendency in liberalism to think that freedom involves independence from unchosen commitments. Sandel thinks that our identities are actually constituted in large part by things we don't choose. We don't choose the nation or family into which we are born, yet these are a very important part of our identity, our sense of self. Sandel argues that we would be better off if we began with the commitments and ends we have as members of various communities and deliberated about how these might be improved and refined. What we know about the history of our country and our past political traditions should be the starting point for debate instead of being set aside.

4.46   Will Kymlicka has defended much of Rawls's approach while remedying perceived deficiencies in his treatment of people as members of groups. (We discuss Rawls's *Political Liberalism* and Kymlicka's views on multiculturalism in Chapter 9.) Kymlicka argues that the root intuition in liberalism is not that we are disembodied selves with no history or communal attachments. We never have to imagine ourselves like that. But we do need to see ourselves as people who are capable of revising, and even rejecting, some of the attachments we inherit. We might change our religious beliefs or immigrate to another country, for example. We may have little desire to do either, but we can imagine such a thing and would not be less of a "person" if we did. Liberalism does defend people's right to alter their attachments.

The device of the original position is a way to illustrate why we think that the ability to revise these commitments should be protected by the law.

A different critique of Rawls come from Michael Walzer. He argues that Rawls is too universalistic. Instead of assuming that we can have a universal list of "primary goods" that people distribute from behind a veil of ignorance, Walzer argues that different cultures value different goods in different ways. Behind the veil of ignorance there would be no way to know how a particular good should be distributed, because we would not know the social meaning of the good in question. For example, Walzer thinks that membership in a community carries with it a commitment to provide for the needs of fellow members. But what are needs? Walzer says that this varies greatly from one community to another, hence different communities are obligated to provide different types of goods for their members. **4.47**

In his later work Rawls appeared to back away from some of the universalistic claims he made in *Theory of Justice*. Instead of a theory of justice for all people at all times, he argues that his theory reflects how people who live in western cultures should think about justice, given the fact that we do live in cultures where we value freedom and equality and where people with different beliefs and convictions must tolerate each other and cooperate. Nonetheless, Rawls would still say that justice defines limits and that societies that don't protect basic rights and opportunities will be *unjust*. **4.48**

Cosmopolitan Critique: The Demands of Global Justice

If Rawls is right and economic resources should be redistributed to maximally benefit the worst off group, what are the implications, when we think globally? Rawls was imagining transferring money from the rich in one country to the poor in another. The wealth gaps are even more vast, however, if we look globally. **For example, the bottom 5 percent in the United States are wealthier (in purchasing power) than 68 percent of the world's population. By some measures, the poorest 5 percent (by income) in the United States has more purchasing power than the top 5 percent in India.** Note that this is not the same as saying the poorest in America are wealthier than the richest in India, which is clearly false. If we were to compare the top 1 percent with the bottom 1 percent, the numbers would be very different. But any way you look at it, global inequalities are huge. **4.49**

While cross-cultural measures of poverty are complex and contestable, it is clear that there are vast gaps in wealth between different countries. For **4.50** most people around the world, the sort of health, education, and work opportunities they can expect are determined by the country in which they were born. **This has led some people to ask whether we should apply Rawls's logic to the issue of global justice**. Imagine a new original position where we adopted rules for global justice without knowing which country we would inhabit. The same logic that prompts us to maximize the plight of the worst off domestically in Rawls's theory would now give us a reason to try to make the poor in the worst of countries as well off as possible. The implications of this attitude, if implemented, would be vast. **There are more than 2 billion people in the world who live on less than \$2 per day**. Making them as well off as possible would require massive transfer of resources from wealthy nations to poorer ones.

4.51   Rawls has resisted this argument. He tries to find a middle ground between a nationalist view, which says we have no obligations to those in other countries, and the cosmopolitan view that national boundaries are irrelevant to justice. Rawls argues that the difference principle applies only within a nation, not between nations. Within a nation people are engaged in a cooperative enterprise and need fair terms of cooperation. Ideally they will have democratic institutions. But vast disparities in wealth can cause the poor to be marginalized from political power. The poor in foreign countries are not cooperating with people in rich countries in the same way, nor do they share the same political institutions.

4.52   Nonetheless, it is also true that states (and the people and companies within them) do interact with each other and that there are some obligations of justice toward other countries. Rawls claims that well-ordered societies should provide aid to what he calls "burdened societies" that lack the resources to be well-ordered. Once these burdened societies reach a sufficient minimum and become well-ordered, no further redistribution is required. This means that there could still be significant differences in wealth between countries once there are fair and just governments that provide basic opportunities for their citizens. Could Rawls's view of international relations be considered a version of sufficientarianism?

4.53   Often arguments about global justice depend on benevolence: what should the rich give to the poor because the rich are rich and the poor are poor? Thomas Pogge has tried to develop a different argument, namely that rich countries owe compensation to poor countries because they have wronged them. Rich countries, he claims, have *caused* poverty in the developing world. They have done this through trade policies whereby rich countries place higher tariffs on goods from poor countries than vice versa, and by recognizing and loaning money to ruthless dictators who have plundered poor countries.

On the other hand, one critic of Pogge argues that it is not obvious that poor countries would be rich if the rich countries didn't exist. Through most of world history, poverty has been very common. The best prediction about where poor countries would be without the rich countries is that they would still be poor. It is not so much that rich countries have made poor countries poorer as that capitalism has generated a lot of wealth in rich countries that makes the plight of the poor look much worse by comparison (Risse, 2005). Is this view plausible? Would the poor countries of the world be better off or worse off in the absence of the wealthier and more developed nations? 4.54

Conclusion

For more than forty years, much of the debate about justice in political philosophy has consisted of critiques, modifications, and defenses of Rawls's position. As this chapter demonstrates, that was not because most people actually agree with Rawls's position. His critics outnumber those who support his entire theory. Nonetheless his position has shaped the debate by placing matters of rights and fair distribution of resources at the center of discussions about justice. These matters are crucial because so much rides on how we answer the question: "What am I entitled to?" We think of progressive taxation differently if we think that it's taking from the rich what was rightfully theirs, as opposed to thinking of it as a way of giving the poor something they are entitled to. Debate about distribution and redistribution tends to be at the center of political debate, and partisans on both sides frequently invoke justice to defend their position. The arguments considered here provide a framework for understanding and evaluating those claims. 4.55

References and Further Reading

Berlin, Isaiah. 1955–1956. "Equality." *Proceedings of the Aristotelian Society*, 56: 301–326. An introduction to a wide range of meanings of "equality."

Cohen, Gerald Allan. 2009. *Rescuing Justice and Equality*. Cambridge, MA: Harvard University Press. Cohen argues that Rawls's difference principle is insufficiently egalitarian, and that justice requires more.

Kymlicka, Will. 2000. *Multicultural Citizenship: A Liberal Theory of Minority Rights*. Oxford: Oxford University Press. Kymlicka argues that pluralistic societies should provide special protections for minority cultures, and presents managing cultural pluralism as a central problem of justice.

Nozick, Robert. 1974. *Anarchy, State, and Utopia*. New York: Basic Books. Nozick's book is the most famous contemporary defense of libertarianism.

Nussbaum, Martha. 1995. "Human Capabilities, Female Human Beings." In *Women, Culture, and Development: A Study of Human Capabilities*, edited by Martha Nussbaum and Jonathan Glover. Oxford: Clarendon, pp. 61–115. In this essay Nussbaum provides a concise and accessible defense of the "capabilities approach" as a component of a theory of justice and as a theory of human development.

Nussbaum, Martha. 2011. *Creating Capabilities*. Cambridge, MA: Harvard University Press. This is a contemporary defense of Nussbaum's capabilities approach.

Pogge, Thomas. 2008 [2002]. *World Poverty and Human Rights: Cosmopolitan Responsibilities and Reforms*. Cambridge: Polity. A defense of the claim that rich countries must help poor countries because the former have harmed the latter.

Rawls, John. 1971. *A Theory of Justice*. Cambridge, MA: Harvard University Press. Rawls's *Theory of Justice* develops a contractarian and egalitarian account of justice as a property of political institutions. It is widely regarded, even by people who disagree with Rawls, as the most important treatment of justice in contemporary political philosophy.

Rawls, John. 2001. *Justice as Fairness: A Restatement*, edited by Erin Kelly. Cambridge, MA: Harvard University Press. In this shorter book, Rawls integrates his ideas from several works and modifies some details of his theory in response to criticisms.

Risse, Mathias. 2005. "How Does the Global Order Harm the Poor?" *Philosophy and Public Affairs*, 33(1): 349–376. A critique of Pogge's claim that rich countries have caused poverty in poor countries.

Sandel, Michael. 1998. *Liberalism and the Limits of Justice* (2nd edn.). Cambridge: Cambridge University Press. Sandel articulates a communitarian critique of contemporary liberal theories of justice.

Sen, Amartya. 2009. *The Idea of Justice*. Cambridge, MA: Harvard University Press. This book extends Rawls's liberal theory of justice, then moves beyond Rawls to argue that justice is a much broader concept than Rawls appreciated.

Tomasi, John. 2013. *Free Market Fairness*. Princeton, NJ: Princeton University Press. Tomasi argues that strong property rights (and the inequality they permit) will in the long run make the poor better off.

Walzer, Michael. 1983. *Spheres of Justice*. New York: Basic Books. Walzer argues that different principles and different "norms" appropriately apply in different areas of public life. This book is written in a more accessible style than most philosophy books.

Williams, Bernard. 1973. "The Idea of Equality." In Bernard Williams, *Problems of the Self*. Cambridge: Cambridge University Press, pp. 230–249. Williams argues that the starting point of equality creates a presumption for equality and that we must show a relevant reason for departing from equality.

Young, Iris. 1990. *Justice and the Politics of Difference*. Princeton, NJ: Princeton University Press. Young's book dramatically expands the scope of the concept of justice, arguing that Rawls inappropriately restricts his attention to problems of distribution.

Online Resources

1 https://www.youtube.com/watch?v=5-JQ17X6VNg
2 https://en.wikipedia.org/wiki/List_of_countries_by_income_equality
3 http://plato.stanford.edu/entries/nozick-political/
4 https://www.youtube.com/watch?v=13DVXzGG6AM
5 http://www.thenation.com/article/why-it-matters-women-do-most-housework/
6 http://plato.stanford.edu/entries/feminist-power/
7 http://economix.blogs.nytimes.com/2011/01/31/the-haves-and-the-have-nots/?_r=0
8 http://plato.stanford.edu/entries/international-justice/
9 http://www.worldbank.org/en/topic/poverty/overview

Part II

PROBLEMS OF AUTHORITY AND LEGITIMACY

5

DEMOCRACY

JUSTIN   Sophie, our democracy is just a mess. The politicians aren't responsive to the people: ever since the Supreme Court set loose the corporations, corporate money speaks louder than anyone else.

SOPHIE   I heard about those cases. Weren't they about free speech? They were about people's ability to spend money to express their support for candidates or policies they prefer.

JUSTIN   They're *sort* of about free speech: free speech for *corporations*, not for individuals. What really bothers me is that big rich corporations now have the right to spend huge amounts of money on campaigns. The democratic process can't work properly when some people just have more power to influence electoral outcomes than others. And it *really* can't work when rich corporations can manipulate the process so that things turn out their way.

SOPHIE   Justin, I hear you. But I think it's much more complicated than you imply. When, as you say, "corporations" spend money for political campaigns, it's really the people *in* those corporations who are spending that money. And surely you don't deny that campaign ads are a form of speech. Democracy needs free speech more than just about anything else. What's more, when people put out political ads, it's *political* speech. How can you have an effective democracy if Congress has the right to control political speech?

This Is Political Philosophy: An Introduction, First Edition. Alex Tuckness and Clark Wolf.
© 2017 John Wiley & Sons, Inc. Published 2017 by John Wiley & Sons, Inc.

JUSTIN   Campaign ads may be political speech. But does that mean
          that *money* is speech?

SOPHIE   If I spend money to support my favorite candidate, then
          yeah, I think money is speech. You know what they say:
          "Money talks!"

JUSTIN   In this case, *as they say*, "Money doesn't talk. It *screams!*"
          And if we let people's influence on election outcomes depend
          on their income or their wealth, then we don't have a democ-
          racy any more. We have a *plutocracy*, where the people who
          have all the wealth have all the political power too.

SOPHIE   I know people said that when the *Citizens' United* and
          McCutcheon cases came through the Supreme Court. But
          it hasn't worked out that way, has it? People said that the
          big corporations would all support the Republican can-
          didates, since people think the Republicans are more
          sympathetic to business interests. But *both* parties have
          raised huge amounts of money, and candidates from
          both parties have benefited from the money that has
          been spent on elections. These decisions don't seem to
          have had the effect on elections that people predicted
          they would have.

JUSTIN   You're right that both of the major political parties have
          spent huge amounts of money trying to influence cam-
          paign outcomes. But that doesn't mean that this money
          hasn't warped the democratic process. In this case, it
          means that *both* parties have sold out. They're both so
          deeply in debt to their wealthy political donors that nei-
          ther one of them cares about the interests of the rest of us.
          Instead of listening to people, trying to find out what our
          interests are and what they could do to earn our votes,
          they're viewing us as *consumers*, as *pawns* to be manipu-
          lated. Instead of being influenced by the people who vote,
          they spend all their time trying to influence *us*, to tell us
          what to think.

SOPHIE   I don't think it's nearly as bad as you imply. Politicians posi-
          tion themselves so that they will appeal to as many voters
          as they can, and when they decide on how to do it they
          certainly look at polls and try to gauge what people want.
          It's true that they work to influence and persuade other

people, once they've defined their position. But they're much more responsive to people's values and interests than you imply.

JUSTIN   I think it's much easier, these days, to *manipulate* public opinion than it is to respond to people's real interests. Democracy only works if money and market forces are kept out of the political process. People may not be equal in wealth, but we should be equal in our ability to influence the outcome of elections: one person, one vote! A nation that doesn't preserve democratic equality isn't really a democracy any more at all.

SOPHIE   By that logic, the United States has *never* been a democracy. And Canada isn't either: in Canada there are all sorts of special provisions that give rights to indigenous peoples. The structure of voting in the United States *ensures* that people from different states don't have equal influence on the Senate. These things might mean that people have different influence on democratic outcomes, as you say, but it's just silly to say that they mean that the United States isn't a democracy.

Democracy and Political Self-Governance

Who should hold ultimate political power? One popular answer today is 5.1 "the people." While most governments today claim to be democracies of one form or another, democracy has not always been a favored form. Traditional alternatives are monarchy (rule by one), oligarchy (rule by the few who are rich), aristocracy (rule by the elite), or some combination of these. Through most of human history democracy has been rare, and often unpopular. Even in eighteenth-century America the founders vehemently denied that what they proposed was a democracy. This chapter will consider the forms and justification of democracy. We will find that some of democracy's popularity comes from vagueness: people mean different things by this term. We will also see that there are a variety of ways to justify democracy. Some appeal to benefits that democracy will bring about, while others claim that democracy is intrinsically valuable.

What Is Democracy?

5.2 Democracy means "rule of the people." People who celebrate democracy often emphasize that democratic institutions are a form of *self-rule:* instead of having laws and rules passed down from some authority, in a democracy citizens govern themselves, either directly or through representatives.

5.3   Three questions arise for any democratic state: first, who are "the people" who are to rule themselves? That is, who gets to participate in the public decision process, and who is excluded? Second, how are the contributions of different people aggregated into a collective decision? Must votes have equal weight and consideration, or is it permissible for different people's votes to count differently? Finally, are there areas that are *excluded* from democratic decision making? Or should all issues of public concern be decided through a democratic process?

Who Gets to Participate?

5.4 In ancient Athens citizens involved in public decision making were "free-born" landowning males over the age of 20 who were not foreigners. In the United States there were vigorous debates about who should be allowed to vote and about how political power should be organized. John Adams, one of the US founders, thought that it was obvious that *women* should not be allowed to vote. He argued that voting rights should be restricted to landholding men, since (as he claimed) people who don't own property lack the necessary judgment and are not likely to take an interest in public affairs:

> But why exclude women? You will Say, because their Delicacy renders them unfit for Practice and Experience, in the great Business of Life, and the hardy Enterprises of War, as well as the arduous Cares of State. Besides, their attention is So much engaged with the necessary Nurture of their Children, that Nature has made them fittest for domestic Cares. And Children have not Judgment or Will of their own. True. But will not these Reasons apply to others? … [I]f you give to every Man, who has no Property, a Vote, will you not make a fine encouraging Provision for Corruption by your fundamental Law? Such is the Frailty of the human Heart, that very few Men, who have no Property, have any Judgment of their own. They talk and vote as they are directed by Some Man of Property, who has attached their Minds to his Interest. (Adams, 1776, p. 3)

Until the Civil War, the United States excluded slaves from voting and political action. It was **not until 1920** that women were able to participate in national elections. Some people argue that the United States was not a real democracy until the mid-twentieth century, after women and African Americans demanded and won a meaningful right to vote. But all democratic institutions exclude some interested parties from participation: children and nonnaturalized aliens are still excluded from voting in US elections. Does their exclusion raise similar questions? Perhaps "democracy" is a matter of degree, some states or institutions being more democratic than others. If so, maybe we should ask: "*How* democratic are our institutions?" instead of asking: "Are we a democracy?" Then we can consider whether our institutions would be improved if they were made more democratic (if 17-year-olds were permitted to vote, for example) or whether democracy should sometimes be constrained.

The American experience shows that merely formal possession of a legal right to vote is not enough for democratic participation. African Americans had the legal right to vote for many decades before they could effectively *exercise* that right. Formal legal rights may have little value if people's rights are consistently violated or if some people use force to prevent others from exercising their rights.

Most democracies use voting procedures to combine individual judgments into a collective judgment. So anyone who is allowed to vote is included, and everyone gets one vote. But is voting enough? On some models, democratic decision making must be *deliberative*. According to advocates of deliberative democracy, people should have an opportunity to talk and to reason with one another before votes are cast. Deliberative democracy of this sort is a philosophical ideal, but it is difficult to achieve in practice. Even when elections are small and local, it is difficult for people to get together to discuss the reasons for alternative policies or candidates. If votes merely reflect people's uninformed preferences, why should we take elections seriously?

Equality is sometimes taken to be necessary for democracy: if different people's inputs are counted differently, then democratic outcomes won't be the rule of the people, it will be the rule of those people whose input counts most. But in actual democracies equality is difficult to achieve. In the United States, for example, the weight of your vote in national elections **may depend on the state in which you live**. Americans who live in a low-population swing state have a vote that "counts much more" in national elections than it does for those who live in a populous state, where elections are reliably won by one political party or the other. Is this inequality in votes a flaw that makes the United States less democratic than it could be? Is it so egregious that it makes the US something other than a democracy? Or can this state of affairs be justified with good reasons and reconciled with democratic ideals?

Constitutional Democracy and Rights

5.8　It is difficult to separate the idea of democracy from the rights that motivate democratic ideals and from the rights that make democratic institutions possible. For this reason, we will begin our discussion of democracy with a brief introduction to rights.

5.9　　Well-functioning democracies are often instituted to support an underlying right to self-governance, which will be discussed in a later section of this chapter. But other rights are necessary in order to ensure that democratic institutions will function appropriately: participants in a democracy should have a right to contribute to democratic decision making (in many cases, this means a right to vote) and rights against manipulation or distortion of democratic outcomes.

5.10　　Constitutional democracies insulate *some* rights against democratic control: under the US constitution, for example, it is impossible to overturn fundamental constitutional rights by democratic vote. Even if a majority of citizens were to vote to put in place laws that prevent the "free exercise of religion," or to institute "cruel and unusual punishments," those laws would have no effect. Constitutionalism both protects and denies rights: if we have a fundamental constitutional right to freedom of assembly, this means, by implication, that, as citizens, we have *no right* to enact legislation that would deny other citizens the right freely to assemble.

5.11　　By contrast, in a direct democracy, all matters of public concern can in principle be settled through a public vote. Constitutionalism was motivated in part by concern that unregulated direct democracy would impose a *tyranny of the majority* on minority groups. In a constitutional democracy democratic majorities will not always get their way. According to constitutionalism, the fundamental rights of a minority take precedence over majority rule. For example, the state of Virginia had laws prohibiting inter-racial marriage until 1967. A majority of Americans were *opposed* to inter-racial marriage in 1967. But in the aptly named case *Loving v. Virginia* of that same year, the US Supreme Court ruled that the majority had no right to deny inter-racial couples equal protection of the law, and that Virginia's law did just that. In this as in other cases, the court ruled that the rights of the individual cannot be violated even if a majority of citizens votes to enact legislation.

In some constitutions even fundamental rights can be changed: the 5.12 United States could add amendments to the constitution to *remove* rights of freedom of speech or religion. Under other constitutions, some rights are *entrenched*: they cannot be changed by any constitutional means. The German constitution, for example, specifies in Article 79 Section 3 that some constitutional amendments are inadmissible.

Sources of rights

Political theorists usually distinguish between *legal rights* and *natural* or 5.13 *moral rights*. Legal rights are rights that are created by the legislature. If you were 19 years old when the voting age was lowered from 21 to 18, then you had a right to vote after the law was changed—but not before. There is nothing inherent in the moral fabric of the universe that says 18 is the correct age to begin voting, as opposed to 18 years and 2 days. Some prefer to use the terms "institutional" and "noninstitutional" to get at the same idea. Institutional rights are recognized by an institution, such as Congress or the United Nations. Noninstitutional rights are claimed independently of that recognition. In practice, these terms can overlap. Something might be both a legal right and a natural right. Something can be both an institutional right and a noninstitutional right. Torturing the innocent might be intrinsically wrong, and also illegal in a particular country.

When people urged that former slaves have a right to vote, they often 5.14 argued that former slaves had a natural or moral right to vote and that the law should acknowledge that natural right. Consider the following statement:

> One of the reasons slavery was wrong is that people's rights were systematically violated by bad laws. Equal democratic representation is a *right*: Oppressed American slaves had a right to vote, even if unjust laws prevent them from exercising that right.

This statement can't refer to *legal* rights: it was bad *laws* that denied people the right to vote. If the claim makes sense, it must mean that slaves had a natural right, or a moral right. To say that they had such a right, one need not believe that rights are part of the natural order of the world, in the way the laws of physics are natural laws. To say, in this sense, that a person has a natural or moral right to vote is to say, minimally, that there are good moral reasons supporting that person's claim to vote. For example, one might argue that there are compelling moral reasons why people should be able to influence the political institutions that govern them, and that this reason explains and justifies the right to vote. On one view, moral or natural rights are reducible to the reasons we have for providing people with whatever they have a right to. On this view,

> Person P has a moral right to A just in case there are conclusive moral reasons why other people should honor P's claim to A.

The idea that some rights are preconstitutional has a long history. For example, when Thomas Jefferson wrote, in the Declaration of Independence, that all people (he actually wrote all "men") are endowed with "inalienable rights to life, liberty and the pursuit of happiness," he did not mean that there were laws in place protecting those rights. On Jefferson's view, natural rights may not be *secure* if people are not able to protect them. One of the purposes of government, as Jefferson wrote in the next sentence of the declaration, is to make our natural rights *secure:* "To secure these rights, governments are instituted among men, deriving their just powers from the consent of the governed."

5.15   Jefferson did not invent this view of rights. One of his sources was the political philosopher **John Locke**. According to Locke, people have natural rights just by virtue of being human. If a random group of people found themselves suddenly washed ashore on a deserted island where there were no laws, Locke would have said that each person still had a natural right to life and that murder violates a person's rights even if there is no legal system in place.

5.16   There are other terms people sometimes use to get at this same idea. Sometimes people use the phrase "human rights" in a way that makes it similar to "natural rights." On this view, *human rights* are rights that people have just by virtue of being human. If a country's legal system does not recognize these human rights, the legal system is flawed.

5.17   People can also disagree about how to characterize a right. Sarah and Tom might both agree that war crimes violate people's rights, but Sarah might think that this is true because international law forbids war crimes (a legal–institutional explanation), while Tom might think that such actions violate moral rights people have regardless of whether international law condemns such actions.

It is possible to see democracy as something required by natural rights or to see the power of majority as constrained by natural rights. It is also possible to argue the reverse: that rights gain their authority from the majorities that enacted them. 5.18

Claim and liberty rights

Not all rights restrict the power of the majority in the same way. Philosophers and lawyers have developed a sophisticated vocabulary for differentiating various kinds of rights. The claim "I have a right to life" could mean several different things. It might mean that other people have a duty not to kill me. This is sometimes called a *claim right*, because the person asserting the right makes a claim on others to act or not act in a certain way. But someone might also invoke his "right to life" in a case where he is accused of killing another person. The person accused might say that he should not be charged with murder because he killed in self-defense and the right to kill in self-defense flows from a right to life. This sort of right has several different names: a privilege, a *liberty right*, or a bare liberty. A person has a *liberty* to do something just in case there is no valid moral or legal reason why she should not do it. If you have a liberty to do something, then you cannot rightly be blamed or punished for having done it. Thomas Hobbes argued that the right to self-defense is a liberty right. No one can be blamed for doing what they must do to preserve their own life. 5.19

Imagine the following scenario: a man walks into a hospital and demands to be treated for a life-threatening health problem. This hospital has a policy, allowed by the law, of refusing to treat people who are unable to pay. The man is unable to pay, so the hospital refuses to treat him. The man then pulls a gun and threatens to kill a doctor unless the doctor saves his life. The doctor, who is also well trained in political philosophy, might respond, "I can't blame you for what you are doing since I happen to believe a person is always justified in doing whatever is needed to save his own life."

That same doctor, without contradicting herself, could give the man a lethal dose of medicine, in self-defense. If there is a right to self-defense, then in this case both the patient and the doctor may have a "right to life" in the sense of a liberty right. Each is at liberty (within limits) to do what is necessary to save his or her life. A liberty right doesn't place any obligations on other people, it merely blocks moral or legal condemnation of the action one is at liberty to perform.

5.20   Some philosophers question whether bare liberties can properly be called "rights." Some have urged that a liberty must be accompanied by claims (against others' interference) before it is properly a right. A bare liberty right does not obligate the majority to provide anything to help a person attain her goal. Normally when we think of rights we think of claim rights, since these place a positive obligation on others to see that our right is respected. In the history of philosophy, however, there are philosophical traditions (notably Hobbes) in which liberties are identified with rights.

Interest and choice theories of rights

5.21 There are two popular theories about the *function* of rights, which are associated with underlying views about what it is that rights protect. *Interest theorists* hold that rights serve to protect important interests of those who possess them. For example, if we think that a person has an important interest in being able to choose which religion, if any, she will follow, we might conclude that because this interest is so important there should be a right to protect it, such as a right to the free exercise of religion.

5.22 *Choice theorists*, by contrast, hold that rights serve to protect our ability to exercise autonomous judgment as we make decisions about what to do. While interest theories of rights are closely allied with utilitarian values, choice theorists urge that rights serve to protect our right to autonomy. An example may make it clearer what choice theorists have in mind: suppose a suspected criminal is told: "You have the right to remain silent." That means that the criminal has a choice between exercising that right by remaining silent or waiving that right by speaking.

5.23 Both theories face difficulties. Interest theories have difficulty accounting for rights that protect interests that are relatively trivial. (If I purchase a lemonade, I have a right to it. Is the interest that this right protects really a high-priority interest?) Choice theory implies that only persons who can exercise autonomy can have rights. (But most people think newborn babies have rights even though they are not able to make choices yet. Some people think animals have rights too.)

5.24 Do we need to choose between these theories? Maybe they are both wrong: perhaps different rights serve different functions, some making space for our choices, others protecting our interests. A third view of rights holds that rights are valid moral claims, so if I have a right I can demand that other people respect my claim (Feinberg, 1970). On this view, the right of free speech is a claim against others who might prevent you from speaking; a right of freedom of conscience is a claim against anyone who would force you to do what violates your basic values. But either interests or choices may be the subject of a valid claim.

Different accounts of rights may have important implications for social 5.25 justice and law. When proponents of democracy claim that adults should have a right to vote, they might think that the right to vote is justified because the vote is the best way for people to protect important interests from government interference. Alternatively, they might think that it is crucial that people can choose whether or not to vote and whom to vote for. The latter view might oppose mandatory voting, while the former view could support it.

Benefits of Democracy: The Instrumental Case

Would a kind dictator be a bad thing?

Democratic decision making is time-consuming and often messy. Voting 5.26 takes time we might devote to other projects, and justifying our judgments to others requires that we speak, listen, and reason with people who may disagree with us. It's not always pleasant to do this. It would be much more neat and efficient for decisions to be made without all this fuss, perhaps by an individual dictator. If a dictator cared about the interests of citizens and tried to make decisions to promote the public good, would that be a better alternative?

One concern is that dictators usually aren't like this: even dictators who 5.27 try to be benevolent will be followed by others who may be worse. Mark Twain once wrote: **"As a perishable perfect man must die, and leave his despotism in the hands of an imperfect successor, an earthly despotism is not merely a bad form of government, it is the worst form that is possible"** (Twain, 2003–2012 [1889], Chapter 10). We might share this doubt about the good intentions of dictators and despots. Perhaps Mark Twain's quip contains a good argument against "benevolent" dictatorship as a stable form of governance. But defenders of democracy have argued that democracy has other beneficial effects as well.

Defenders urge that democratic institutions provide benefits that other 5.28 forms of governance cannot provide. Sometimes the value of democratic institutions is justified by reference to these benefits. These arguments imply that democracy is *instrumentally valuable*—valuable because it produces other things we value. It is sometimes argued that democracy is *intrinsically valuable*—valuable not merely because of benefits it promotes or creates, but for its own sake as well. This section will address some of the instrumental arguments for democracy, and the next section will briefly outline an argument for the claim that democracy is also intrinsically valuable.

Do the people know best?

5.29 James Surowiecki opens his book *The Wisdom of Crowds* with the story of a man at a fair where people could guess the weight of an ox after it was slaughtered and dressed (Surowiecki, 2005). Some of the people there were experts, but most of them were not. He was interested in the analogy between the knowledge of crowds in cases like this and in cases of democracy: how much do the average people actually know? He totaled up the 787 guesses and found that the average guess was 1,197 pounds. The actual weight was 1,198 pounds. Perhaps the collective wisdom of the people might sometimes be better than the wisdom of the most educated experts!

5.30 To verify this thought, of course, we would want to have more than an anecdote: we would need to collect evidence that crowds are a reliable source of knowledge, or to identify circumstances in which collective wisdom is reliable. *Epistemology* is the branch of philosophy that studies knowledge and belief. According to *epistemic theories of democracy*, democratic outcomes are justified because they are more likely to be true or right than the choice of an individual. Epistemic theories of democracy note that voting combines the knowledge of different people, so that a democratic choice reflects the collective knowledge of a community.

5.31 Is it true that democratic procedures are more likely to generate better outcomes? Perhaps this depends on the specific procedures employed and on the information available to individual voters. If one wanted to know about the structure of subatomic particles, it would be better to ask an expert physicist than to aggregate the views of the general public. If democratic procedures are appropriate for public policy and representation, then there must be a significant difference between those cases and the physics case.

5.32 One possible explanation is that public policies need to be responsive to the values and interests of citizens, while the laws of physics obviously don't accommodate themselves to our interests. Suppose that most voters know little about particle physics and have a very low chance of answering questions about it correctly. On the other hand, suppose that most voters are right more than half of the time about what would be in their interests. Even if each had only a 51 percent chance of being right, if they all vote independently and there are millions of them, they will almost certainly choose the right option.

In cases like guessing the weight of the ox, it is crucial that each person 5.33 makes an independent judgment about what she thinks the answer is. If people are not deciding independently and everyone is just listening to a few voices, the above logic doesn't hold any more. One of the questions confronting democracy is how you set up a system so that you are more likely to get good answers.

Can representation help?

How much of your day would you like to spend at the city hall? Voting may 5.34 be a way to gather information from voters, but it is time-consuming for voters to become informed and it takes effort to get people together to vote. Even online voting will require secure logins to prevent fraud, greater security being needed as the votes become more important. Moreover, the number and complexity of the issues is very great. Most democracies today are not direct democracies of the sort ancient Athens had. Instead of voting directly on laws, people normally vote on representatives.

Elected representatives are *accountable* to the voters who put them in 5.35 office and, while voters may not be able to control their representatives directly, at least they can vote people out when they do things that are unfortunate or unpopular. Perhaps democratic institutions will result in better public decisions, since they are supposed to be responsive to the interests and ideals of voters. If people think independently about whether a representative is doing a good job, then perhaps the "average" voter whose views determine elections will lead to good judgments. Voters pick good representatives, and those representatives work through the details.

Yet there is something lost in the shift to representation as well. While 5.36 both direct and representative democracy give citizens opportunities to vote and discuss, direct democracy provides people with unique experiences. People get to actually govern themselves rather than merely choose their governors. Even if representative democracy is more efficient, how does it affect us? In the next section we look at the intrinsic values of democracy— how being in a democracy might make us better or happier independently of whether we actually make better decisions.

Is Democratic Self-Governance Intrinsically Valuable?

5.37 Some defenders of democracy have argued that democratic institutions make their citizens better people: because democratic citizens are more engaged in public decision making, they may develop public-spirited values and virtues of self-reliance and assertiveness. When citizens participate in collective decision making, they may regularly be called upon to justify themselves and to explain their judgments and choices. As they engage in public deliberation, they may also learn to listen to others and to compromise, accommodating their own values and interests to the different values and interests of other citizens. Because of this, some defenders of democracy (including John Stuart Mill, Jean-Jacques Rousseau, and Thomas Jefferson) argue that democracy is a good form of governance; as they argue, participation in the democratic process causes citizens to become more self-reliant, independent, reasonable, and public-spirited.

5.38 But democracy is also defended as a way to ensure that people govern *themselves* and are not obliged to take commands from a ruler who is not accountable to them. When representatives are elected, their continued success depends on their ability to satisfy their constituents, which is one of the ways democratic institutions involve *self*-governance. While individuals don't direct the course of the government, the voters as a group are in a sense responsible for the laws they must obey and for the decisions made on their behalf. To this extent, democratic institutions put people in charge of their own collective fate, so that the people are responsible for the legal rules that bind them.

5.39 This idea is the core of another theory of democracy, often called *civic republicanism*: the theory that democratic institutions are valuable because they promote the autonomous self-governance of the people who participate in them. Just as individuals have a right to autonomy—a right to decide for themselves what goals to pursue and how to live their lives—this view holds that groups of people also have a right to govern their collective lives by participating in a democratic process. Democratic political institutions should give people opportunities to participate in self-governance.

5.40 In *The Social Contract* (3.15), Rousseau argues that relying on others to deliberate for you is a sign of vice:

> Once public service ceases to be the chief business of the citizens, and they prefer to serve with their wallet rather than with their person, the state is already near its ruin. Is it necessary to march to battle? They pay mercenary

troops and stay at home. Is it necessary to go to the council? They name deputies and stay at home. By dint of laziness and money, they finally have soldiers to enslave the country and representatives to sell it. (Rousseau, 1987 [1762], Book 3, Chapter 15)

Here we see a particular version of human virtue. The citizen who actually participates in governing himself is free and equal in a way in which those who are simply ruled by others are not. This creates another reason why democracy might be intrinsically valuable. Even people who are not as extreme as Rousseau and have a higher opinion of representative democracy might still think that voters get to exercise some of the same virtues.

Is There a Right to Democratic Self-Governance?

One of the arguments offered to defend **the US-led invasion of Iraq** in 2003 was that it would promote democracy in an area of the world where democracies were scarce. Set to the side questions about whether this was the real motive behind the war. Whatever one thinks about the Iraq War, it is worth thinking hard about the argument. If democracy is such a good thing, shouldn't everyone enjoy it? If it is a universal right, do we have duties to help people around the world enjoy it? 5.41

The arguments that democratic institutions are necessary to ensure liberty or autonomy can quickly generate an argument that all people have a right to live under such institutions: 5.42

1. All people have basic rights to liberty (or autonomy).
2. Because people have this basic right, they have a right to live under institutions that will secure their liberty (or autonomy).
3. Only democratic institutions can secure people's right to liberty (or autonomy).
4. Therefore, all people have a right to live under democratic institutions.

When faced with an argument of this sort, it is important to ask whether the premises are true and to consider how strongly they would support the conclusion if they were true. It is also worth considering what the conclusion would imply if it were true.

It is worth noting that the argument is not based on the claim that people who live under undemocratic governments must be badly off: people 5.43

might be happy living under a monarchy, or even under a benevolent dictatorship. But people may be well off, in an ordinary sense, even if their rights are systematically violated. The institution of slavery would be regarded as a violation of a slave's right to liberty even if masters were benevolent and just.

5.44   While this argument is defensible and may be widely accepted, there are several reservations to note about it. Each of the premises can be questioned: what does it mean to say that people have a basic right to liberty, or to autonomy? Possession of a right does not always imply that one has additional rights to whatever they need in order to exercise the first right. The right to self-defense does not automatically imply the right to a handgun, even if there are situations where it might be necessary to make the right to self-defense effective. A right to autonomy, similarly, may not automatically generate a right to democracy. More argument is needed. And is it true that *only* democratic regimes can enable people fully to exercise this right? Nonetheless, this argument (and its close relatives) is often used to argue in favor of a universal right to democratic self-governance.

What Are the Implications of a Right to Democratic Self-Governance?

5.45 We will deal with the topics of war and revolution in Chapters 6 and 7. For now, let us assume that there are cases where a revolution is justified and cases where military intervention is justified. What violations of rights are sufficiently important to justify revolution or military intervention? The most common answer is: genocide or crimes against humanity. If people are being slaughtered on a massive scale, the case for revolution seems strongest. But what if the government is generally respecting life and maintaining order and the main thing its citizens lack is the right to democratic self-governance?

5.46   The people living in America's 13 colonies in 1775 were not exactly the most oppressed people on earth. No one accused George III of trying to wipe out the Americans. In some ways the most famous grievances seem small: relatively small taxes on tea and stamps. Proponents of revolution were making a different claim, that America should be able to govern itself and not depend on the will of a king who could tax them without their consent. They were asserting a right to democratic self-governance. Are democratic rights sufficiently important to justify the violence that a revolution will bring?

Does it matter whether we are considering a case where a third party 5.47
intervenes? If people have a right to revolt, do other countries have a right
to intervene to assist them? The Americans benefited from French assistance
during the Revolutionary War.

One obvious reservation about the claim that third-party democracies 5.48
have a right to impose democratic institutions where such institutions do
not exist is that this principle would justify *too much* intervention. There
are many undemocratic governments in the world, but a determined effort
by the world's democratic nations to intervene to overthrow them all would
lead to global war. A second concern is closely related: can institutions be
institutions of self-government if they are imposed from the outside?

The achievement of democratic self-governance may be something that 5.49
people must come together to forge for themselves. If these institutions are
externally imposed, this may hinder the goal. Finally, democratic institutions
may lack legitimacy, or perceived legitimacy, when third parties impose them.
To say that democratic institutions are *legitimate* is to say that their existence
is justified and that the powers exercised under these institutions appropriately protect the interests and rights of the people who live under them.
Institutions have *perceived* legitimacy when people who live under them
accept them and *believe* that they appropriately protect their interests and
rights. Legitimacy and perceived legitimacy do not always go together: people
can believe that their institutions are just, but they may be wrong. Is the reverse
also possible? Can institutions be legitimate if people believe they are not?

Perhaps institutions cannot be fully legitimate unless they are accepted 5.50
as legitimate by those who live under them, or at least by most of those who
live under them. In this context, perceptions matter: it is not enough for
institutions to intend to secure basic rights and to facilitate democratic public decision making if they are not also understood to achieve these goals by
the people who live under them. It is often reasonable for people who live
under imposed institutions to doubt that these institutions protect their
rights and their autonomy, or that these institutions effectively secure democratic self-governance. Under such circumstances, people may even regard
themselves to have a right, based on the underlying right to democratic
self-governance, to overthrow and replace imposed institutions. If people
have a right to democratic self-governance, perhaps this is a right people can
only secure for themselves. If that is true, was France unjust in helping
America during its revolution?

This leaves several important questions unanswered: are there *other* 5.51
reasonable steps that democratic nations and their citizens might take to

promote democracy and self-government more broadly? And when, if ever, is third-party humanitarian intervention justified as a way to protect people from their own governments? We will return to some of these questions in Chapter 7.

Voting and Representation: Interests or Ideals?

5.52 Voting presents a number of interesting ethical questions: what if your own interests differ from the public good? What if your values are different from the values of the people you represent? In a representative democracy, representatives are supposed to have more time to consider proposed legislation and to negotiate with other representatives, whose constituents may have different interests. It's worth asking what a representative should do when the interests of constituents appear to be at odds with what she thinks is right. Some people hold that, in that context, representatives should "represent" the interests of their constituents by voting in a way that will promote those interests.

5.53   But this view is by no means universal. The British theorist Edmund Burke, for example, eloquently argued in a **"Speech to the Electors of Bristol" (of November 3, 1774)** that representatives should vote according to their conscience, whatever the views or opinions of their constituents: "Your representative owes, you not his industry only, but his judgment; and he betrays, instead of serving you, if he sacrifices it to your opinion" (Burke, 2000 [1987]). There is some debate over what Burke meant by this, but it is clear that he believed that representatives should sometimes act in ways that might disappoint their constituents: they should vote according to their ideals and judgments, even when those who voted them into office would not approve.

5.54   A similar question arises for voters: when you go to the ballot box, should you vote for whatever (or whomever) will, in your judgment, best promote your private interests? Or should you vote instead for whatever will best achieve your values and ideals, such as the public good? In 1984 Ronald Reagan's campaign slogan was: "Are you better off than you were four years ago?" His opponent, Walter Mondale, countered with: "Is America better off than it was four years ago?" Mondale alleged that the economic growth had been fueled by huge budget deficits that would haunt the nation in years to come. Mondale asked voters to set aside self-interest—and he won only in one state. Different democratic theorists are at odds on this question: while Rousseau urged that voters should vote according to their public-spirited ideals, Condorcet assumed that they will vote according to their preferences. This disagreement lives on in contemporary discussions of democracy and citizen obligations.

Does Democracy Rest on a Paradox?

We normally assume that, if we have a fair vote, the side that wins represents 5.55 the views of the majority of the people. The reality is more complicated than that. Voting works best when there are only two choices, but often there are many choices. Here are some ways the results of a vote may not reflect the will of the people.

1. THE RUN OFF PROBLEM. If there are more than two candidates for an office, it is possible that no one will win a majority. Some countries simply declare the person with the most votes the winner, but it is possible that the people who supported the other candidates would have joined forces and had a majority. For that reason, many other countries have a runoff election. The top two candidates after the first poll face each other if no one has a majority. There is no guarantee here either. Suppose the candidate who is second picks up enough votes in the runoff to win the election. Suppose the parties that finished first and second in the first election loathe each other. The party that was first after the first poll might have given its support to the party that was third, in order to block the party that was second. It is possible that in a straight-up vote the third-place party would have beaten the second-place party and then beaten the first-place party in a subsequent straight-up vote!

2. PARTIES. Some countries utilize proportional representation. Each party gets a percentage of seats equal to its percentage of votes. The difficulty is that the same problem can reappear at the next level. When the parliament votes to elect a prime minister, there will often be more than two candidates, so the runoff problem can reappear. Also, a small party might end up with a disproportionate amount of power if its votes are desperately needed to form a majority coalition.

3. KILLER AMENDMENTS. In the 1950s a law was working its way through the US Congress to fund school construction, and it looked like it had majority support. Then Congressman Adam Clayton Powell proposed an amendment: any school district that refused to desegregate its

schools would not receive money. This created a dilemma: a majority of Congress supported desegregation, and so it would be very difficult for those members of Congress to vote against the amendment. On the other hand, if the amendment passed, proponents of segregation would now oppose the bill. Their support was needed. Thus a bill that had majority support was defeated.

4. NONVOTING STAKEHOLDERS. Many people don't vote, so their interests are not reflected in democratic outcomes. Perhaps some people don't vote because they don't have an interest in the outcome of an election. But one might ask whether people *ever* truly have an interest in voting. The only case in which your vote makes a difference to an electoral outcome is when the election is decided by a *single vote*. But in large democracies it is vanishingly unlikely that any electoral outcome will be this close. It has sometimes been argued that this shows that voting is always, or almost always, irrational: voting involves significant costs (the cost of registering in advance, of bringing oneself to the polling place, and of spending the time required to cast a ballot). If the probability that *your vote* will make a difference to the electoral outcome is near zero, does it really make sense to bear these costs? Is voting irrational?

However, there are reasons to think that this simple argument misrepresents people's reasoning. Some people *enjoy* taking part in the political process. Some directly *value* their involvement in this process, or value voting as an expression of their commitment to democratic institutions. For such people, voting may be rational in the straightforward sense that the costs are counterbalanced by greater benefits. Other people may not even frame the decision to vote as a matter of correlated costs and benefits. They may regard themselves to have an obligation to vote *even if* the costs to themselves are not counterbalanced. Such people's choices will not appear to be rational from the cost–benefit perspective. But it is not at all clear that they are irrational in a more substantial sense.

5.56 From these and related problems, some people conclude that the results of an election don't ever properly reflect the "will of the people." At best, elections provide an opportunity for voters to get rid of representatives they strongly dislike. But perhaps this conclusion is too strong: the problems described arise only when voter preference profiles are structured in special ways. In many actual elections, the results are far less perverse than they are in the examples given above.

Deliberative Democracy as a Solution?

Most people think that the American Constitutional Convention went better 5.57
because of the deliberation that took place face to face. What if the whole
convention had been done online, where all that people could do was submit
proposals and vote on them? What would have been lost? Because of the
problems discussed in the previous section, it's clear that majoritarian voting
systems won't always result in the election of the candidate who has majoritarian support. You might think that this *structural* problem undermines the
idea that democratic elections represent the "will of the people."

Is democracy really just a matter of counting votes? Isn't democracy in 5.58
large part a place where citizens gather together and have to persuade each
other? Some political theorists distinguish between "aggregation conceptions"
and "deliberative conceptions" of democratic legitimacy (Cohen, 1996, p. 19).
"Aggregation" means massing individuals together in a collection, which is
just what voting systems do. The problems with voting systems are real (and
interesting!), but democratic institutions might be preferred because they
provide better opportunities for citizens to discuss important issues, offer
reasons, and to try to persuade one another.

This alternative view of democracy is called *deliberative democracy*. Cass 5.59
Sunstein makes the case for deliberative democracy in this way. In the
aggregating approach voters just have preferences, and whoever has the
most votes wins. In many ways this is just a version of might makes right:
each side has a preference and the stronger side gets its way. Sunstein coined
the phrase "naked preferences" to describe situations where one group
simply imposes its preferences on another group without giving reasons
that the other side could plausibly accept. In order to put clothes on our
preferences, so to speak, we actually have to get together with the people we
disagree with and offer reasons for our policies and listen to their reasons.
When people deliberate in this way, even the side that loses comes away
feeling that it has been treated with respect.

Critics of deliberative democracy have questioned how it is that we can 5.60
know whether the reasons we are giving are ones that our opponents should
accept as reasonable. Deliberative democracy requires not just giving reasons, but giving reasons that the other side thinks of as legitimate. If I give
you reasons for a policy, but they are based on my religious views, does that
count as deliberating? What if I appeal to a philosophy that you think
is deeply misguided? In Chapter 9 we take up the question of religious
arguments in politics.

Distorting Democracy: Persistent Minorities and Electoral Inequalities

5.61 However we conceive the relationship between democratic institutions and the justification of political authority and power, actual institutions are likely to fall short of ideal conceptions of democracy. Can democratic institutions be imperfect without becoming *un*democratic?

Persistent minorities

5.62 Democracies support *pluralism*. But pluralism means that there will be different groups, and usually some of them will be minority groups. What if some groups are *always* in the minority? Persistent minorities might vote, election after election, but might always see their candidates lose out to other candidates supported by the majority. In one sense, this might seem fair enough: everyone gets their vote, and if some people lose out that's not unfair, it's just the way it is. On the other hand, members of minority groups who never see their candidates elected might not have good reasons to support the democratic system. If they always lose, why should they want to stay? It is often said that public institutions should be justifiable to the people who live under them. But can democratic institutions be justified to members of minority groups who always lose elections? Such groups might have good reasons to leave and try to form a smaller nation, where they would no longer be a minority. But if they have reason to do this, pluralist democracies may be *unstable*.

Electoral inequalities

5.63 Joseph Stalin was not a supporter of democracy. But he recognized that elections can increase the perception that public actions are legitimate. He is supposed to have said that the important power is not the power to vote but the power to decide how the votes will be counted. Stalin had in mind a system where people vote, but their votes don't really count at all, since the outcome is determined in advance. If this is an extreme case, consider an only slightly less blatant way to undermine the integrity of a democratic electoral system: consider a "democracy" where everyone gets to vote, but where some people's votes count for three. (John Stuart Mill proposed extra voting power for the well-educated.) Is this a real democracy at all? Or does democracy become a sham when citizens and votes are not equal in number? If citizen equality is a *condition* for democracy, then democracy is lost or undermined when that equality is not in place.

One kind of democratic failure occurs when some people are denied   5.64
voting rights: it wasn't until 1920 that women could vote in US elections. While African American citizens gained a legal right to vote in 1869, it wasn't until much later that they could effectively exercise that right. **The Nineteenth Amendment** to the US constitution, passed in   🖵
1920, says: "The right of citizens of the United States to vote shall not be denied or abridged by the United States or by any State on account of sex." But what if the US had decided not to *count* women's votes? Or what if it had decided to count them, but had ruled that the votes of a woman should represent one-tenth of the vote of a man? It's not just that such a rule would be *unjust*, as it clearly would be. Would it undermine the idea that the United States is a democracy? For this reason, one *could* argue that the United States was not a democracy at all before 1920, or before effective guarantees were in place to ensure a broader right to vote.

And what about the equality of votes? Does the principle "one person,   5.65
one vote" mean what it seems to mean, if different people have votes that are weighed differently in the democratic decision-making process? There are different ways in which votes can "count" differently. Because of the Electoral College system in the United States, voters in "swing" states (states that do not always go, predictably, to the same party in national elections) have much more influence than voters in states that have strong majority representation for one party or candidate over another. By some measures, voters in these states have votes that count over ten times more than the vote of someone in a nonswing state. So individual voters in Ohio "matter more" to an election's outcome than voters in California or Georgia.

In the US Senate there are different reasons for the unequal weight of   5.66
votes: since each state gets two senators whether it has a small or a large population, the number of voters per representative is very different in Wyoming (around half a million residents) from its counterpart in California (around 40 million residents). A Wyoming voter has over 70 times more influence on the US Senate than a voter from California.

Should we say that the United States is *not a democracy at all* because of   5.67
these inequalities? Perhaps, as suggested earlier, it makes more sense to think of "democracy" as a matter of degree. A nation may be more or less democratic, depending on the way votes are counted and weighted. Ronald

Dworkin holds that what matters is not whether everyone has mathematically equal influence but whether the inequalities show disrespect for some citizens. These sorts of inequalities do not show disrespect in the way that Jim Crow laws did.

Do Democracies Decline and Fall?

5.68 Voting is not the only way to influence electoral outcomes; if you have money or political power, there are other ways to do it. The Greek philosopher and historian Plutarch is sometimes quoted as attributing the demise of the Roman republic to the inappropriate force of money and power in the democratic process:

> The abuse of buying and selling votes crept in and money began to play an important part in determining the elections. Later on, however, this process of corruption spread to the law courts and to the army, and finally, when even the sword became enslaved by the power of gold, the republic was subjected to the rule of the emperors. (Plutarch, 1965, *Coriolanus*, 1.14)

Plutarch saw money as poison for democracy. But money provides an alternative possibility for voters who live in Georgia or California and whose vote therefore doesn't weigh much in the presidential election. Presidential candidates don't spend much time in either of these states, because the outcome is determined, or at least highly predictable. But voters in these states can still try to influence the electoral outcome by campaigning in a swing state or by using money to support or undermine a candidate. Those who are *very, very* wealthy can pay for political advertisements. And they have a constitutionally protected right to do so.

5.69   The US Supreme Court ruled in the 1974 controversial case *Buckley v. Valeo* that people's right to spend their own money on political advertisements is a form of constitutionally protected free speech. More recently, in 2012, the Supreme Court ruled in the case *Citizens United v. Federal Election Commission* that the constitution also protects the right of *corporations* to spend money in support of (or opposition to) political candidates.

5.70   Is money speech? Does speech that comes from corporate interests merit the same constitutional protection as the speech of individual citizens? Corporations don't vote. Should they still have a right to use their money to influence elections? Still, corporate decisions are made by individuals who do have a right to vote and who have unambiguous rights to free expression. Some people judge these recent cases to have undermined American democracy. Others defend these decisions as necessary protections of free speech. Since some citizens are multibillionaires while others live in poverty, this form of free speech is not equally distributed. And when corporations have free-speech rights to use corporate funds in elections, then this form of speech comes to promote still more inequality.

While these are very *practical* problems involved in democratic 5.71 governance, they also raise important philosophical questions: what circumstances undermine or support the legitimacy of democratic institutions? And at what point does it become sensible to question whether institutions are sufficiently democratic to count as a "democracy?"

Not all philosophers have liked or defended democracy. Plato argued 5.72 that democracy was a form of government in which the ignorant majority rules over the educated and enlightened few. More interestingly, perhaps, Plato argued that democratic governments are doomed to fail. In democracies, he argued, people are free to do as they wish, since no one has the authority to constrain them. He argued that democracies generate disorder, which provides an opportunity for people who are unscrupulous and power-hungry. Eventually one such person will manage to gain power and to become a tyrant. Democracy, argued Plato, devolves into the rule of those who want power for its own sake.

But Plato also believed that democracy was itself a degraded political 5.73 state, descended from oligarchy and even worse. Modern democratic institutions and contemporary democratic theories are quite different from the dystopian ideal described by Plato, but perhaps Plato was right to warn that democratic institutions can be undermined and may disappear altogether where inequalities of wealth or power play the wrong role in politics.

The coming decades will test the ability of democracies to survive and 5.74 flourish. Can democracies keep their debt to a manageable level? Can they solve environmental problems that often transcend the borders of particular states? Will economic inequalities fatally undermine democratic equality? Can democracies adapt to changes in technology that alter the way we learn about politics and discuss it? Can democracies respect the freedom of political expression while ensuring fair representation for both the rich and the poor?

References and Further Reading

Adams, John. 1776. "Letter to James Sullivan, May 26." http://historytools.david
jvoelker.com/sources/Abigail-John-Letters.pdf (accessed February 24, 2016).
John Adams was the second president of the United States, and served as vice
president under George Washington. While Adams's letter, quoted in this
chapter, is clearly sexist, he is also known as the husband of Abigail Adams,
whose articulate advocacy of women's rights, and passionate arguments
against slavery made her an intellectual force to be reckoned with. This selection of correspondence shows early discussions about the expansion of suffrage to various groups around the time of the Declaration of Independence.
Abigail Adams makes a case for women's suffrage, comparing male domination to domination by the British.

Burke, Edmund. 2000 [1987]. **"Speech to the Electors of Bristol, November 3,
1774."** In *The Works of the Right Honourable Edmund Burke.* The University of
Chicago. http://press-pubs.uchicago.edu/founders/documents/v1ch13s7.html
(accessed February 12, 2016). Burke's speech is a classic on the topic of representation. Burke argues that representatives must exercise independent judgment and not simply reproduce the views of their constituents.

Christiano, Thomas. 1996. *The Rule of the Many.* Boulder, CO: Westview Press.
Christiano offers a *normative* defense of democracy, arguing that democratic
institutions are intrinsically valuable.

Christiano, Thomas. 2003. *Philosophy and Democracy.* New York: Oxford University
Press. This collection includes some of the most important contemporary
papers on democracy and public deliberation.

Cohen, Joshua. 1996. "Procedure and Substance in Deliberative Democracy." In
Democracy and Difference, edited by Seyla Benhabib. Princeton, NJ: Princeton
University Press, pp. 95–119. (Also in Christiano, 2003, pp. 17–38.) Cohen
argues that democracy should not be defined in purely procedural terms but
that deliberation about ideas like equality and liberty is central to democracy.

Dworkin, Ronald. 2008. *Is Democracy Possible Here?* Princeton, NJ: Princeton
University Press. An accessible introduction to Dworkin's political philosophy
including his understanding of democracy and its relationship to equality.

Feinberg, Joel. 1970. "The Nature and Value of Rights." *The Journal of Value Inquiry*,
4(4): 243–260. Feinberg's paper is a famous defense of the view that rights are
valid claims.

Landemore, Hélène. 2012. *Democratic Reason.* Princeton, NJ: Princeton University
Press. Landemore defends the claim that the people, taken collectively, are frequently smarter than experts.

Mill, John Stuart. 1958 [1861]. *On Representative Government.* Indianapolis, IN:
Bobbs Merrill. Mill's book is a classic philosophical examination of democratic
institutions.

Plato. 1992. *The Republic*, translated by G. M. A. Grube and C. D. C. Reeve. Indianapolis, IN: Hackett. In Book 8 of *The Republic* Plato presents classic arguments against democracy.

Plutarch. 1965. *Makers of Rome: Nine Lives by Plutarch*, translated by Ian Scott-Kilvert. London: Penguin Books. Plutarch (c. 45–120 CE) wrote historical, moral, and philosophical works but is most famous for his *Lives of Celebrated Greeks and Romans*. His *Coriolanus*, which was adapted by Shakespeare into a tragedy of the same name, tells the story of a general and war hero of the fifth century BCE who was exiled by his own people and then turned against them, seeking the downfall of the Roman republic.

Rousseau, Jean-Jacques. 1987 [1762]. *On the Social Contract*, translated by Donald A. Cress. In Jean-Jacques Rousseau, *The Basic Political Writings*. New York: Hackett, pp. 139–227. Rousseau is an important critic of the idea that voting alone is sufficient political involvement. His version of the social contract places substantial emphasis on the citizen's active promotion of the public good.

Sunstein, Cass. 1993. *The Partial Constitution*. Cambridge, MA: Harvard University Press. Sunstein argues that constitutional systems treat the status quo as neutral but that this reflects an inappropriate understanding of the way the constitution shapes public policy and public debate in a democratic system of government.

Surowiecki, James. 2005. *The Wisdom of Crowds*. New York: Random House. Surowiecki argues that aggregating information from many people often yields better results than asking an expert.

Twain, Mark. 2003–2012 [1889]. *A Connecticut Yankee in King Arthur's Court*. LiteraturePage.com. http://www.literaturepage.com/read/aconnecticutyankee-55.html (accessed February 12, 2016). Twain's *Connecticut Yankee* is a work of fiction, not a work of political theory. But, like most of Twain's writing, it includes biting commentary and criticism of contemporary political and social institutions.

Online Resources

1   https://en.wikipedia.org/wiki/Women%27s_suffrage_in_the_United_States
2   http://www.nytimes.com/2008/11/02/opinion/02cowan.html?_r=1
3   http://plato.stanford.edu/entries/locke/
4   http://www.literaturepage.com/read/aconnecticutyankee-55.html
5   http://www.constitution.org/jjr/socon_03.htm#015
6   http://usiraq.procon.org/view.answers.php?questionID=000873
7   http://press-pubs.uchicago.edu/founders/documents/v1ch13s7.html
8   http://www.archives.gov/historical-docs/document.html?doc=13&title.
    raw=19th%20Amendment%20to%20the%20U.S.%20Constitution:%20
    Women's%20Right%20to%20Vote

6

THE OBLIGATION TO OBEY THE LAW

JUSTIN When did you start watching that show?

SOPHIE A few months ago.

JUSTIN I didn't know you had cable.

SOPHIE Well …

JUSTIN I see. You are a pirate. I know lots of pirates. In fact most of my friends are pirates. Do you mind talking to me about it? I have only done it a few times and always have a guilty conscience afterwards.

SOPHIE Sure. I have actually thought about this quite a bit and I don't think there is anything wrong with downloading copyrighted movies, TV shows, games, or music.

JUSTIN OK, so why not? It seems like the people who make the shows should have the right to sell them on the terms that they choose.

SOPHIE The copyright laws are an unjust infringement of my liberty. You know I think that people should have liberty where their actions don't harm other people, and I don't think my downloading TV shows or music actually harms anyone. Information wants to be free!

JUSTIN What about the company that owns the copyright? Aren't they losing money from the sale?

SOPHIE Not really. If I had to pay I would choose to just do without it. I don't have that much money. It is a common misconception that every illegal download means a lost

This Is Political Philosophy: An Introduction, First Edition. Alex Tuckness and Clark Wolf.
© 2017 John Wiley & Sons, Inc. Published 2017 by John Wiley & Sons, Inc.

sale. Many of the people wouldn't have paid anyway and done without.

JUSTIN   Sounds like rationalization to me. You may not know which of the things you pirated you would have paid for, but probably you would have paid for some of them. But let's say you are right and you wouldn't have bought the things you pirate. Your argument is that, since the owners are still free to sell just as many copies to other people, no one is harmed.

SOPHIE   Right.

JUSTIN   But some of the people who download for free would have bought it. Did those people do something wrong?

SOPHIE   Yes, because in that case the owner really is worse off.

JUSTIN   So does it matter that there is a law saying that what you are doing is illegal?

SOPHIE   Well, it matters in the sense that there is a very small chance of being caught and prosecuted. I have thought it through and decided the chances of getting caught and punished are so small that it is worth the risk.

JUSTIN   But does it matter morally? One reason to obey the law is that you don't want to get punished, but a different reason is that you have a moral obligation to obey the law.

SOPHIE   In some cases, yes. But not in every case. You don't think people had a moral obligation to obey the fugitive slave law before the American Civil War. Do you?

JUSTIN   No, not in that case. I think there is a moral obligation to obey the law, but in extreme cases another moral consideration overrides it. Slavery laws were wrong, and the moral obligation to help the slaves was even stronger than the moral obligation to obey the law. I don't think this really helps your position because you're not protesting injustice, just trying to get free entertainment.

SOPHIE   That's not actually true. Laws that restrict my freedom even when I am not harming anyone else are unjust. So I'm not morally obliged to follow them.

JUSTIN   But your position would not make a workable law. If we say that only people who would have paid can be prosecuted for pirating, there is no way to prove that someone would have paid in court. Even the people who would have paid would go unpunished. I think part of the reason we have an obligation to obey the law is that sometimes we need general rules that apply to all of us.

SOPHIE   Sometimes respecting rights is inconvenient. Since I should have the right to engage in harmless behavior, if some companies lose a little money because respecting my right means allowing a few other people who would have paid to profit, that is the price of justice.

JUSTIN   So do you think everyone should decide for themselves whether laws are just and only obey the just ones? That sounds like anarchy in the making to me.

SOPHIE   Why not? The alternative is everyone always doing what the majority says, and the majority is often wrong. It often tramples on individual freedom. Some of the great figures in history disobeyed the law because they thought it was unjust, people like Mahatma Gandhi and Martin Luther King, Jr.

JUSTIN   So you really think you are a hero for stealing TV shows?

SOPHIE   I am not saying that my cause in any way compares to theirs. I was just answering your question about whether we should always obey the law. I think that I would rather live in a world where disobedience causes a little commotion and inconvenience and where people actually think for themselves than in a world where everybody just goes along with the majority.

JUSTIN   But what if it creates more than just a little commotion? Some people use the same logic to violently overthrow governments.

SOPHIE   There are a lot of countries today that got their start that way. Sometimes we should try to overthrow governments. I admit that my issue doesn't justify a revolution, but I think you are wrong if you are suggesting that overthrowing governments is always wrong.

JUSTIN   So you think that the law doesn't really have any moral authority over you at all. You think each person should decide whether the law is just and should feel free to disobey it if it's not, and in some cases even overthrow the government.

SOPHIE   Right.

JUSTIN   I'm not convinced. I think the law is more than just a threat to punish. I think that there is moral value in having laws that we all agree to abide by even when we disagree with them. I am not denying that there may be extreme cases where breaking the law is right, but your approach says there is no moral obligation to obey the law even when the disagreements are fairly trivial. I wish I had a better way of articulating why we ought to obey the law.

SOPHIE   Do you *really* think that I'm risking the overthrow of our government by downloading *Game of Thrones*?

Breaking the Law

Imagine yourself in the situation of a judge before the American Civil War 6.1 who opposed slavery but thought that the **Fugitive Slave Act** was nonetheless a valid law. It accorded both with the constitution as it was written at the time and with existing statutes. Should the judge uphold the written law or work to undermine the institution of slavery? One of the most famous twentieth-century examples of lawbreaking is **Rosa Parks's** decision to go to jail for refusing to comply with segregated busing. In this chapter we will explore the obligation to obey the law.

Motives for breaking the law

People break the law for many different reasons. Some break the law out of 6.2 *ignorance.* (Perhaps I didn't know it was **illegal to drive while talking on a cell phone.)** Other people break the law knowingly, for *personal gain*, or just for thrills. (A thief steals your bike…) In the dialogue above, Sophie seems to have broken the law because she wanted to watch a show!

In other cases, people break the law as a matter of *principle*. When ordered 6.3 not to talk about philosophy, Socrates refused to comply. In the Bible there is a famous story where the apostles are forbidden to talk about Jesus and they respond that **they will not obey because God has commanded them** to do what they are doing. Principled lawbreakers may break laws they believe to be morally wrong or unjust. Sometimes lawbreakers even question the legality or validity of the "laws" they violate: an invalid law is not properly a law at all, so their behavior isn't really "lawbreaking" at all.

In other cases people break a law even though the law is not itself unjust, in 6.4 order to protest other laws that are. When **Martin Luther King, Jr** wrote his *Letter from a Birmingham Jail,* the law he broke was about holding a march without a permit. He didn't think laws that required permits for marches were illegitimate in principle, but when Birmingham, Alabama refused to issue a permit, King and his followers decided to hold the march anyway, in order to draw attention to the city laws that were enforcing racial segregation.

6.5   Sometimes people break the law because they believe the law in question is foolish. **Some people even make a point of breaking really strange laws that seem to serve no good purpose**. Other times there are laws that have a purpose but seem irrelevant in a specific case. Suppose you are sitting at a stop light very late at night and you can clearly see that there are no other cars coming from any direction. The light is on an excruciatingly slow timer. Now you could just break the law for personal gain—you want to get quickly where you are going, and the stop light is preventing that. But this case may be different. In the theft cases, a person may agree that there are good reasons for there to be a law against theft and still decide to break that law for personal gain, but in this case you might decide that the law itself is misguided. While under normal circumstances traffic lights are very helpful, the law should include an exception for situations like this one. The law is not actually protecting anyone from harm and is inconveniencing you. This is part of Sophie's argument in the dialogue. While there are good reasons for a general rule against pirating TV shows, she thinks that in her particular case the reasons behind the law do not apply: no one is harmed, since she would not have purchased the TV shows anyway.

Ways of breaking the law

6.6 Martin Luther King argued that conscientious lawbreaking should be *open* and that those who engage in civil disobedience should be prepared to accept the punishment associated with it. His goal, and the goal of the civil rights protesters, was not to express disrespect for the law but to protest and try to change laws that were unjust. But some people engage in *secret* acts of disobedience. Others use *violence* in disobeying the law. This could range from an actual revolution to protesters who forcibly resist arrest. In contrast to all three of these alternatives, some would argue that in a reasonably fair democracy you should obey the law until such time as you can persuade others to change it.

6.7   There are several different questions related to breaking the law that are important in political philosophy. First, what should people do if they think that a law is unjust? Is it still morally compulsory to obey? Second, if there are cases where a person may break the law legitimately, are there any moral rules about how to go about it? In other words, is there a right way to break the law but also a wrong way to do it? Third, is there any moral obligation to obey the law at all? If so, what reasons support this obligation?

Unjust laws

The most common moral justification for breaking the law is that the law in 6.8 question is unjust. The phrase "unjust law" implies that we have a standard of justice other than the law itself. *Legal justice* is whatever the law says is just, but *moral justice* has to do with whether the law actually conforms to some standard of justice other than law.

There are different accounts of how we might know that a law is unjust. 6.9 **John Locke's political philosophy** held that, through reason, we can discern natural laws. Human laws that violate natural law are unjust. Do we need natural law theory in order to make sense of the idea that laws can be unjust? Perhaps not: we might consider whether laws are consistent with the values of the society or culture where they apply. But can't laws be unjust even if everyone thinks they're just? Can't we all be wrong? Perhaps the worst forms of oppression take place when oppressed people accept their predicament as justified.

There are different philosophical accounts of justice, but few defend the 6.10 view that justice *just is* whatever a nation's laws may require. Anyone who holds that some laws are unjust, however, must have a standard of justice separate from the law itself, to make the comparison. The **American Declaration of Independence** claimed that by nature all men were created equal, yet the **US Constitution** permitted slavery. Someone might reason that America committed itself to a principle of equality but failed to live up to that standard. Others hold that slavery is simply *unjust* even if it is an accepted practice, and even if some slaves are themselves brainwashed into believing that it is a just system. There are different ways of arguing for such a theory. For example, Robert Paul Wolff argues that political institutions are just only if they support people's ability to exercise autonomous control over own lives (click **here** for Wolff's blog). Other theories of justice are considered in Chapter 4 of this book.

Are we obligated just because it is a law?

According to Wolff, there is never a basic obligation to obey the law. He calls 6.11 his view *philosophical anarchism*. But Wolff doesn't mean that we should never obey the law or that we should abandon our legal systems. His point, rather, is that we have no *moral* obligation to obey the law just because it is the law. If the law forbids piracy and if Sophie also thinks that piracy is unjust and therefore decides to obey the law, she acts autonomously because she is following what her own reason says. The fact that the law forbids piracy is, however, redundant in this case. She already thinks that piracy is wrong on moral rather than legal grounds. On the other hand, if the law forbids piracy but Sophie thinks that piracy is morally permissible, Wolf would say that she should not obey the law. Where the law and individual conscience disagree, the threat of punishment makes it in your interest to obey the law but does not give you a moral obligation to do so. According to Wolff, we should obey the law only when what the law requires is consistent with our autonomous judgment about what we ought to do. But legal punishment may give us reasons to obey the law even when we have no obligation to do so.

6.12   On the other hand, sometimes we may have excellent reasons to follow other people's judgments. If your friend is a mechanic and you are not, you would do well to follow your friend's advice about your car. You don't sacrifice your autonomy when you take into account others' opinions as you decide what to do.

6.13   Perhaps something similar can happen with the law: the law prohibits you from purchasing drugs unless the government has approved them. While you may find this inconvenient, it is also true that untested drugs could pose a threat to your health, or could just waste your money. If you consciously decide to trust the legislators' decision on this question, your decision to trust is autonomous in the same sense.

6.14   Laws are different from advice you receive from your friend the mechanic, because they address whole classes of people—in the case of traffic laws, all the people who drive vehicles. If drivers take them as authoritative (they feel obliged to use their turn signal even when it seems like it doesn't matter), this helps *coordinate* behavior among many different people. Many of the things law does, such as regulating property and contracts, create benefits by helping people coordinate behaviors and expectations, but this mechanism only works if people defer to the law rather than using their own judgment in each case.

6.15   Whether one thinks of unjust laws as laws that violate "natural" laws, as laws that are at odds with society's values, or as laws that conflict with impartial requirements of justice, it is not controversial that law is a fallible human creation. It is inevitable that people will sometimes confront laws that they think are unjust. Do people have a duty to obey laws even when they're not just?

How strong are our legal obligations?

Perhaps we should be more specific about what it means to have a duty to 6.16
obey the law. Some obligations are *absolute*. Philosophers sometimes call
these obligations categorical. An absolute or categorical obligation is one
that always holds, no matter what. If the obligation to obey the law is absolute,
that would mean that, no matter how unjust the law was, you should obey it
because it is the law.

Few people think that the obligation to obey the law is absolute. Most 6.17
people would say that the laws upholding slavery in the American South
were so unjust that people were under no moral obligation to obey them
just because they were the law.

Unlike Robert Paul Wolff, the American philosopher John Rawls (whose 6.18
thought was more extensively discussed in Chapter 4) argues that we have
a basic obligation to obey the law and that this obligation is based on the
underlying principles of justice and fair play. The principle of fair play
requires that, when people benefit from the cooperation of others, they
should themselves be willing to cooperate. As the philosopher H. L. A. Hart
puts it with less economy but much greater precision,

> when a number of persons conduct any joint enterprise according to rules
> and thus restrict their liberty, those who have submitted to these restrictions
> when required have a right to similar submission from those who have ben-
> efited by their submission. (Hart, 1955, p. 185)

On this view, obedience to law is a burden. But a peaceful, productive
society depends on a state of affairs where most people are willing to bear
this burden. If other people are cooperating by obeying the law and we
benefit from their cooperation, then we have an obligation to obey the
law too.

If we participate in the political process, we are involved in the creation 6.19
of legal constraints that will apply to others. According to the principle of
fair play, anyone who participates in this process assumes an obligation to
be similarly constrained *by* others. But Rawls agrees that, in such circumstances, the obligation to obey the law is not absolute. In his discussion
of civil disobedience he frames the philosophical question carefully: "At
what point does the duty to comply with laws enacted by a legislative majority cease to be binding in view of the right to defend one's liberties and the
duty to oppose injustice?" (Rawls, 1971, p. 319). On Rawls's view, the obligation to obey the law is a *prima facie* obligation. *Prima facie* is a Latin

phrase that means "at first glance," "at first sight," or "on the face of it." If I have a *prima facie* obligation to obey the law, then this implies that there is a moral *presumption* in favor of obeying the law and I have a moral obligation to do so unless I have an even weightier reason not to.

6.20   On Rawls's view, the burden of proof is on the person who breaks the law to show that another, even weightier moral reason trumps or overbalances it. This underlying view would apply to both uncivil and civil disobedience. But do people have the right to judge for themselves whether their obligations are overbalanced? Some people find it easy to make exceptions for themselves, especially when they could gain substantial benefits by breaking the law. However, even if the principle of fair play is not enough to motivate criminals to obey the law, we might refer to such a principle when we hold them responsible for violating it.

Breaking the Law: A "How to" Guide

6.21 Perhaps you would like to know how to break the law and get away with it. Sadly for you, this section will not be much help. What we need to do here is to assess the moral considerations that are relevant when a person, confronted with legalized injustice, decides how to respond. One option is to work through the democratic process to change the law by persuading others to vote for a change in the law. You could write letters, conduct legal protest marches, organize boycotts, or pay for advertisements to get out your message. The alternative, "breaking the law," is not really a single option. There are several different ways of going about it.

Civil disobedience

6.22 One can choose to engage in civil disobedience. When people engage in civil disobedience, their goal is not to "get away with it." In fact being ignored by the police would undercut the strategy. Civilly disobedient protesters often *want* to be arrested, or are at least willing to take that risk. There are several reasons for this: when people are arrested, it is more likely that there will be news coverage that will bring more attention to the injustice that motivated the protest in the first place. In addition, breaking the law creates what Henry David Thoreau, in a famous essay titled **"On The Duty of Civil Disobedience,"** called "friction." Thoreau notes that disobedience inconveniences people and increases tension. Keeping people in jail is expensive (**a year in prison in the United States typically costs more than \$30,000** and sometimes **a lot more**). Part of the point of civil disobedience is to increase tensions and to compel the majority to recognize the injustices that motivated the protest.

Finally, by protesting peacefully, activists increase the chance that others 6.23 will be sympathetic to their cause. While the public might lose sympathy with protesters who resisted arrest, peaceful protesters often gain public sympathy and respect. By accepting punishment for their civil disobedience, protesters acknowledge their respect for the overall system of government while proving that civil disobedience need not lead to anarchy. Civil disobedience expresses respect for law and a desire to improve our system of laws, not a desire to overthrow the rule of law.

In his discussion of civil disobedience, John Rawls packs this respect 6.24 for law into the *definition* of civil disobedience: civil disobedience is "a public, nonviolent, conscientious yet political act contrary to law usually done with the aim of bringing about a change in the law or policies of the government" (Rawls, 1971, p. 320). Rawls does not claim that civil disobedience is the only kind of lawbreaking that can be justified. But he argues that disobedience is justifiable when three conditions are met: if (1) disobedience is undertaken in order to protest serious infringements of justice, if (2) alternative legal means to redress these injustices have been tried and have failed, and if (3) the disobedience undertaken will not lead to greater injustices than those protested (or to the general destruction of society itself), then civilly disobedient actions will be justified.

A test for Rawls's theory: can you think of circumstances where these conditions are met, but where there are other reasons why civilly disobedient actions might be unjustifiable? What if the action has no chance of success, but will impose serious disadvantages on others? More generally, what if the social costs of disobedience outweigh the expected benefits?

Violence

A different response to injustice is *un*civil disobedience or *violent resistance*. 6.25 Civil disobedience avoids harming others and is often thought to express respect for law itself. But those who engage in covert lawbreaking or violent resistance hope to avoid the legal consequences of their actions. For this reason among others, uncivil lawbreaking is more difficult to justify than civil disobedience. Violent resistance is an even more extreme response, and there are those who argue that it is never justifiable. Those who fought in the American Revolution, however, clearly believed that extreme circumstances justified an extreme response. In what circumstances (if any) might it be justifiable for protesters to engage in protests that are violent or covert?

6.26   During the US civil rights era, **Malcolm X** rejected the idea that blacks needed to just accept imprisonment without fighting back. One of Malcolm's famous speeches was titled "The Ballot or the Bullet" (click **here** to listen). The speech makes a clear threat: either make equal voting real or prepare for violence. Proponents of violence will argue that, in situations of injustice, the law itself is attacking people unjustly. If the law legalizes slavery and a public official comes to capture a fugitive slave, the slave could reason as follows: "The law authorizing the public official to arrest me is unjust and not morally binding, and therefore I should regard the official's actions as an attack on my person that I am entitled to respond to by means of self-defense." In other words, the victims of legalized injustice are often the recipients of unjustified violence and hence, when they use violence back, they are simply exercising their right to self-defense. Most people agree that self-defense is morally justified; the question is how far one can extend that logic.

6.27   Another possible justification for violent resistance is based on the idea that society is a social contract. This idea was central to John Locke's political philosophy and was popularized in real politics by the US Declaration of Independence. The basic notion (discussed further in the chapter on justice) is that people are naturally free and that governments arise because free people consent to the creation of a government that exists to protect their rights and promote the public good. Since contracts arise by consent, the metaphor of a contract is a frequent way of talking about consent. Contemporary versions of this idea generally do not assume that there was an actual historical event where people entered into a real contract. Instead they use the idea as a thought experiment. For example, people would not have consented to a government that is tyrannical, so a tyrannical government is not legitimate. Once a government loses its legitimacy, the people are free to replace it with a new government and, if necessary, to use force in order to do so. Jefferson added this Lockean idea to the Declaration of Independence when he wrote that the people have a right to "alter or abolish" a government that becomes destructive of people's fundamental rights.

What should be on the menu?

If you want to cause political change, what should you do? One answer is 6.28
that it depends on what would be most effective. If your group is small and
you have little chance of leading a successful revolution, then you should
choose civil disobedience. If your group is large and the chances of leading
a successful revolution are good, then you should go with violent revolution.
This way of framing the question is incomplete, because it assumes that the
only relevant question is that of effectiveness. In political philosophy we ask
whether there are any moral considerations that should come into play.

Moral considerations can be of several different sorts and may be associ- 6.29
ated with underlying views about fair play, harm and risk of harm, and the
justification of violence. A pacifist would argue that we should never resort
to violence. Someone who thought the obligation to obey the law is absolute
would say that both civil disobedience and violence should be off the menu.
If you think that violence should be on the menu, you might think that it
should be employed only as a last resort, only when it would prevent even
greater harms or injustices.

What should we choose from the menu?

Once we have decided what is on the political menu, there still may be 6.30
moral considerations that restrict which options we can choose in a
particular case. For example, some people think there is a requirement of
proportionality, by which they mean that the harm caused by the disobedience should not exceed the expected gain. Minor grievances do not justify
a civil war. If this is a moral requirement, then in some cases it will rule out
violence while in other cases it will not. A revolution that is almost certain
to fail is likely to fail the proportionality test, since it will not bring about a
new regime, would probably result in loss of life, and may lead to even
greater repression. Civil disobedience will normally pass the proportionality test only when other options have been tried and failed, and where the
injustice is weighty enough to justify the stress and friction that civil disobedience will put on the system and on other people.

A second moral consideration is *reciprocity*. Some would argue that 6.31
those who break the law for reasons of conscience are being hypocritical.

On the one hand, if Manuel thinks a law is just, he typically thinks that
Nancy has a moral obligation to obey it as well. On the other hand, if Nancy
thinks the law is just but Manuel thinks it is unjust, Manuel will think he

has no obligation to obey it. The objection is that Manuel is in a sense imposing on others an obligation to obey the law on the basis of his view of justice but does not grant others a reciprocal right to impose obligations on him on the basis of their view of justice. In other words, if we expect others to obey the laws we think just, do we have an obligation to obey laws that other people think just?

Defenders of civil disobedience respond that this is an unfair characterization of their position. First, it conflates the *legitimacy of the law* with the *moral obligation to obey the law*. The legitimacy of the law refers to the actions of government. If the law is legitimate, the government has the moral right to enforce the law. In the earlier example, Manuel is not saying that whether the government has the right to enforce a law depends solely on his own opinion. Whether a law should be enforced will depend on a democratic decision that he participates in with other people. The moral obligation to obey the law, on the other hand, is from the perspective of the citizen. From that perspective, Manuel is willing to grant others the right to act on the same principle he acts on: "Disobey unjust laws." If someone else breaks a law that Manuel thinks is just, he will affirm the legitimacy of enforcing the law against that person. He will also admit, however, that, from the perspective of the person who breaks the law, disobeying a law you consider unjust is acting on the right principle. One question is whether you should obey unjust laws. Whether this particular law is unjust is a separate question.

6.32   Sometimes this dilemma comes up in cases where there is not a democracy. When Mahatma **Gandhi** launched his campaign of civil disobedience in India, the people of that country were living under imperial British rule. They had to hope that they could persuade a government far away to change policy. During the **Arab Spring** protesters tried to overturn governments where democratic governance was weak or nonexistent. Do revolutionaries need to take into account the likelihood that they will be able to create a better political system?

Principles for ideal and nonideal agents

6.33   Another way of talking about this is to note that we can describe a principle like "disobey unjust laws" from two different perspectives. We can choose a principle because it is the principle we would want an ideal agent to act on. In virtue ethics, asking what a wise, knowledgeable, and virtuous person would do in a given case is a common way of answering the question: "What should I do?" In deciding whether to affirm the principle "disobey unjust laws" or not, I should ask whether it is a principle I would want an ideal agent to act upon. A different position states that, when selecting principles for political life, we should ask what principle we would want a nonideal agent to act upon. In the real world many people may be wrong about which laws are unjust, and this might affect which principle we would want. When a legislator votes for a bill, the legislator must imagine how real people in the real world will interpret the law and will apply it. A principle that an ideal agent would use well but that in practice would frequently be misapplied might be rejected.

For example, Martin Luther King wrote in his ***Letter from a*** 6.34 ⌨ ***Birmingham Jail***:

> Sometimes a law is just on its face and unjust in its application. For instance, I have been arrested on a charge of parading without a permit. Now, there is nothing wrong in having an ordinance which requires a permit for a parade. But such an ordinance becomes unjust when it is used to maintain segregation and to deny citizens the First-Amendment privilege of peaceful assembly and protest. (King, 1963)

In this case the problem is not with the law itself, but with the way people are interpreting and applying it.

The same could be true of a moral rule: it could be fine in principle but 6.35 applied wrongly. This is part of what King replied to those who objected that he was inconsistent when he broke the law but then criticized segregationists for ignoring Supreme Court decisions. He continued:

> I hope you are able to see the distinction I am trying to point out. In no sense do I advocate evading or defying the law, as would the rabid segregationist. That would lead to anarchy. One who breaks an unjust law must do so openly, lovingly, and with a willingness to accept the penalty.

Notice what King has done. He considers a principle—"break laws you think are unjust however you like"—and rejects it. That principle might be acceptable if people were always right about justice and the appropriate means of pursuing it; but they are not. He realizes that, since people disagree about which laws are unjust, such a principle would create "anarchy." Instead he modifies it so that the consequences will be better when people misapply it.

6.36   The reason why this distinction is important is that the moral principles that people invoke in order to justify breaking the law normally involve contested terms. People disagree about what is morally right, what is just, and what promotes the common good. Since people who affirm the same principle will often come to different conclusions, and since all of us are fallible, we are faced with a dilemma. When asking what principle we would want ourselves and others to act on, should we take human fallibility into account or not?

6.37   If we do, we might reason as follows: "If I would not want other people, including those I disagree with, to adopt a given principle as a principle of action, then I should not adopt that principle either." This gives us a way to acknowledge both our own fallibility and that of others and to uphold the idea of reciprocity by acting on a principle we would want other people to act on as well. If I don't want others to impose on me what they think the true religion is, then I should not impose on them what I think the true religion is. This strategy also allows us to do it while still believing that we have good reasons for thinking that our interpretation of "true" or "unjust" is better than the interpretations of others. In other words we do not have to be skeptics about morality or the public good.

6.38   The other strategy is to ask what principle we would want for an ideal agent who is particularly wise about the public good, justice, and so on. Proponents of this strategy will object to the previous strategy that it leads to the following unwelcome conclusion: the fact that other people misapply a principle becomes a reason for me to reject it even if I believe I can apply it correctly. The fact that people misapply the principle reflects a problem with the people, not with the principle. We should ask instead which principle we would want an ideal agent to act on.

6.39   For example, when there are calls for intervention to stop crimes against humanity, some people may object that this principle could be misused. Some nations might use "crimes against humanity" as a mere pretext for intervention. But if there really is a situation where clear crimes against humanity are being perpetrated, should we let people die just because in another case someone might misuse the principle?

6.40   Let's take a step back now. We have noted that there are various different practical strategies for responding to unjust laws. We can obey the law and work through the political system for change. We can engage in civil disobedience. We can use violence to overthrow the system. One question is: Which of these options should be on the menu? Another question is how to decide which one to pick out of those that are on the menu. Proportionality and reciprocity are examples of principles that might apply to the more detailed question of what specific principle we will use for deciding whether to break the law and how to go about doing so. With reciprocity we noted that we can imagine either other people who disagree with us applying the principle or an ideal agent acting on the principle. Something has been missing from this whole discussion. So far we have more or less assumed that there is some *prima facie* moral obligation to obey the law. But is that the case? Are there good moral arguments for thinking that we do? In the last section we take up this question—the one that has generated the most discussion among political philosophers.

Do We Have an Obligation at All?

Most people intuitively think that we have a moral obligation to obey the 6.41 law. A number of philosophers have considered this view to be mistaken, while others have sought to vindicate our initial intuition. One of the earliest defenses of the obligation to obey the law was articulated by Plato more than two thousand years ago. Many of the arguments we will discuss below originate in Plato's dialogue **Crito**.

Historically, one argument in favor of the obligation to obey the law was 6.42 theological. We have a *prima facie* obligation to obey the law because God has imposed that obligation on us. The main objections to this position today are that not everyone believes in God and that not everyone who does believe in God thinks that God has placed a *prima facie* obligation on people to obey human laws. It is beyond the scope of this chapter to explore these questions further here. As we will see, this is not the only argument that faces big objections.

Consent

One of the more common reasons people will give for having a moral obli- 6.43 gation to obey the law is *consent*. This answer was popularized by John Locke in the seventeenth century and by the American Declaration of Independence in the eighteenth century. It rests on the intuitively appealing idea of an analogy with a promise. Promising is a way to put yourself under an obligation. If I promise to meet you for pizza, I now have an obligation (probably only a *prima facie* one) that I did not have before. Similarly, if a person consents to be under the authority of a government, that consent would create a moral obligation to obey the law. This view of consent derives from an underlying view of human autonomy: when we voluntarily consent, we make an autonomous decision to undertake an obligation. When we hold people to the obligations they have consented to undertake, we are honoring their autonomy.

6.44   But when is consent truly voluntary? Several objections to the consent account call into question whether the consent we give to our government and its laws can be truly autonomous. Suppose a robber comes up to you with a gun and a contract and tells you to sign over all your possessions to him or he will kill you. If you sign the contract, this is not an act of true consent because the robber coerced you. Consent needs to be *voluntary*. If someone decides that, if you wear a blue shirt on a certain day, you thereby consent to give her $100 but she never tells you about it, this is not consent because consent must be *informed*: you have to understand the choice you are making and know your other options. If she says that unless you jump 10 feet in the air you consent to give her the $100, your failure to jump is not an expression of consent. Consent creates obligations only when nonconsent is *possible*.

6.45   What if nonconsent involves great costs? What if someone says: "I'll cut off your hand if you object." When consent is given under duress, nonconsent is *possible*, but it *is too costly*. In order for consent to generate a moral obligation, it needs to be informed and voluntary and the consenting person or party must be able to withhold consent without unreasonable cost.

6.46   If these are the standards of consent, how many people have actually consented to their government in a way that meets those standards? Some say: "You consent because you choose to live in the country." But most people don't believe or assume that, if they choose to remain in the country where they were born, they acquire a moral obligation to obey the law from that time forward. Most people don't view the day they turn 18 as the day on which they will decide whether to leave or to acquire a moral obligation to obey the laws of the land.

6.47   Second, the choice would have to be real. If someone lacks the financial means to leave the country and provide for himself in another country, the decision to stay is not a choice, it is a necessity. There are also people who do not have other countries willing to accept them as permanent citizens.

6.48   Third, the choice would need to be a voluntary one, and the cost of nonconsent should not be too high. Many people might prefer to lose a limb than to be forced to leave the place where they grew up and all the friends and family members who live there. Is it reasonable to require that people incur such a cost? And where would they go? Arguably the cost is just too high, and the range of better alternative countries too small for this option to count as a real choice.

"You consent when you vote." Do people know that, when they vote, they 6.49 are incurring that obligation? What about people who are not allowed to vote (legal aliens, minors, some felons)—do they have a moral obligation to obey the law? If I choose to quit voting, can I withdraw my consent and free myself from the moral obligation to obey the law?

"You consent when you say a pledge of allegiance." Children are asked 6.50 to recite this at school, but we don't think of children as being able to give consent: they lack the necessary capacity. On the occasions when adults say it, how many of them think that their set of moral obligations changed after saying it? Are there cases where there is so much social pressure to say it that the action is coerced rather than voluntary? If the pledge is compelled, does it really constitute consent? Further, when people say the pledge, they do not typically understand themselves to be taking on an obligation. Can it be an act of consent if people don't intend it as an act of consent?

"You consent when you take an oath as part of becoming a naturalized 6.51 citizen, serving in the military, or holding a public office." Naturalized citizens are probably the best case where there really is consent: in most cases they voluntarily choose to become a member of a political society, knowing that by doing so they receive new obligations as well as new rights. But if we take that as the template, we see that there are few other cases that match the theory equally well. A soldier or a public official may take an oath of allegiance, but typically they do not think of themselves as acquiring a new obligation as citizens. Instead they are just reaffirming something that was already true, or they are acquiring a new obligation related to their new position.

We could continue with the examples, but you see the basic pattern. 6.52 A. John Simmons is a consent theorist who is also a philosophical anarchist. He thinks that consent generates an obligation to obey but that very few people have really consented. Other consent theorists argue that we can understand the conditions of consent far more loosely. They would say that, even if there were not a specific moment in time when a person knew that they were giving consent, if most people think they have an obligation because they choose to live in the country, this means that most people consent. Still others would claim that looser ways of identifying oneself with a country should count as consent.

Gratitude

6.53 Not everyone agrees that consent is the right explanation. A second justification for our having an obligation to obey the law is that we have an obligation of *gratitude*, which is based on the benefits we have received. Governments provide police and fire protection, roads, schools, national defense, clean water, and a variety of other goods. We receive these goods and therefore have an obligation to obey.

6.54 The counterargument to this position is that people are often unable to refuse these gifts without leaving the country and renouncing citizenship. The government is making us an offer that we literally cannot refuse. The government will protect you from foreign armies whether you want it to or not. Thus, from a consent standpoint, the idea that someone can impose an obligation on us just by giving us a gift we literally cannot refuse is questionable.

6.55 Even if we could refuse it, it still doesn't follow that this gift giving creates an obligation. Imagine that someone gives you a birthday present. Does that create a moral obligation for you to give them one back? While it might be polite to do so, some would say that the reason to give a gift is that you want to do it, not that you are obligated to do it. If gifts generate obligations, then they are not as free as we think they are.

6.56 Defenders of the gratitude view might hold that receiving a gift actually does create an obligation, although only a *prima facie* one. They would also question the individualist assumptions of the consent theory. It is true that we cannot refuse some benefits, but many of our most important obligations are things we did not consent to. If you think you have obligations to your family, did you choose to have them as family members? We don't choose our parents or siblings or grandparents, for example. If we have obligations to them, these obligations must be based on something other than consent. One explanation is gratitude. We have obligations to them because of the benefits we received from them even if we were in no position to refuse those benefits.

Fairness

6.57 A third possible justification for the obligation to obey the law appeals to the value of *fairness* or the principle of *fair play*, discussed earlier. This justification may be related to gratitude—the previous justification—in that it includes the idea that we receive benefits from the rule of law and owe something in return. But the argument from fairness also includes the idea that our participation in shared governance imposes constraints on others. To impose such constraints without accepting them yourself would be *unfair*. There is a sense in which one who doesn't obey is "free riding" on the obedience of others.

Consent theorists will, again, object that people should be able to opt out 6.58 of these schemes of cooperation if they want. As before, they would say that a benefit we cannot refuse does not generate obligations. Another criticism of the fairness account is that in many cases our disobedience to the law doesn't really harm others, and so we are not treating them unfairly.

Defenders of the fairness view will respond by stating that most people 6.59 willingly accept the benefits in question, even if they didn't have a good way to refuse them. Suppose there are three doors and I must go through one of them. I want to go through the first door and I do so. It turns out that, unbeknownst to me, the other two doors were locked. We might still say that I freely chose to go through the first door, even though I could not have done otherwise. Similarly, many people very much want to remain in their country and see themselves as doing so willingly even if they could not have left easily.

Duty

A fourth justification for obeying the law is the idea that we have a *natural* 6.60 *duty to support just institutions*. One criticism of the previous accounts is that they seem to assume there are not duties unless we create them ourselves through consent, or someone else creates them by conferring a benefit, or some combination of the two. If we start from the assumption that we have certain positive duties to one another, it is not implausible that one duty is to help maintain just institutions. Just governments are extremely important for how peoples' lives go. If justice is itself an obligation, it seems plausible that it is not enough to refrain from unjust acts, but that we should also act in ways that promote just governments. Therefore, if the government is just, we have a duty to help maintain it, and obeying the law helps maintain the law.

Critics of the natural duty approach reply that we can support just insti- 6.61 tutions in other countries as well, and many of them may need the support more. If there is just a generic duty to support just institutions, why do I have special obligations toward my own government? Also, there is still the problem that many acts of disobedience don't undermine just institutions in any measurable way. Does your going a little over the speed limit really threaten the national government?

Membership

6.62 The last approach we will discuss grounds the duty to obey on *membership*. We mentioned earlier that many people think they have obligations to their parents even though they didn't choose their parents and couldn't refuse the benefits their parents gave them. More than that, some people would say they have obligations to their parents even if the latter were not particularly good to them. In other words, our duties to our families can't be explained just through the benefits we receive or the consent we give. A different explanation is that there are certain relationships that become a part of our very identity. Membership in a family creates duties because of the kind of relationship it is.

6.63 Similarly, people typically have a sense of connection to members of their nation, with whom they share a common political culture and history. This argument tries to reverse the burden of proof. Instead of assuming that we don't have political obligations and asking what proof there is that we do, the membership view assumes that we naturally have duties toward those we have close affinity with and that this is enough to create a *prima facie* obligation. The burden of proof is on others to show cases where our obligations to our fellow citizens are outweighed by something stronger.

6.64 Critics of this view argue that, while membership may create feelings of attachment, these do not necessarily constitute real moral obligations. They also argue that the relationship one has with one's parents is quite different from the relationship one has with one's government. The level of attachment is just not strong enough to create the moral obligation needed. Moreover, the state is not the same as the nation. Switzerland has people whose nationality is French or German but who are citizens of Switzerland. Some states have a number of different ethnics or tribal groups. Often these attachments are much stronger than the attachment people feel toward the state.

Conclusion

6.65 One big question in this chapter has been how to reason about cases where you think that a law is unjust. If you think the law is just, you have a moral reason to abide by it regardless of whether there is a moral obligation to obey the law. But what if the law is unjust? We have seen that there are many different moral considerations related to how you break the law: What options should be on the menu? How should proportionality and reciprocity shape your choice of means? There are also many explanations of why there is a moral obligation to obey the law at all. All of them seem to have flaws. Some have suggested that our mistake is thinking that there is only one explanation for the obligation to obey the law, when in fact we may need several different justifications to work together in order to explain this obligation.

References and Further Reading

Dagger, Richard and David Lefkowitz. 2014 [2007]. **"Political Obligation."** In *Stanford Encyclopedia of Philosophy*. http://plato.stanford.edu/entries/political-obligation (accessed February 12, 2016). A thorough but still introductory exploration of the problem of political obligation.

Hart, Herbert Lionel Adolphus. 1955. "Are There Any Natural Rights? *Philosophical Review*, 64(2): 175–191. This paper addresses the problem identified in the title but also includes a classic statement and defense of the principle of fair play.

Hart, Herbert Lionel Adolphus. 2012. *The Concept of Law*, 3rd edn. Oxford: Oxford University Press. A classic but still very helpful overview of law, what it is and in what sense it is obligatory. Hart's book set the standard for jurisprudence since its first publication in 1961.

King, Martin Luther. 1963. *Letter from a Birmingham Jail*. https://www.africa.upenn.edu/Articles_Gen/Letter_Birmingham.html (accessed February 27, 2016). A classic defense of civil disobedience.

Klosko, George. 2008. *Political Obligations*. Oxford: Oxford University Press. A careful defense of the fairness view.

Rawls, John. 1971. *A Theory of Justice*. Cambridge, MA: Harvard University Press. Rawls argues that we have a natural duty to uphold just institutions, which typically provides an obligation to obey the law.

Sandel, Michael. 1998. *Liberalism and the Limits of Justice*, 2nd edn. Cambridge: Cambridge University Press. Sandel articulates a communitarian critique of contemporary liberal theories of justice and a membership theory of political obligation.

Simmons, A. John. 1981. *Moral Principles and Political Obligations*. Princeton, NJ: Princeton University Press. A classic and quite complete discussion of arguments for obedience to law, including an articulate defense of philosophical anarchism by consent. Simmons offers thorough critiques of the various possibilities for why there is an obligation to obey the law.

Tuckness, Alex. 2002. *Locke and the Legislative Point of View*. Princeton, NJ: Princeton University Press. Chapters 1–2 explore whether we should modify our principles on the basis of how others might misapply them and discuss Martin Luther King, Jr as an example.

Wellman, Christopher and A. John Simmons. 2005. *Is There a Duty to Obey the Law?* Cambridge: Cambridge University Press. Wellman provides an extended argument justifying the right of the state to coerce, while Simmons argues against the view that people have a general obligation to obey the law.

Online Resources

1   http://www.history.com/topics/black-history/fugitive-slave-acts

2   http://www.archives.gov/education/lessons/rosa-parks/

3   http://www.ghsa.org/html/stateinfo/laws/cellphone_laws.html

4   https://www.biblegateway.com/passage/?search=Acts%204&version=HCSB

5   https://en.wikipedia.org/wiki/Martin_Luther_King,_Jr.

6   https://www.africa.upenn.edu/Articles_Gen/Letter_Birmingham.html

7   http://www.penguinrandomhouse.com/books/169423/you-can-get-arrested-for-that-by-rich-smith/

8   http://plato.stanford.edu/entries/locke-political/

9   http://www.archives.gov/exhibits/charters/declaration_transcript.html

10   http://www.archives.gov/exhibits/charters/constitution_transcript.html

11   http://robertpaulwolff.blogspot.co.uk/

12   http://www.gutenberg.org/files/71/71-h/71-h.htm

13   http://www.cbsnews.com/news/the-cost-of-a-nation-of-incarceration/

14   http://www.nytimes.com/2013/08/24/nyregion/citys-annual-cost-per-inmate-is-nearly-168000-study-says.html?_r=1

15   http://malcolmx.com/biography/

16   https://www.youtube.com/watch?v=D9BVEnEsn6Y

17   https://en.wikipedia.org/wiki/Mahatma_Gandhi

18   https://en.wikipedia.org/wiki/Arab_Spring

19   http://classics.mit.edu/Plato/crito.html

7

POLITICAL VIOLENCE
WAR, TORTURE, AND PUNISHMENT

SOPHIE   I've been writing a paper about the so-called "war on terror." I'm amazed—do you have any idea how far we went, abandoning fundamental constitutional principles in an effort to pursue the terrorists and to get information out of the people we captured?

JUSTIN   Sophie, as far as I'm concerned those people got what they deserved. Anyone who organizes attacks on innocent civilians deserves the worst—whatever people did to them, it can't be worse than what they did to other people.

SOPHIE   I can't believe you're saying this, Justin. American operatives *tortured* people we captured. They violated the international conventions governing the treatment of prisoners, and violated the laws of warfare.

JUSTIN   It's not *torture*. They used water and made them think they were drowning.

SOPHIE   When other nations did that to American soldiers during World War II, we regarded it as torture. Japanese soldiers were *executed* after the war for waterboarding Americans. Apparently our government thinks waterboarding was OK when we did it, but that it's not OK when other people do it.

JUSTIN   Still, these are things people did during war. How can warfare be governed by laws, anyway? Haven't you heard the saying "all's fair in love and war"? War is horrible, yes. But the point of war is to *win*. It's only reasonable to predict

This Is Political Philosophy: An Introduction, First Edition. Alex Tuckness and Clark Wolf.
© 2017 John Wiley & Sons, Inc. Published 2017 by John Wiley & Sons, Inc.

that people will resort to any methods whatsoever in the effort to win, if their fundamental values are at stake.

SOPHIE   If we were willing to do *anything at all* to win, then I think we'd be no better than the terrorists. And I hope you don't really believe that love justifies anything a person might do in its name. Even in war there are things no one should ever do. Besides, the treatment of prisoners isn't a matter of military strategy. Once they're prisoners, they are no longer a threat.

JUSTIN   But the organization they're working with is still a threat. What if we need the information they have in order to protect ourselves? What if the only way we can prevent a tragic disaster is to get information out of them? We shouldn't second-guess our military experts in circumstances like this. If they think these enhanced interrogation techniques are needed, they're in a better position to make that judgment than we are.

SOPHIE   But our military experts did *not* agree that so called "enhanced interrogation methods" were needed. Expert interrogators argued that these techniques weren't needed to get the information and that they produce unreliable information anyway. Justin, some things are *always* wrong, and torture is one of them.

JUSTIN   Even if you're right about that, extreme circumstances require extreme measures. And war is an extreme case. I don't think we can blame or convict people for taking extreme measures in circumstances like that.

SOPHIE   You're changing the subject: it's one thing to say that it's OK to torture captured prisoners. I think that's obviously and always wrong! But it's entirely another thing to consider whether people who have tortured prisoners should be convicted and punished. I agree that, when people commit crimes under stress or duress, courts should take this into account. But that doesn't mean we shouldn't bring them to trial, where they can answer to the charges against them. It just means that the courts should take all mitigating circumstances into account. Of course courts should do that. But we need to hold people who commit crimes accountable. Torture is a crime.

JUSTIN   But the people who did this were following orders from other people who told them that what they were doing was legal. If anyone is responsible, it's the politicians and legal advisors who gave the orders.

SOPHIE   Following orders doesn't always get people off the hook. If people are given illegal orders, they have a duty not to comply.

JUSTIN   That's so easy for you to say, Sophie. But if you were in the military you would know that soldiers are not really in a position to refuse to comply with an order from a superior officer. Maybe they have a legal right, or even an obligation to do it. But the idea that they're free to act on their own judgment in that circumstance is just silly.

Umkhonto we Sizwe

On March 21, 1960, in the South African township of Sharpeville, a crowd of unarmed demonstrators converged on the police station. They were there to protest a new law that required black South Africans to carry a passbook for identification. The protesters arrived unarmed and without their passbooks, to offer themselves peacefully for arrest. Reports say that the crowd started with several thousand people but grew much larger over the course of the day. Protesters became increasingly angry and divided. The police officers in the station were afraid. They called in reinforcements, and these arrived with armored cars and submachine guns. As the crowd grew more restive, tempers rose. Protesters threw stones and the police responded with tear gas. It is not clear exactly how the conflict progressed from that point—different participants tell very different stories, but there is general agreement that the crowd was increasingly threatening. At about 1:00 p.m., the police opened fire into the crowd. As many as 69 people were killed, including 10 children, and 180 people were injured. People who examined the bodies reported that many of those killed were shot in the back, gunned down as they tried to run from the police.

Across South Africa, the response to the Sharpeville Massacre was powerful. In retrospect, some historians see the event as the tipping point that prompted other nations to isolate South Africa. And, within the nation, many South Africans concluded that change could not be accomplished through passive, peaceful resistance. The African National Congress (ANC), one of the main political organizations working to free South Africa from the racist policies of apartheid, faced internal division. Some members urged that peaceful resistance was the only way to effect permanent change. Others urged that such methods could not be effective against a government that had shown itself to be shameless and ready to slaughter unarmed civilians and children.

7.3   Long before Sharpeville, Nelson Mandela had been working toward political change in South Africa, but up to that point he had been committed to peaceful change. In the wake of the Sharpeville massacre, Mandela began to question his commitment to nonviolent change. Together with others in the ANC, Mandela founded an organization called Umkhonto we Sizwe, which means "Spear of the Nation." Umkhonto was conceived as an armed wing of the ANC. Members published a **manifesto** that indicated a change in policy:

> The time comes in the life of any nation when there remain only two choices: submit or fight. That time has now come to South Africa. We shall not submit and we have no choice but to hit back by all means within our power in defense of our people, our future, and our freedom. The government has interpreted the peacefulness of the movement as weakness; the people's nonviolent policies have been taken as a green light for government violence. Refusal to resort to force has been interpreted by the government as an invitation to use armed force against the people without any fear of reprisals. The methods of Umkhonto we Sizwe mark a break with that past. (African National Congress, 2011 [1961]; click **here**)

Mandela was later arrested as a terrorist. In a **famous speech** at his defense trial he explained his reasons for forming Umkhonto:

> Firstly, we believed that as a result of Government policy, violence by the African people had become inevitable, and that unless responsible leadership was given to canalize [direct] and control the feelings of our people, there would be outbreaks of terrorism which would produce an intensity of bitterness and hostility between the various races of this country which is not produced even by war. Secondly, we felt that without violence there would be no way open to the African people to succeed in their struggle against the principle of white supremacy. All lawful modes of expressing opposition to this principle had been closed by legislation, and we were placed in a position in which we had either to accept a permanent state of inferiority, or to defy the Government. We chose to defy the law. We first broke the law in a way which avoided any recourse to violence; when this form was legislated

against, and then the Government resorted to a show of force to crush opposition to its policies, only then did we decide to answer violence with violence. (Mandela, 2011 [1964]; visit http://www.anc.org.za/show.php?id=3430)

According to Mandela, the transition to armed resistance was undertaken thoughtfully. Members of the group considered what kinds of actions would be undertaken by the group and decided to take only one step away from peaceful resistance:

> Four forms of violence were possible. There is sabotage, there is guerrilla warfare, there is terrorism, and there is open revolution. We chose to adopt the first method and to exhaust it before taking any other decision. In light of our political background the choice was a logical one. Sabotage did not involve loss of life, and it offered the best hope for future race relations. Bitterness would be kept to a minimum and, if the policy bore fruit, democratic government would become a reality. (Mandela, 2011 [1964])

Asked by the court to renounce violent resistance, Mandela refused. "I have dedicated myself to this struggle of the African people," he said. "I have fought against white domination, and I have fought against black domination. I have cherished the ideal of a democratic and free society in which all persons live together in harmony and with equal opportunities. It is an ideal which I hope to live for and to achieve. But if needs be, it is an ideal for which I am prepared to die" (Mandela, 2011 [1964]).

The transition of the ANC from a policy of peaceful resistance to the 7.4 Umkhonto policy of armed resistance is historically important, but this is also an opportunity for philosophical reflection: when, if ever, is violence justified? Are there conditions that must be met before one resorts to violence as a means of effecting political change? We are fortunate to have documented sources that record the deliberation of ANC members who formed Umkhonto, just as we have similar documents recording the deliberation of the signatories to the US Declaration of Independence. They too decided that the time for peaceful resistance had passed.

What Is Violence?

One way to investigate a concept like violence is to consider instances where 7.5 it takes place and then try to discover what they all have in common. Another way is to begin with a *definition* or an *analysis* of the concept and then test it against principles or potential counterexamples, to see whether it captures the meaning it should. The World Health Organization (WHO) uses a definition of violence that contains three individually necessary and jointly sufficient conditions:

> An action or event is an instance of *violence* if and only if (1) It involves the intentional use, or threat to use physical force or power, (2) This power is directed against oneself, another person, or a group or community, (3) The consequences of this use of power is [*sic*] highly likely to result in injury, death, psychological harm, maldevelopment, or deprivation. (World Health Organization, 2002)

Philosophical questions cannot be settled with a definition: it is worth noting that this definition is controversial and that not everyone would accept it. But philosophical analysis often *starts* with a definition of a concept that is then tested and evaluated. As analyzed here, each of these three conditions is presented as *necessary* and, together, they are *jointly sufficient* for violence. If we want to ask whether an action is an instance of violence, we would need to show that each of these three elements is present.

7.6   For example, this account excludes actions that are reckless or negligent: if a person is struck by a car driven by a careless driver, or by a stray bullet recklessly fired by a person who didn't actually intend harm, the action will not count as "violence" even if it is deadly. Force can also be exerted recklessly or negligently if people who have power use it to push others around, without concern for the effect their actions will have on others. And power can be negligently employed if people just don't care enough to think about the consequences of its use.

7.7   It is interesting that this definition counts *psychological harm, maldevelopment, and deprivation* among the consequences of violence: this opens the possibility that some acts of violence may extend over the long term and may not involve a direct assault or an immediate event, but instead a long-standing condition.

7.8   When Nelson Mandela and the ANC founded Umkhonto we Sizwe, it must have made perfect sense to think of the poverty and deprivation in black South African townships as reflecting a form of violence. Poverty was the result of intentionally racist policies that were implemented through the use of brutal force, directed at communities that were defined in South African law as "black" and "colored". All of the elements of the WHO definition of "violence" were fully satisfied.

When (If Ever) Is Violence Justified?

Mandela evidently believed that there is a *sequence* from sabotage to guerilla 7.9
warfare to terrorism, and finally to open revolution. Perhaps each stage
represented, to him, a logical next step in a sequence. It does not follow
from what Mandela said, however, that he believed that each of these
sequential steps would be justified. Mandela argued that members of
Umkhonto should avoid actions against people and should instead pursue
sabotage against infrastructure. But, after Mandela was captured and
imprisoned by the South African government, Unkhonto members moved
to increasingly violent actions. This exemplifies one of the dangers that
attend acts of violence: sometimes violence is not an *act* but a path. Like
fire, violence often sets in motion a process that is difficult or impossible to
control once it gets started.

The members of Umkhonto we Sizwe believed that the time for peaceful 7.10
resistance had passed, but, because they still hoped for reconciliation with
the South African government, they decided to take action against infrastructure, not against people. Their first action was to sabotage an electric
power station. Other early actions were directed at government posts and
machines.

Then, in 1964, Nelson Mandela was imprisoned. ANC members became 7.11
increasingly frustrated with their lack of progress: if anything, the South
African government seemed to become even *more* oppressive and brutal. In
response, Umkhonto members took yet another step, ordering actions that
aimed to kill and injure military targets: in 1983 a bomb that exploded
Church Street targeted the South African Airforce Headquarters and
resulted in 19 deaths and many injuries.

Still later the group undertook actions that expressly targeted civilians. 7.12
In 1985, under ANC orders, an Umkhonto member named Andrew Zondo
detonated a bomb in a shopping center in Natal. Zondo targeted Christmas
shoppers. Five civilians were killed and 40 were injured.

This progression of increasingly harmful actions exemplifies one of the 7.13
problems with violent movements: once violence begins, it is often difficult
or impossible to control. Mandela suggests that there are different *levels* of
violence. Even when people become convinced that the time for peaceful
protest has passed, he urged, they should minimize harm and avoid targeting civilians. Nothing in Mandela's writing on this topic would justify
targeting Christmas shoppers. That action, however, was undertaken when
he was in prison.

7.14   One might think that actions against objects, while serious in themselves, require a level of justification different from that of actions against persons. Guerilla warfare, whether in the context of Umkhonto's actions against the South African Airforce or in that of colonial American revolutionary actions against British troops, involves actions against military targets. But are there *any* circumstances that can justify actions taken against civilian noncombatants? The world community condemned the 1985 shopping center bombing and, as a result of this and other actions, the Umkhonto movement lost significant international support. Perhaps this means that those actions were *strategically* inappropriate and ill advised. But it is also reasonable to think that they were morally wrong: perhaps there are actions, or kinds of action, that *cannot* be justified under any circumstances whatsoever. The needless targeting of innocent civilians might be one of these.

7.15   Targeting civilian shoppers is an act of *terrorism*. In the case of Andrew Zondo, the action may have been self-defeating—in addition to being morally wrong in other ways. But it is worth considering the motives of people who pursue terrorist actions: on one definition, terrorist actions are actions that aim to create fear—terror—in order to motivate change. But are all efforts to motivate other people by fear acts of terrorism? If a teacher threatens to give students a surprise exam if they don't buckle down to work, has she committed an act of terrorism? Other definitions of "terrorism" focus on the idea that terrorist actions harm some people—their direct targets—in an effort to influence others—their indirect targets.

7.16   Terrorist actions are sometimes committed by people whose ultimate goal is a good one: perhaps Andrew Zondo's ultimate goal was to end the evil of racial oppression in South Africa. Those who regard such actions to be indefensible even when they are carried out in support of a laudable goal need to be able to explain the reasons—perhaps nonconsequentialist ones— why the actions in question are wrong.

Pacifism

7.17 Some people argue that violence is *never* justified. *Pacifism* involves a commitment not to perpetrate violence. There are two different kinds of pacifist: some pacifists are committed not to do violence, but regard this as a *personal* commitment. They do not argue that violent actions are always wrong. A stronger pacifist view holds that violence is always wrong, even when it is necessary for self-defense or the defense of others. There are various reasons one might offer in favor of such a view.

First, violence is intrinsically harmful and undesirable. To *initiate* vio- 7.18
lence is always wrong, so the best case in favor of justified violence would be violence in self-defense or in defense of others. But, second, as pacifists sometimes point out, when we respond to violence with violence we tend to *escalate* a conflict rather than resolving it. To initiate violence is to put in motion a process that cannot be controlled and that has a tendency to grow and become extreme over time.

Gandhi's pacifism

Mahatma Gandhi, perhaps the most celebrated pacifist in recent history, 7.19
argued that recourse to violence involves escalation and that people who are the victims of violent assault should respond in a way that expresses concern for the welfare of the person perpetrating the assault. In this spirit, he is reported to have said that an eye for an eye leaves the whole world blind. Instead of responding to violence with yet more violence, Gandhi recommended that we respond with nonviolent resistance. The goal of such resistance is to bring about a change in the hearts and minds of those who *do* use violence: when aggressors find themselves brutalizing people who are brave enough not to retaliate, they will eventually come to understand that they are in the wrong.

In an essay titled "**The Doctrine of the Sword**," Gandhi (2016 [1920]) 7.20
wrote: "I do believe that where there is only a choice between cowardice and violence I would advise violence." But it is clear that Gandhi didn't believe that we need to make a choice between the two: passive resistance as Gandhi conceived of it is not cowardly, but heroically brave. It seems evident that Gandhi believed that violence is a sign of weakness: we need *never* be so weak as to have to resort to violence.

Russell's "relative pacifism"

But it is one thing to adopt a doctrine of pacifism and accept the conse- 7.21
quences of others' violence onto oneself, and quite another thing to stand by while others are victimized. While the philosopher Bertrand Russell also considered himself a pacifist, his pacifism was less absolute than that of Gandhi. For example, Russell supported the war against Nazi Germany in World War II because he believed (1) that passive resistance would be

ineffective against the Nazis, who were willing to exterminate people without a qualm, and (2) that fighting Germany was bad, but that it would be even worse if Germany were to win the war. Russell seems to have held the view that it's not worth fighting *most* wars, but in extreme circumstances it's better to fight than allow others to be slaughtered.

7.22   We might question whether Russell's position really counts as a form of *pacifism*. People who are not pacifists don't favor fighting in useless wars either! On the other hand, Russell spent a significant amount of time and energy speaking and writing against war and against resorting to violence, and he was at one time *imprisoned* as a pacifist. His convictions were not absolute, but they appear to have been both powerful and sincere.

7.23   A more significant question concerns the *justification* of pacifism: do we have sufficient reason to adopt pacifist principles in our own lives? Or should we instead adopt a view that permits or advocates recourse to violence in circumstances where a pacifist would demur? Nelson Mandela, Martin Luther King Jr, Gandhi, and Bertrand Russell offer different answers to these important questions.

Ius ad bellum: "Just War" and the Justification of Large-Scale Violence

7.24 Russell believed that war is sometimes justified. But when? And if some wars, or some actions in war, are unjustified, how should we decide? In moving to a policy of *armed resistance*, Nelson Mandela seems to have been guided by principles that required that peaceful means of change should be tried first and that more forceful resistance can only be adopted as a last resort. He also urged that actions should involve the least imposition of harm that was possible while the objectives would still be achieved. The principles he employed are very similar to those that have been adopted and refined over many centuries. *Just war theory* holds that some wars are just, but that certain conditions must be met before one decides to start or enter a war. These conditions are embodied in the principles of just war theory.

7.25   **Just war theory** has been around for a long time and there is a rich and ancient literature articulating and offering justification and revision of its principles. It has roots that trace back to the works of Aristotle, the Roman philosopher, orator, and lawyer Cicero, and Christian theologians like the Neoplatonist Augustine and the Peripatetic Thomas Aquinas. It has changed and developed over the centuries and now enjoys some formal recognition in international law.

Classical just war theory distinguishes the conditions that must be met 7.26 before one enters or starts a war (often referred to by the Latin phrase *ius ad bello*: one's "right to wage war") from the principles that restrict the actions that can be undertaken once one is *engaged* in war (*ius in bello*: one's "right during war"). More recent discussions also include requirements of justice after hostilities have ended (*ius post bello*: one's "right after war"), which govern the treatment of a conquered nation and the negotiation of treaties designed to gain and preserve the peace after war.

1. JUST CAUSE. It is only permissible to enter a war as a means to *resist aggression*. Aggression, in turn, is the military use of force in violation of someone's basic rights.
2. RIGHT INTENTIONS. A state's *reason* for entering a war must actually *be* this just cause. A state cannot legitimately enter a state of war for reasons that are *ulterior* to the motive to resist aggression.
3. PROPORTIONALITY. A just war must not be *disproportionate* by comparison with the acts of aggression and injustice to which it is a response.
4. LAST RESORT. If there are other means to address an act of aggression, they must be tried first, unless circumstances require immediate action.
5. LIKELIHOOD OF SUCCESS. Entering into war is not permissible if it is *futile*, or if it can be expected to have no significant effect to change the situation for the better. A futile action is one that has no chance of success.
6. LEGITIMATE AUTHORITY. An action to enter the state of war is justified only when the decision to go to war has been made by the proper authorities within the nation.

To test these principles, consider what they require. The *just cause* requirement prohibits wars of aggression or imperialist acquisition. It does permit a nation to go to war in self-defense, however, and is also understood to permit entry into war for the sake of preventing humanitarian catastrophes. The *right intention* principle makes it impermissible for a nation to go to war under the *pretext* of a just cause when its *real* reasons are different. For example, suppose Rwanda attacks its neighbor, the Democratic Republic of Congo, under the pretext that the civilian population of the Kivu province needs to be protected from humanitarian catastrophe. Perhaps the *real* reason why Rwanda undertook military action was to *annex* Kivu! If so, then Rwanda's action would fail to satisfy the *right intention* requirement.

7.27   *Proportionality* is a broad principle that applies in many different contexts. In this case, it prohibits a decision to go to war when the consequences incurred through war would be grossly out of proportion with the causes that justify that decision.

7.28   The *last resort* principle requires nations to try nonmilitary means for dispute resolution before resorting to war. Only when other resources have *run out* is it legitimate for a nation to enter armed conflict. The *last resort* principle also prohibits *preventive* wars.

7.29   The principle that prohibits war unless there is a *likelihood of success* might be thought to be a peculiar one: what nation would enter a war unless the leaders at least *believed* that success is likely? To enter a futile war would seem to be futile at best. But this requirement might also be considered unreasonable in some circumstances: if a nation is violently attacked by an aggressive neighbor, surely it would seem permissible for the victims to respond in self-defense. When people are pressed to the wall defending their homes and families, they can be expected to fight even if there is no reasonable chance of success. It is for this reason that the *likely success* requirement does not appear in international law, and also because it is sometimes seen as an unfair burden on small states.

7.30   Finally, the *legitimate authority* principle specifies that a state may go to war only if war has been properly declared in the way specified by the state's constitution, its governing documents, or its customary decision procedures. If a state's government has broken apart, or if a state does not have institutions that support legitimate decision making by public authorities, that state may be unable to meet this requirement. In that case, the state will simply lack the *right* to go to war.

7.31   Sometimes these requirements may be closely related to one another and violation of one principle may be evidence that other principles have been violated as well. If a state goes to war precipitously (in violation of the *last resort principle*), or if its response to another state's offense is *disproportionate*, this may be good reason to think that the supposedly just cause for entering the conflict is a mere pretext and that there are other ulterior motives at play.

Testing Just War Theory

7.32 Some people object to just war theory on the grounds that war can never be just: by its nature, war involves massive and uncontrollable violence. The decision to enter into a state of war implies acceptance that rights will be violated and that civilian noncombatants will suffer and die. One might hope to *minimize* such costs, but entry into a state of war involves the creation of circumstances no one can hope fully to control.

If the requirements of *just war theory* are the right ones, then it will be 7.33 *morally* justifiable for a nation to enter a state of war when (but only when) they are all satisfied. The requirements are taken to be individually necessary and jointly sufficient to justify the decision to go to war. To test the theory, look for a counterexample. There are two different kinds of counterexample that would make an adequate test: (1) can you think of a case where all the requirements are satisfied, but there are reasons to think that the decision to go to war would be unjustified? Or (2) can you think of cases where *not* all of the requirements are satisfied, but the decision to go to war would nonetheless be justifiable? Test the theory against your own moral judgment by trying to describe a case that fits either of these descriptions.

Vagueness

But there is another important problem with just war theory as described 7.34 above: the requirements all are vague and stand in need of interpretation. It is highly likely that any state that perceives itself to have *interests* that would be served by going to war could find a way to interpret the principles to have been satisfied.

Manipulability

The principles of just war theory can be used to provide public justification 7.35 or "cover" for actions that are in fact unjustified and unjustifiable. In the worst case, we might imagine a state that enters a war for revenge, or from an imperialist goal to gain territory, but uses the principles of just war theory to concoct a plausible rationalization for its actions. Before intervening in such a conflict, third-party nations would also need to have *just cause* and should move to armed intervention only as a *last resort*. It is conceivable that a manipulative aggressor nation might be able to use other nations' compliance with the requirements of just war theory as a way to prevent interference with its own wrongful conflicts.

The vagueness and manipulability of these provisions may be problem- 7.36 atic, but perhaps there is no way around this problem. All regulations require interpretation and deliberation, and many systems of rules can be misused and abused. The principles may still be appropriate and useful in several contexts: at an individual level, we can use the principles of just war theory to evaluate conflicts taking place in other parts of the world, or to evaluate the actions of our own state. Many US citizens urged that the invasion of Iraq in 2003 was an unjustified *preemptive* attack that violated the longstanding requirement that armed conflict should be a *last resort*. Others, including President Bush himself, argued that the situation in Iraq was itself evidence that the requirements of just war theory were obsolete and outdated. We can use the principles of the theory in retrospect, to make judgments about the moral justification of such actions.

7.37   At an international institutional level, the principles of just war theory have acquired new force and meaning with the rising power of the International Criminal Court in the Hague. Where nations enter into questionable or wrongful conflicts, their leaders may now be brought to account in an international tribunal invested with the authority to extradite and punish wrongheaded decisions. In the International Criminal Court many of the requirements of just war theory gain the force of law and have been refined and interpreted through negotiation and court rulings.

Ius in bello: Justice in the Conduct of War

7.38 Just war theory also specifies standards that are to apply to the *conduct* of war. It is not enough that a nation has adequate justification for going to war; there are restrictions that apply to soldiers, decision makers who make tactical decisions, and others who must make swift decisions in the context of battle. The principles of just conduct in war—usually referred to by the Latin phrase *ius in bello* (literally "right/law in time of/during war")—are supposed to provide guidelines in both contexts.

1. PROPORTIONALITY. Force used in battle must be proportional to the legitimate military objective pursued. It is impermissible to use force *beyond* that which is necessary for the achievement of a legitimate military objective.
2. DISCRIMINATION. In the conduct of war, participants are required to discriminate between *legitimate targets* and *noncombatants*. Weapons may only be used against legitimate military, political, or industrial targets of strategic significance. The principle of discrimination is not violated when there are *some* collateral noncombatant casualties, but it expressly prohibits actions that *target* civilians.

3. AVOIDANCE OF WRONGFUL MEANS AND PROHIBITED WEAPONS. Traditionally, some means of war were prohibited as wrong in themselves. These included poison, treachery, and the use of force to compel soldiers to fight against their own army. The principle of prohibiting wrongful means also forbids the use of terror, rape, ethnic cleansing, and genocide. More recently this requirement has been extended to the use of chemical and biological weapons and, more generally, of weapons that are indiscriminate in their effects.

4. SAFE AND BENEVOLENT DETAINMENT FOR PRISONERS OF WAR. Once prisoners are captured, they are no longer combatants and must be given humane treatment. They may, however, be confined until the cessation of hostilities.

5. NO REPRISALS FOR VIOLATION. In cases where one party violates the requirements of just conduct in war, the *no reprisals* principle forbids the other party to respond with violations of its own.

Like the principles of *ius ad bellum*, these principles are an attempt to specify proper behavior for people who are in intolerable circumstances. Even in the context of combat, some actions and weapons are unjustifiable. To test these principles, ask yourself: (1) can you conceive of circumstances in which a person or a state might be morally justified to violate the requirements specified? Then (2) is it possible that one might satisfy all of the requirements listed but still be morally guilty of misconduct in the context of war?

If you can think of circumstances that satisfy the first of these questions, 7.39 you will have reason to question whether each of these requirements is truly *necessary*. In that case, perhaps a better theory would eliminate or revise some of the principles stated. And, if you can think of circumstances that satisfy the second question, you will have reason to think that the principles stated are *incomplete*. In that case you might consider what other principles we might add to make the list more satisfactory.

For example, suppose a villain is firing bombs on a town from a civilian 7.40 area. The only way to get the bomber is to counterstrike, but to do so would kill civilians. Is it permissible for those who are targeted to launch a counterstrike? The answer is complicated: according to the principle of proportionality, they should consider the military significance of the counterstrike. How effective is the villain? If his bombs are ineffective in any case, then the military significance of the counterstrike will be minimal. And what would be the effect of the counterstrike? If it can be expected to yield extensive civilian casualties, or if it is unlikely to stop the villain, then the negative consequences of the counterstrike are *disproportionate*. In that case, a counterstrike is prohibited under the rules of *ius in bello*.

Cultural Conflicts and the Laws of War

7.41 One of the difficulties with the principles of *ius ad bellum* and *ius in bello* is that they are themselves bound to cultural traditions that have not always been universal. In World War II, Japan and China did not share traditions that included the classical European rules of conduct in war. Japan did not regard itself as having an obligation to treat captured prisoners with respect. While the Europeans were shocked by the treatment of prisoners in imperial Japan, perhaps it was unreasonable to have expected Japanese commanders to understand and accept the principles that had been passed down in the Western European tradition.

7.42 In other contexts it was the Europeans who shocked their opponents by violating longstanding customs that governed warfare. When native Americans fought against European settlers in the early years of the European colonization of North America, some native American groups were shocked that Europeans would resort to the use of fire as a weapon of war. Within their communities fire was regarded as an immoral and indiscriminate weapon. Its use by the settlers was taken as evidence that Europeans were ruthless and unprincipled. This in turn led some Native American groups to adopt different and less constrained methods of warfare in subsequent conflicts.

7.43 With globalization and the growing presence of effective institutions of international law, some of these cultural differences have diminished over the course of the past century. After World War II, Japanese soldiers were held responsible for their actions during war, just as the German soldiers and leaders were held responsible at the Nuremberg Tribunal. The post-World War II tribunals provided individuals accused of war crimes with an opportunity to defend themselves in court. But where there was evidence of individual "wrongdoing" that violated accepted (European) principles of conduct, these courts held people responsible for their actions. Those found guilty were imprisoned or executed. As a result of these World War II tribunals, there is now global international acceptance of treaty-based principles of conduct in war and an international court that holds people to account when these principles are violated (though not all nations are parties to the International Criminal Court).

Pushing the Limits, I: Preemptive War

There have been more recent tests of the requirements of just war and of 7.44
justice in the conduct of war. In the context of the so called "war on terror,"
US leaders, including President George W. Bush, were led to conclude that
the standards that had governed war in the past were obsolete and that new
principles were needed for modern times. The US invasion of Iraq in 2003
was one case in point: while the principle of *last resort* is usually understood
expressly to prohibit *preemptive warfare*, the invasion of Iraq was not a
response of resistance to aggression but an attempt to remove Iraq as a
threat to the United States and US interests.

At the time of the invasion, many critics urged that the United States and 7.45
its allies had an obligation to continue to pursue diplomatic attempts to
disarm Iraq. The decision to go to war was led by the United States and
followed, after intense parliamentary debate, by Britain.

In the case of the Iraq War, it is widely agreed that the decision to wage 7.46
preemptive war was unjustified. The reasons given by the Bush administration to justify the action were (1) that war was necessary in order to prevent
Iraq from further developing and using weapons of mass destruction, and
(2) that Iraq had been involved in the terrorist attack on the World Trade
Center Towers in New York City. In the aftermath of the invasion, there has
been wide agreement that both of these reasons were spurious. The US
invasion of Iraq does not seem to be a difficult test case for the rule that
prohibits preemptive strikes. Defenders of the Bush administration might
argue that our information is clearer now than it was to the agents at the
time and that many of them did believe that Iraq had weapons of mass
destruction. Just war theory judges people on whether they acted rightly
with respect to the information reasonably available at the time.

But the broader question remains: are there circumstances in which a 7.47
preemptive attack might be justifiable as the only way to prevent aggression? Consider an enemy who commands a superior military force, which
could be defeated only if action were taken before these forces were strategically placed. Might the rule against preemptive war prohibit a nation
from taking action at the only moment when such action might be successful? If the principles of just war require a nation to wait until it is too
late, do these principles consign some innocent victims to the fate of being
conquered?

Or perhaps this hypothetical example will confuse rather than clarify 7.48
our understanding of the requirements of just war. Aggressor nations have

often claimed that the decision to "strike first" was justified by necessity. Perhaps such claims should always be dismissed as disingenuous and pretextual.

Pushing the Limits, II: When Are Captured Combatants "Prisoners of War?"

7.49 The principles of *ius in bello* have also been put to the test in the twenty-first century. Terrorists do not obey the rules of war: terrorist actions frequently target noncombatants and are not sanctioned by a state authority. On the other hand, members of Al-Qaida have certainly taken themselves to be at war and have been regarded as "enemy combatants" by the United States and its allies.

7.50 Some people have urged that actions against terrorists should not be called war, but should instead be pursued as a police action that aims to bring to justice those who perpetrate terrorist acts. But in some respects Al-Qaida seemed very much like an army: it had training camps, practiced military exercises, and took strategic action against American military targets.

7.51 Since those who fight for Al-Qaida are not fighting on behalf of a state and are not authorized to fight by a recognized state authority, can captured fighters properly be regarded as prisoners of war? The Geneva Conventions require soldiers to wear recognizable uniforms. This makes it much easier for soldiers on both sides to discriminate between combatants and noncombatants, but it also puts the soldiers at greater risk (for that very reason). The Geneva Conventions deny some of the protections that would otherwise be granted to combatants who are not in uniform. Since terrorists frequently dress as civilians in order to keep their identities secret, some have argued that this justifies treating them differently from enemy soldiers who bear arms openly. If they are not prisoners of war, does this mean that the requirements that mandate humanitarian treatment—the normal requirements that apply to captured prisoners—do not apply? The principles of *ius in bello* require that prisoners must be released after the end of hostilities. But what does this mean in the context of a conflict against a variety of disparate groups, a conflict that has no obvious end-point when hostilities come to a close? Can prisoners be held *indefinitely* in such a situation, or should new rules be adopted to accommodate this unfamiliar situation?

Pushing the Limits, III: Torture, "Enhanced Interrogation," and Ticking Bombs

In the early twenty-first century, the United States decided not to treat 7.52
people captured on the battlefield in Afghanistan and elsewhere as prisoners of war. John Yoo, legal council to President Bush, argued that the international requirements of the Geneva Convention were quaint and obsolete
and that they did not apply in the context of a "war" of this kind. On legal
advice from Yoo and others, American intelligence officers were told that
they could employ "enhanced interrogation techniques" on captured prisoners, as a means to get information from them. Accordingly, a number of
prisoners were subject to *waterboarding*, a technique that had been called
"the water torture" in World War II. In waterboarding the prisoner has a
cloth placed over his mouth. Then water is poured over the cloth, making
it impossible for the victim to breathe. People who have been subject to
this treatment report that it is excruciatingly painful. This technique can
cause permanent damage due to oxygen deprivation, as well as damage to
the lungs.

Between 2005 and 2007, the United States used waterboarding, among 7.53
other *enhanced interrogation techniques*, to question several different high-
value prisoners. The decision to use these techniques is still among the
most controversial actions to have been undertaken by any US
administration.

Are there any circumstances that could justify the use of torture? Consider 7.54
the following widely discussed hypothetical example:

> The ticking bomb: A time bomb has been set to go off somewhere in
> a crowded public place. You have in your custody the person who
> planted this bomb, but he won't talk. The only way to get from him
> the information that will save lives is to torture him.

One line of reasoning about this case runs as follows: "While torture is a
terrible thing, extreme circumstances call for extreme measures. If the only
way to prevent the deaths of hundreds of innocent people is to torture one
person—a person who is, in any case, guilty of having planted the bomb
that would kill these innocents—then it is permissible to extract information by torture."

This case is designed to test our intuitions about torture as a form of 7.55
treatment that is always and invariably impermissible, but it was also used

as a way to justify the actions of CIA interrogators who used torture techniques in the effort to get information from captured prisoners. Does the argument work?

7.56   A number of different responses might be made to this argument. The most direct response is simply to assert that torture is always invariably and categorically wrong, that it is one of those actions that can never be justified, even if it were necessary for the prevention of some horrific consequences.

7.57   Of course, one who offers such a response must be willing to explain *why* torture has this categorical status. One may need to say more than simply to observe that the actions violate the prisoners' rights, or that torture treats a person as a mere means—as if he were a thing instead of a person. These arguments may be correct and rationally persuasive, but they have not always persuaded skeptics.

7.58   Some interrogators objected to the practice of torturing captured prisoners on the grounds that, as they urged, intelligence gained through torture is unreliable. Under duress, most prisoners will say whatever they believe will persuade their tormentors to stop the pain. In such circumstances none of us can be trusted to tell the truth.

7.59   Still others objected that the widely known fact that the US engaged in torture in the course of interrogations put American soldiers at risk. Even though the rules of *ius in bello* forbid reprisals, the fact that Americans employed torture during interrogations made it more likely that captured American soldiers would endure torture at the hands of their captives.

7.60   In a widely read paper, the philosopher David Luban argued that we cannot simply think of torture as an individual act. If torture is permitted, then it becomes a *practice* that is undertaken whenever the circumstances that justify its use are met. In order to sustain such a practice, argues Luban, we might need "a professional cadre of trained torturers" (Luban, 2005, p. 1445) and many other bureaucratic incidentals. According to Luban, we should not accept the normalization of torture as a practice of our institutions. But this means that we cannot sanction individual torturous interrogations, even in the case of the ticking bomb.

7.61   Another, closely related argument against torture is based on our ideals as a society: to sanction torture would be to turn our back on longstanding ideals that reflect our deepest values. Our institutions should reflect these values, the argument goes, and we should preserve them not merely because their implementation has the best consequences, but also because these practices make us the kind of people we are and express our hopes for what we can be.

In a similar manner, these practices and constraints make our nation the kind of nation it is. On this view, the decision to permit officially sanctioned torture is not a one-time decision, made to promote the best consequences. It is a decision about the kind of people and the kind of nation we want to be.

Finally, it is sometimes argued that torture not only violates principles of justice and humanity that should govern out *institutions*, it also harms those who carry it out. People who are involved in the infliction of torture report that it is horrifically painful for those who *do* the torture, as it is for those who suffer it. When people engage in brutal behavior, they can quickly become deadened, more callous, and indifferent to others' suffering. While this may start as a "coping" tactic, eventually habits of indifference to other people's suffering might become permanent features of one's personality. Might torture be wrong, in part, because it harms the torturer? 7.62

Are these arguments successful? Do they effectively address the predicament of the person who hopes to prevent catastrophe in the case of the ticking bomb? 7.63

Punishment

Many people react very differently to the following two scenarios: 7.64

> SCENARIO 1: The government tortures a known terrorist who has planted a bomb in a large city in order to get him to disclose its location before many die.

> SCENARIO 2: Thinking that there is not enough time for scenario 1 to be successful, the government tortures the 5-year-old son of the terrorist, who is in front of him, until the terrorist discloses the location of the bomb.

Even people who think that torture is right in both cases tend to feel greater uneasiness about it in the second case. Why? If we are only concerned about future consequences—in this case, stopping the bomb from killing many people—the difference shouldn't matter. For many people it matters because we think violence is justified if it is deserved—if it is a fitting punishment for a crime. In scenario 1 we know that the one who suffers is a terrorist, hence he seems to deserve the punishment. In scenario 2 someone other than the criminal suffers.

7.65   This tension is at the heart of another perennial debate in political philosophy: the proper justification and use of punishment. While the case above is extreme, the basic dilemma occurs in more mundane questions related to punishment. For example, are there people whose crimes are so wicked that they justify a death sentence even if that would bring no benefit in reducing future crime? Suppose someone is serving a long prison sentence for armed robbery, but it seems clear that the prisoner's character has changed so that he is no longer a threat to others (the person has been rehabilitated). Should the prisoner be released for that reason?

7.66   Must punishments be equal? In the case of **Skinner v. Oklahoma**, (316 US 535 [1942]), Skinner had been sentenced to mandatory sterilization when he committed his third serious crime (twice for armed robbery and once for stealing chickens). While stealing chickens was on the list of serious crimes, embezzling money was not, even though a bank employee might take far more money than a chicken thief. Is this fair? Is there a requirement that equally serious crimes get equally serious punishments? There was some support from the Supreme Court for the idea that the inequality of punishment was grounds for overturning Skinner's punishment.

Rationales for punishment

7.67   There are several competing rationales for punishment. Some theories claim that a single rationale is sufficient, while others claim that several are needed.

7.68   *Positive future consequences*:   Punishments can help deter other people from committing the crime, protect society from dangerous criminals, reduce the chances that the criminal will recidivate after release, and minimize the cost of administering the criminal justice system. *Consequentialist theories* are greatly influenced by utilitarianism, which requires that we maximize human happiness. Jeremy Bentham argued that we should see crime and punishment in just this way.

7.69   If we take this argument as our rationale, it does provide clear answers to important questions.

QUESTION: When should we criminalize something?

ANSWER: When criminalization will improve lives more by reducing crime than enforcing the law will make life worse.

For example, do drug laws reduce harmful behavior enough to justify the cost of all the law enforcement and prisons they require? If legalization would reduce the power of drug cartels and drug-related violence and would increase government revenue, those consequences would also go on the plus side. If legalization led to a society full of heroin addicts, that would go on the negative side. There would still be difficult empirical questions, but at least we would have a philosophical framework for knowing what questions to ask.

QUESTION: Should governments employ capital punishment?

ANSWER: Yes, if it the extra deterrence it provides is enough to offset the higher court costs, the pain to criminals and their families, and any other negative consequences it might bring.

Consequentialists are divided on this question. Some think that it is the certainty of punishment, not its intensity, that is key to deterring crime. If you were certain you would spend your life in prison, would you commit the crime? The problem is that people think they will not get caught (or they are just not thinking clearly to start with). Capital punishment thus adds little deterrence. Others argue that both certainty and intensity are important for deterrence and that capital punishment is (or can be made) efficient.

7.70 The consequentialist approach provides a way of answering questions like these, but other approaches worry that its simplicity is just the result of oversimplification. There are morally relevant considerations that are being ignored.

Desert: *Retributive theories* claim that it is a mistake to think that punish- 7.71 ment is justified by future benefits. Punishment requires that people undergo "hard treatment" *because* they did wrong. We might quarantine someone with a contagious illness who has done nothing wrong because we think that future consequences would demand it, but we would not call that *punishment*.

7.72 Retributivist theorists see several problems with the consequentialist approach. Bentham himself admitted that, on the basis of his theory, if there were a way only to *pretend* to punish criminals, this would be better than actually punishing them, so long as the secret never got out. As long as people *think* that prisoners are getting punished you get your deterrence (on the positive side of the ledger), and if there is no actual suffering of the prisoners then there is no pain on the negative side of the ledger. For Bentham, inflicting pain on anyone, even a criminal, is never a good thing in itself and is only justified if it is needed for the purpose of preventing even greater harms. Thus, pretending to punish would be ideal if secrecy could be kept.

7.73   Retributivists disagree. They think there is something fundamentally right about wrongdoers being punished, that this is actually a fundamental part of justice. Punishment is another instance of the general principle that justice is giving people what they deserve. That is also why retributivists think it wrong to ever punish an innocent person. What if we use the consequentialist rationale and discover that framing innocent people sometimes has very positive consequences? Lastly, retributivists note that consequentialism reduces criminals to mere tools for promoting the good of society.

7.74   One way to combine retributive and consequentialist approaches was suggested by the legal philosopher H. L. A. Hart: perhaps the overall practice of punishing is justified by consequences—that is why we have the law and how we decide the content of the law and how severe punishments will be. The application of punishment to individual criminals, however, must be done on the basis of desert. We can only punish those who are actually guilty of a crime.

7.75   *Sending a message*:   A third group consists of theories that focus on punishment as a way of sending a message; these are *communicative theories*. There are several versions. In one, the point of punishment is for society to communicate to the criminal "you have done wrong." In another version, the point is to communicate to the victim (or the victim's family) that the victim is still considered valuable and important. The communication could also aim at bringing the criminal to take responsibility for the harm caused, or at reconciling the criminal with the victim (and the larger community).

7.76   Communicative approaches to punishment are attractive because they can capture many of the insights of retributivism while avoiding some of the objections. It is essential in communicative theories that the punishment is directed at a wrongdoer, not just at someone whom it is advantageous to punish. These theories also address the wrongdoer as a moral agent rather than simply treating the criminal as means to an end. Thus, in these respects communicative approaches are similar to retributivism.

7.77   But there are also differences. One of the criticisms of retributive theories is that it is hard to know how to fit the punishment to the crime. What punishment should correspond to stealing chickens? For communicative theorists, this is less important. For the message of punishment to make sense, more serious crimes should get more serious punishments, but the absolute level isn't fixed in any particular place. The punishment need not be "an eye for an eye." Many retributive theories insist that murder be punished with death, but a communicative theory would not need to hold this—only that more serious crimes get more severe condemnation.

The big problem for communicative theories is this: if punishment is 7.78
about sending messages, why do we need to send the message by fining or imprisoning people? In other words, why is the "hard treatment" that prisoners normally experience necessary for the communication? Could not a resolution passed by a respected governmental body on behalf of the people communicate to the criminal "you have done wrong" and make the point? That would be much less expensive than years in prison.

Again, one option is to create a hybrid theory. Perhaps the goal is both to 7.79
protect society (thus imposing hard treatment for the sake of deterrence) and to communicate a message (thus punishing only those who have done wrong). One might even try to combine all three theories. While this may sound like the easy solution, it has its own problems. The three theories do not always agree in their recommendations as to who and how to punish. A hybrid theory must explain how these differing perspectives will be reconciled.

War, Torture, and Punishment in Political Context

While earlier chapters addressed political *ideals*, the topics covered in this 7.80
chapter are all associated with problems that arise when we fail to meet our ideals. War and rebellion arise when political institutions are threatened or break down, when they cease to protect rights and welfare, and when public actions violate rights or perpetrate harms. The debates about torture exemplify one context where right-violating actions are perceived to be justified as part of an effort to protect the state. In a similar vein, the question of punishment arises when people break the law, not when they submit to it.

Philosophers and political theorists sometimes distinguish between 7.81
ideal theory and *nonideal theory*. Ideal political theories develop political ideals under the assumption that people will all comply with the rules that maintain institutions over time, such that each participant does her or his part to keep public institutions running smoothly. Nonideal theories assume that people will only *partially* comply with social requirements and

will sometimes break the rules—namely when it is personally advantageous to do so. The real world is nonideal. Does this mean that ideal political theory is just wrong, or that it is useless?

7.82 Perhaps not. When we evaluate our institutions we should not be blind to their faults, or to the human weaknesses of the people who participate in them. But, in order to see where our institutions go wrong or in what ways they might be improved, we need ideals that provide a standard of comparison. In the real world we should not assume that everyone will comply with social rules. But we may be able to think sensibly about the rate of compliance that is necessary to keep institutions functioning. Different institutions may inspire different levels of compliance: perhaps people are more likely to break the law in some circumstances rather than in others. We might seek to prevent lawbreaking by adopting increasingly harsh penalties and punishments, so as to give people a disincentive for misbehavior. In practice this has not worked very well, but it is easy to see why people have found such a strategy appealing. On the other hand, we might seek to increase the level of compliance by improving our institutions, so that people have more confidence that their interests and rights are respected. If lawbreaking is more likely when institutions are (or are perceived to be) unjust, perhaps compliance is more likely when people can see that their institutions are effective at protecting rights and welfare.

References and Further Reading

African National Congress. 2011 [1961]. "Manifesto of Umkhonto we Sizwe Leaflet Issued by the Command of Umkhonto we Sizwe." December 16. ANC. http://www.anc.org.za/show.php?id=77&t=Umkhonto%20we%20Sizwe (accessed February 12, 2016). In this Manifesto, founding members of Umkhonto we Sizwe articulate their reasons for resistance, and call for unity in the struggle against the racist South African government.

Card, Claudia. 2010. *Confronting Evils: Terrorism, Torture, Genocide.* Cambridge: Cambridge University Press. This book presents a clear discussion of terrorism, torture, and genocide, including historical and contemporary legal analysis.

Feinberg, Joel. 1965. "The Expressive Function of Punishment." *Monist*, 49: 397–423. In this controversial paper Feinberg argues that one of the central functions of punishment is to express people's moral disapproval of the action for which other people are punished.

Fotion, Nicholas. 2007. *War and Ethics: A New Just War Theory.* New York: Continuum. This book is an accessible presentation and expansion of just war theory.

Gandhi, Mahatma. 2016 [1920]. "The Doctrine of the Sword." *Young India* (Ahmedabad), August 11, 1920. Gandhi website. http://www.mkgandhi.org/nonviolence/D_sword.htm (accessed February 12, 2016). This paper presents a brief defense of Gandhi's complex view of nonviolence.

Hart, Herbert Lionel Adolphus. 1959. "Prolegomenon to the Principles of Punishment." *Proceedings of the Aristotelian Society*, 60: 1–26. Hart argues that retributivism determines who should be punished and consequentialism determines how much.

Krug, Etienne G., Linda L. Dahlberg, James A. Mercy, Anthony B. Zwi, and Rafael Lozano, eds. 2002. *World Report on Violence and Health*. World Health Organization:Geneva.http://whqlibdoc.who.int/publications/2002/9241545615_eng.pdf (accessed February 12, 2016). This widely cited report provides a definition of violence and reports on the indirect effects of violence on people's health.

Luban, David. 2005. "Torture and the Ticking Bomb." *Virginia Law Review*, 91: 1425–1461. Luban offers a famous argument against the view that torture should be permitted in extreme extenuating circumstances, by arguing that "ticking bomb" cases should not be used to define public policy regarding torture.

Mandela, Nelson. 2011 [1964]. "Nelson Mandela's Statement from the Dock at the Opening of the Defence Case in the Rivonia Trial." http://www.anc.org.za/show.php?id=3430 (accessed February 12, 2016). This may be Nelson Mandela's most famous speech, offered during the trial for which he was imprisoned.

McMahan, Jeff. 2009. *Killing in War*. New York: Oxford University Press. McMahan's book questions traditional views on when it is permissible for soldiers to kill enemy combatants in time of war.

Morris, Herbert. 1968. "Persons and Punishment." *Monist*, 52: 576–601. Morris offers an articulate defense of a *retributive* theory of punishment, referring importantly to the principle of fair play.

Rodin, David and Henry Shue. 2008. *Just and Unjust Warriors: The Moral and Legal Status of Soldiers*. New York: Oxford University Press. This book collects contemporary papers on the morality of combat and on the moral and legal status of soldiers.

Russell, Bertrand. 1943. "The Future of Pacifism." *The American Scholar*, 13: 7–13. This brief essay contains Russell's defense of pacifism. Russell is not a categorical pacifist, since he believes that it is sometimes justified to fight in a war.

Walzer, Michael. 1977. *Just and Unjust Wars: A Moral Argument with Historical Illustrations*. New York: Basic Books.Walzer's book renews discussion of just war theory and provides a careful moral evaluation of war and the use of military violence.

Online Resources

1 http://www.anc.org.za/show.php?id=77&t=Umkhonto%20we%20Sizwe
2 http://www.anc.org.za/show.php?id=3430
3 http://www.mkgandhi.org/nonviolence/D_sword.htm
4 http://plato.stanford.edu/entries/war/
5 http://www.nybooks.com/account/signin/?msg=Password+changed+for+jwc
   wolf.+You+may+now+sign+in
6 https://www.law.cornell.edu/supremecourt/text/316/535

Part III
SPECIFIC TOPICS

8

WHO COUNTS?

SOPHIE	Justin, I can't believe you eat that stuff.
JUSTIN	What?
SOPHIE	*Dead animals.* You're eating *dead animals.*
JUSTIN	Soph it's *salami*! And it's really good salami too. Surely you don't think I'm a bad person just because I eat a salami sandwich?
SOPHIE	Justin, we're friends. I don't think you're a bad person. But yes: I *do* think eating meat is wrong. I think you do it because you're thoughtless about the pain and suffering that is involved in the production of the food you eat. To tell the truth, I think you're *willfully* thoughtless: you don't think about it, because you like eating meat and deep inside you know that if you thought carefully about the implications you'd have to stop doing it. So you don't think about it.
JUSTIN	So you *do* think I'm a bad person, in spite of what you say!
SOPHIE	This isn't about you, it's about your sandwich. If I thought you were a bad person, I wouldn't try to *reason* with you. Justin, animals—and especially pigs!—are raised in inhumane conditions. The dead animals in your salami were intelligent social creatures, but they probably lived their entire miserable lives in a filthy, sunless confinement facility where they were packed tightly into pens much too small for them. Then they were put on trucks that schlepped

This Is Political Philosophy: An Introduction, First Edition. Alex Tuckness and Clark Wolf.
© 2017 John Wiley & Sons, Inc. Published 2017 by John Wiley & Sons, Inc.

them, terrified and traumatized, straight to a slaughter-house where they could smell the blood and hear the screams of the other pigs as their throats were slit. Is all that suffering really worth it, just so that you can eat salami?

JUSTIN   So are you arguing that eating meat is always wrong, or just that it is wrong if animals have bad lives before they are killed?

SOPHIE   I think eating meat is always wrong because one should not kill mammals, but I think the fact that so many animals suffer so much makes the case much stronger.

JUSTIN   I think you are overstating the suffering of animals. People need different things to be comfortable—different from the things pigs need. What's comfortable for a pig would not be comfortable for a person. But, even more importantly, people are smarter: we anticipate the future. People would know what's coming and would be made miserable by fear. Pigs don't have any idea what's coming, so they can't be miserable in the same way.

SOPHIE   Pigs are smarter than you think they are, Justin. But even if they weren't, suppose you knew that your child would be mentally disabled so that her intelligence and conscious-ness would be similar to what you ascribe to pigs—she couldn't predict what's coming and wouldn't have anticipa-tory fear. Could we kill her?

JUSTIN   Why on earth do you think comparing children to pigs is relevant?

SOPHIE   People who study pig behavior say that they are **about as intelligent as a three-year-old child**. It would *certainly* be wrong to do these things to a three-year-old. So it must be wrong, and for the same reasons, to do these things to an animal that is as intelligent and aware as a three-year-old.

JUSTIN   Your hyperindividualism goes even farther than I thought! You think the moral status of a person is merely a function of the capacities of that particular person. But our identities are more complicated than that. It matters that a three-year-old human is a member of a group, human beings, who typically have capacities that far exceed those of the pig.

SOPHIE   I never said that an individual's capacities are the *only* thing that matters, but it seems pretty clear that they matter a lot. Besides, judging people by their group rather than as

individuals is exactly what racists do. Giving rights to
humans but not animals when they have the same capabilities is species bias. We could call it "speciesism."

JUSTIN   Sophie, I know you think you are standing up for animals,
but you are actually undermining the very concept of
human rights. You are opening the door to treating the
most vulnerable human beings—infants, the handicapped,
and so on—as if they had no more rights than animals!

SOPHIE   I am not saying that there is no moral difference between
animals and humans, but I am saying that some animals do
have rights. Should we just say nothing while millions of
animals suffer?

JUSTIN   I agree with you that animal cruelty is wrong, though I am
not sure animals are suffering in all the cases you think
they are. I would even support laws against animal cruelty.
But I think human beings have rights that animals do not,
just by virtue of being human.

SOPHIE   Obviously I believe in human rights. But I think we have
the rights we have because we have the capacities to exercise them, not just because we're members of our species.
Any other creature with interests and capabilities like ours
would have the same rights we have, even if it were a member of a different species. But I'm not arguing that animals
have human rights. I'm arguing that they have rights that
match their capacities. They have a right not to be treated
with cruelty. If we agree about that, maybe the next step is
to look at the circumstances of life for the animals you're
eating. I think you'll be shocked.

JUSTIN   So I think we agree that the issue is cruelty but it seems like
we disagree about what counts as cruelty.

Who Gets Justice?

Debates over animal rights are just one part of the larger debate about who   8.1
is entitled to justice. Should the life of a fetus be protected by the law? Does
it matter whether it is two months old or eight months old? Do children have
rights? If they do, are they the same rights as those of adults? What about the

handicapped and those with disabilities? What about future generations who must live with the consequences of the environmental decisions we make today? In all of these debates there is a difference of opinion about moral standing.

The Guano Ring

8.2 Blue-footed boobies are seabirds that live on the Galapagos Islands, far off the coast of Ecuador, and along the coast of South America. At nesting time, blue-footed booby pairs gather stones and place them in a circle to make a nest, which eventually becomes surrounded by a larger ring of guano (bird poop). The biologist Stephen Jay Gould reports that there is an invisible boundary about halfway into this guano ring: when he moved the toe of his shoe just beyond the invisible boundary, the parent birds pecked at it to chase him away. But if he remained on the far side of the boundary they ignored him entirely. The same rule applies to chicks: if you take a blue-footed booby chick and put it inside the ring that marks the boundary of the nest, the parent birds will feed, shelter, and protect it. If the same chick is placed just outside the ring, the parent birds will peck at it and chase it away as an alien intruder. When food is scarce, bigger chicks will sometimes push their smaller siblings out of the center of the nest, just beyond the invisible boundary. Gould writes:

> As human mammals, our first reaction might be: so what? The younger sibs are not physically hurt and they end up but a few inches from the ring, where parents will surely notice their plaintive sounds and struggling motions and gather them quickly back. But a parental booby does no such thing… Parental boobies work by the rule: if a chick is inside the ring, care for it; if it is outside, ignore it. Even if the chick should flop, by happenstance, upon the ring, it will be rejected with all the vehemence applied to my transgressing toe. (Gould, 1994, p. 50)

What sits inside the guano ring is protected, what sits beyond the limit is *other*, to be ignored or chased away as a threat. But the bird's behavior is *stereotypical* thoughtless behavior. It would be a mistake to blame the parent bird for pecking and chasing off its own chick. It's simply what blue-footed boobies do. They have no moral responsibility for this behavior, and it would be inappropriate *anthropomorphism* to blame them for it.

Human beings, too, make choices about who and what lies within their 8.3
own metaphorical guano ring, but, unlike blue-footed boobies, we are *responsible* for our discriminatory choices. The ring we use is not made of guano: it is made of concepts and reasons and ideas. We apply these concepts when we make judgments about whether it is wrong to kick soccer balls or kittens, whether we can make salami out of pigs or three-year-olds, whether it is permissible to use mice or chimpanzees or children in scientific experiments.

If we *favor* people who are members of our own group, we are *biased* 8.4
toward them and, if we *disfavor* them, we are *prejudiced against* them. Bias and prejudice are not always reprehensible or irrational, but they are discriminatory behavior and thus stand in need of justification. Where discrimination is unjustified and disadvantages those who are discriminated against, it *is* morally wrong. For example, if sex and race are not a relevant reason for discrimination, then sexual and racial prejudice are morally wrong. Where membership in a nation or tribe are not good reasons for bias or prejudice, nationalism and tribalism are wrong.

Animals

What about animals? As a matter of course, we treat animals very differently 8.5
from the way we treat people: we capture and hunt them, we keep them as *pets*, we eat them, we wear bits of them, we use them in scientific experimentation, and we regularly overrun their homes when we make houses or clear fields. To treat people in these ways would clearly be wrong. But if the differences between humans and animals are significant from the moral point of view, then these differences in treatment might be justified. **Is it inhumane to keep whales in captivity? Should laws require pet stores to obtain animals from shelters rather than from commercial breeders?**

Do animals matter? Do they "count" as individuals whose interests we 8.6
need to take into account? It's hard to *prove* that animals matter from the moral point of view, but, as Robert Nozick points out, it's just as difficult to prove that *people* matter (Nozick, 1974, p. 35). To test your own intuitions, consider the following (regrettably gross) thought experiment designed to test your intuitions on this question:

Suppose your philosophy professor brings to class a pumpkin, a kitten, and a baseball bat. Announcing that she intends to put moral questions on an empirical footing by conducting an experiment in class, she first whacks the pumpkin with the baseball bat, causing it to explode in little splattered bits. "This was messy," she admits, "but was it wrong? Is it wrong to whack a pumpkin?" She searches among the gooey pumpkin pieces for evidence of "wrongness." Failing to find any, she concludes that it was not wrong to whack the pumpkin. Then, still brandishing the bat, she approaches the kitten. She raises the bat back for a strong swing, and then …

Splat. Smashing a pumpkin (if it's your own) might be fun. And if a pumpkin is a mere *thing* with no moral standing, then surely whacking the pumpkin isn't objectionable from the moral point of view. We still might wonder why this empiricist experimental ethicist believed that she might find "wrongness" among the gooey shards. But if your professor whacked a kitten in class *you would think differently of her.*

8.7   If you agree, then you hold that a kitten *counts*. We should take the interests of kittens (and other relevantly similar animals) into account when we decide what to do. This does not imply that a kitten has the same moral status as a human being; but it's not a mere *thing* like the pumpkin either. Not everyone feels this way, of course. But people who lack empathy and compassion for animals, as it turns out, are often people who lack empathy and compassion for other people as well. The fact that every US state has laws prohibiting animal cruelty is good evidence of wide agreement that such actions are wrong and unacceptable. If these laws are justified, then animal cruelty must be wrong in a sense that makes it *legally prohibitable.*

8.8   What is it about the difference between a kitten and a pumpkin that makes it OK to pulverize one but not the other? We might begin by listing characteristics that are possessed by kittens but not by pumpkins, to consider which ones seem significant. Kittens are cuter than pumpkins. But is cuteness relevant? Would it be permissible to whack an animal that wasn't cute? (Perhaps a deformed kitten or a mole rat?) What we find cute may be arbitrary and culturally relative: different people may find different things cute. Kittens are more closely related to us than pumpkins. But kittens are also are more closely related to us than dolphins are. Is cruelty to dolphins less wrong than cruelty to kittens? Some of the differences between kittens and pumpkins are morally irrelevant.

8.9   Other differences seem more relevant. Kittens have conscious mental states, while pumpkins do not. They are intelligent, sensitive to suffering and pleasure, and have the ability to make decisions on their own. Pumpkins do not suffer when they are mistreated, and they never make decisions or choices. Perhaps we can come to a better understanding of our own views about who counts from the moral point of view by thinking more carefully about the characteristics that we would pick out to explain and justify our different treatment of pumpkins and kittens.

Moral Standing and Moral Personhood

To regard an individual as having *moral standing* is to see it as something— 8.10 or rather as someone—we need to take into account from the moral point of view. To think that we shouldn't whack a kitten *because of what that does to the kitten* is to think of kittens as creatures with moral standing. On the other hand, to think that the only reason why we shouldn't whack kittens is that *other people will be disturbed if we do* is to think that kittens do *not* have moral standing. If the pumpkin belongs to an eager child who hopes to make it into a jack-o-lantern, then smashing it might be wrong—wrong to the child. But if pumpkins don't have moral standing, then smashing is not wrong to the pumpkin.

Perhaps "standing" is a matter of degree: if different individuals have dif- 8.11 ferent moral status, then perhaps they matter *differently*. If so, then to say that a kitten or a pig has moral *standing* does not imply that it has the same moral standing as an adult human being. To say that we should take their interests into account doesn't imply that they have the same rights as a human person. We can use the idea of *moral personhood* to refer to the level of moral standing normally thought to be possessed by a human being. A *person*, in this case, is any individual who has that level of moral standing. We can formulate three important questions associated with these concepts of moral standing and moral personhood:

1. What characteristics of individuals are sufficient to confer moral standing, such that those who possess them need to be taken into account?
2. What characteristics of individuals are sufficient to confer *full* moral standing, such that those who possess them should be regarded as full moral *persons?*
3. If different individuals have different moral standing, what characteristics are relevant in case we wish to identify and characterize these differences?

Notice that this way of speaking leaves it open for some nonhumans to be "persons." For example, it makes sense to ask whether dolphins or nonhuman great apes (orangutans, chimpanzees, bonobos, and gorillas) are *persons* in this sense. There is a movement—the **Great Apes Project** (GAP)—that seeks to guarantee basic rights for these creatures, including the right to life and liberty, the right not to be used in scientific experiments, and a right against torture. Some advocates of this project point to similarities between human beings and the other great apes, arguing that these similarities justify affording them a higher moral status than we normally do, including basic rights. Some people claim, more contentiously, that these animals should be regarded as morally equal to human persons. These people believe that great apes are *persons* in the full moral sense of the word. Perhaps these people are wrong. What evidence would we use to evaluate such a claim?

8.12   We are very similar to the other great apes—indeed humans are often classified as the fifth species of great ape, or as the third species of chimpanzee. Other animals might also turn out to be persons: for example, **research on dolphin psychology** might reveal that the psychological and emotional lives of dolphins are similar to our own, which might lead us to conclude that we ought to treat them differently from the way we typically do. On the other hand, **research might reveal** that dolphins have much *less* rich psychological lives than we thought, which might lead us to conclude that they are not persons. While the question whether these animals are *persons* in the relevant sense is a moral question, empirical research may be relevant, since it may give us insight into the capacities of these nonhuman creatures.

8.13   One strategy would be to identify the characteristics of human beings that constitute our reason for treating human beings as moral persons. Then we could consider whether any nonhuman animals possess these same characteristics. If there are some who do, then it might be reasonable for us to conclude that they are nonhuman persons.

8.14   So what are the characteristics that are relevant for determining personhood, and how can we know who has them? In a famous article, Mary Anne Warren suggests the following:

1. CONSCIOUSNESS (of objects and events external and/or internal to the being), and in particular the capacity to feel pain;
2. REASONING (the *developed* capacity to solve new and relatively complex problems);
3. SELF-MOTIVATED ACTIVITY (activity which is relatively independent of either genetic or direct external control);

4. THE CAPACITY TO COMMUNICATE, by whatever means, messages of an indefinite variety of types, that is, not just with an indefinite number of possible contents, but on indefinitely many possible topics;
5. THE PRESENCE OF SELF-CONCEPTS, AND SELF-AWARENESS, either individual or racial, or both. (Warren, 1973, p. 55)

Warren does not argue that these characteristics are individually necessary or jointly sufficient for personhood. Her claim is more modest, though (as we will see) still controversial: she argues that we may reasonably conclude that any individual who has *none* of these characteristics is *not* a person in the moral sense. This may correspond well with some people's intuitions: in some states, a physician who encounters a patient who has irreversibly lost all of these characteristics could pronounce her patient "dead."

In a similar vein, Joel Feinberg offers the following as a starting point to identify who the *persons* around us are: 8.15

> What makes me certain that my parents, siblings, and friends are people is that they give evidence of being conscious of the world and of themselves; they have inner emotional lives, just like me; they can understand things and reason about them, make plans, and act; they can communicate with me, argue, negotiate, express themselves, make agreements, honor commitments, and stand in relationships of mutual trust; they have tastes and values of their own; they can be frustrated or fulfilled, pleased or hurt. (Feinberg, 1992, pp. 42–43)

The characteristics Feinberg picks out here are similar to those on Warren's list, though we might take him to be suggesting that we add *emotionality* and *possession of tastes and values* as additional members. There is nothing magical about these lists from Warren and Feinberg: perhaps they are mistaken and have listed the wrong elements. Other philosophers have offered different lists of characteristics—Joseph Fletcher's list contains 15 characteristics, while others consist of only one.

For example, Immanuel Kant argued that it is our human *reason* that gives us moral standing. Reason, according to Kant, involves reflecting on the principles that guide our actions and choices and deciding whether we would recommend those reasons to other people. Such mental activity is highly complex: in order to reflect on my principle I need to be able to *articulate* it, and this requires language. In order to consider whether I could recommend principles to others, I need to "put myself in their shoes"   8.16

and to consider what the world would be like if they followed my principle. According to Kant, human beings are the only animals capable of such a complex thought process. He concluded that human beings are the only ones that have moral standing.

8.17   Kant's view has some counterintuitive implications: according to Kant, we don't have any obligation *to the kitten* not to treat kittens cruelly. We do, however, have obligations to other people, who might be upset if they saw us engaged in animal abuse. And we have an obligation not to corrupt ourselves: Kant argues that cruelty to animals desensitizes people so that they will no longer be concerned—or as concerned as they should be—about the pain. He claims that we ought to avoid such cruelty on the grounds that we might become more complacent about cruelty to other people if we allow ourselves to become desensitized to animal cruelty.

8.18   It's plausible to think that one of the reasons why we shouldn't be cruel to animals is that it would upset others, or that it might make us inappropriately indifferent to the suffering of other *people*. But is it plausible to think that these are our only reasons? That the actual suffering of the animal itself has no moral significance? Jeremy Bentham thought not. Responding to Kant's view, he wrote: "The question is not Can they *reason?* nor Can they *talk?* but Can they *suffer?*" (Bentham, 1988 [1789], p. 311). According to Bentham, the fact that a creature is sensitive to pain and pleasure is entirely sufficient to give that creature at least *some* moral standing.

8.19   The fact that different people regard different characteristics as relevant does not mean that such lists are arbitrary, or that they are simply a matter of taste. Different people may have different views of standing and personhood, but this is another case where differences require justification and explanation.

8.20   Consider one of the items included on both lists: the capacity to communicate. Is it reasonable to suppose that this capacity is a necessary feature, without which one would not have moral standing? Some people are horrified by the fantasy that some disease might strike them immobile, unable to move a muscle. It is terrifying to think that we might be trapped in our own body, unable to communicate with other people around us! But, if we were in such a situation, surely we would still be *persons*! What makes this fantasy terrifying is precisely that such a person still *is* a person but *can no longer communicate that fact to others*. While the capacity to communicate may be crucial in that it enables us to persuade others that we are persons, it does not seem to be a *defining* characteristic of personhood—that is, one without which a person would not be a person. If this argument is a good one, then the ability to communicate should not be a member of the list of capacities necessary for moral standing.

To be fair to Warren and Feinberg, it is worth remembering that neither 8.21 of them claims that the ability to communicate is an essential necessary characteristic that confers moral standing on those who possess it. Feinberg expressly identifies communication as an ability that *convinces him* that other people are persons. And Warren doesn't claim that any of the elements on her list are necessary conditions for moral standing. But, even more importantly, we can evaluate different lists by considering the reasons for including different capacities.

Degrees of Moral Standing? The Constitutive View

What is the relationship between the characteristics that confer standing 8.22 and the degree of moral standing possessed? One suggestion would be to put these characteristics on a scale so that we can compare individuals with one another. For example, perhaps individuals have higher moral standing if they possess more intelligence, or more sensitivity to pain and pleasure. These characteristics are almost always included, in one form or another, on lists like those of Warren and Feinberg, though they are rarely the only items listed. Is it plausible to think that possession of one of these is sufficient for basic moral standing? Perhaps individuals who are not rational in Kant's sense but are sensitive to pain and pleasure have standing, but less standing than individuals who are both rational and sensitive.

Comparative Moral Standing: The Constitutive View

1. There is a set of characteristics that constitute the basis for moral standing.
2. Moral standing varies, so that individuals who have more of these characteristics, or have them to a higher degree, have a moral standing that is *higher* than the moral standing of those with fewer of these characteristics, or those who have them to a lower degree.

The constitutive view is a simple view: it simply makes a correspondence between an individuals' characteristics and its moral standing. We will point out ways in which this view may get some things right—it may account for many of our judgments about moral standing. But keep in mind that this view may be incomplete. In order to account for the moral significance of some of the things and individuals who matter to us, it may be necessary to go beyond this simple theory.

8.23   The constitutive view, or something very similar to it, may lie behind the common belief that nonhuman animals have lower moral priority than human beings. Justin, in the dialogue that introduced this chapter, appears to hold the common view that it is morally permissible to raise animals for food and eat them but that it would be horrible to treat human beings in the same way. Those who hold this view must believe that animals have less moral standing than human beings. If not, our interest in eating them could not justify raising and slaughtering them for food. Such a view would also explain why we might feel differently about dolphins or bonobos if we were to discover that they were more "like us" than we usually believe. For example, if chimpanzees really do have psychological capabilities similar to those of a five-year-old human child, then perhaps we should accord them the same rights we accord a five-year-old human.

Comparing Characteristics and Abilities

8.24 While different people use different characteristics in making such comparisons, the differences range over some important areas of agreement. There is wide (though not universal) agreement (1) that individuals who are sensitive to pain have at least some minimal moral standing—we ought not to cause pain or discomfort if we can help it, even to relatively simple creatures. There is similar agreement (2) that conscious intelligence and the ability to reason are significant from the moral point of view. On this view, perhaps intelligent, reasoning beings have a higher moral standing than others, who are sensitive but are conscious to a different degree. Perhaps these qualities are a matter of degree, so that some are more (or less) sensitive to pain and pleasure than others, some more (or less) intelligently conscious of their surroundings, and some better (or worse) at reasoning and deliberate choice.

8.25   It would be difficult to make the comparisons implied by such a view: it is notoriously difficult to compare the intelligence of chimpanzees to the intelligence of a child, no matter what age. Chimpanzees have *different* capabilities from humans: they find language more difficult than we do, but there is evidence that they are even better than humans at **some complex**

cognitive tasks. This doesn't necessarily mean that it will be *impossible* to develop a scale of abilities that might correspond with a scale of moral standing, but it does mean that doing so will be difficult.

On the other hand, the fact that some comparisons are difficult doesn't 8.26 mean that no comparisons can be made at all. Perhaps it is safe to say, for example, that normal humans are better at calculus than cats are, that chimpanzees have language abilities that far exceed those of mice, that mice are more responsive and social than roaches and worms. We might be wrong about these comparisons, of course: we might discover that worms and roaches have rich and complicated emotional and intellectual lives. (In the *Hitchhiker's Guide to the Galaxy*, Douglas Adams suggests that humans are the *third* most intelligent species, after mice and dolphins. In Adams's universe, the mice have been using *us* in experiments while deceptively leading us to believe that we are using them.) But, if so, that would call into question the comparative moral standing of these different creatures. Suppose we discover that these animals have richer emotional and rational lives than we believed. If this information led us to conclude that they have higher moral standing than we thought they did, we would be *using* the theory, not rejecting it.

Objections to the Constitutive View

One objection to the constituitive point of view is that it undervalues *future* 8.27 *potential*. A young child and an animal might be similar in certain ways at the moment, but the child will continue to grow and will develop mental abilities that far exceed those of the animal. There is an ambiguity in the first principle of the constitutive point of view. Does "characteristics" designate only things that are true of one now, or does it also refer to the capacity to become other things in the future? This question has important implications not just for animal rights, but also for abortion debates. We can go a step farther and ask whether future generations, who don't even exist yet, have "characteristics" that bestow moral standing on them. The answer to this has major implications for environmental policy and resource use.

A different objection is to the second premise. It claims that the constitu- 8.28 tive view overstates the importance of variations in characteristics among members of the same group. If we make the characteristic of intelligence the basis of moral standing, does that imply that more intelligent people should count for more in our moral calculations? And what about human beings who are handicapped and will never develop higher level capacities? Opponents of the constitutive view could argue that rights come from the characteristics of the group to which one belongs, not from the individual characteristics. The notion of "human rights" seems to imply this.

8.29   Defenders of the constitutive view can respond in several ways. They can either include future potential as a characteristic and adjust judgments about moral standing accordingly, or they can deny that future characteristics are relevant to present moral standing. If the latter, they can argue that some of our initial moral judgments are wrong and need adjustment. In responding to the charge that they overemphasize individual differences within groups, they can argue that the designation of groups is arbitrary. Is having a certain number of chromosomes really morally significant? In response to the objection from the concept of human rights, advocates of the constitutive view have typically argued that all individuals who pass a *threshold* fully possess these rights. We will explore these objections and responses in more depth as we look at some hard cases.

Hard Case I: Fertilized Ova and Fetuses

8.30 Different views about abortion are often based on underlying different views about the moral status of the fetus. Some people urge that "life begins at conception," while others regard a newly fertilized ovum as a mere collection of cells. Because of this, members of one group may regard the decision to have an abortion as a decision to end a life, while members of the other group may regard it as the decision not to start one. Can this disagreement be resolved? The constitutive view would suggest that we resolve it by considering the properties of a newly conceived fetus.

8.31   A newly fertilized ovum—a conceptus—is not conscious, rational, or sensitive to pain or pleasure. At this early stage, it is not even certain that the ovum would develop into a single individual or more than one individual: twinning is still possible until the nervous system begins to develop. By the 28th day, an embryo has usually developed a head and tail, and limb-buds may have begun to form. After 35 days the embryo will be 4–5 mm long and will have hands, feet, and eyes. After 42 days some brainwaves are sometimes detectable, though nervous system structure is still relatively simple. More than a month later, after around 82 days, the nervous system may be sufficiently developed for the fetus to experience pain or irritation. The first perceptible fetal movement—quickening—occurs around day 124. Under

US law, day 140 is the latest stage when abortion is still a legally protected woman's right (Schoenwolf *et al.*, 2014).

According to the constitutive view, the status of the fetus will depend on 8.32 its possession of morally relevant characteristics. Mary Anne Warren argues that an early-term fetus possesses *none* of the relevant characteristics and that it therefore cannot count as having moral standing that could compete with a woman's right to make her own decisions about her body. But perhaps there are other characteristics that are relevant: even if one accepts Warren's view that a fetus is not yet a person with moral standing, it is a *potential* person. Unlike other collections of living human cells, a new conceptus can develop, in the natural course of events, into a person with a life like our own.

If a fetus is a potential person, should we treat it as a person now, in 8.33 advance? In general, being a potential *x* does not qualify one as presently having the rights of an *x*. Joel Feinberg quotes the philosopher Stanley Benn, who notes: "A potential president of the United States is not on that account Commander-In-Chief [of the US army and navy]" (Feinberg 1992, p. 48). You may right now be a potential president, but you don't presently have the right to order US troops into battle. By implication, Benn urges, the fact that a fetus is a potential person does not mean that it now has the rights it will have if it becomes a person.

An opponent could respond with the following scenario: suppose agents 8.34 of a foreign country assassinated the president-elect. Would such an action be viewed that differently from the assassination of a sitting president? It is true that the president elect cannot exercise the powers of the presidency (just as a child cannot vote or drive a car as an adult could), but the future status of the president-elect affects how we would view his or her death.

While many people are potential presidents in the sense that they meet 8.35 the constitutional requirements and are conceivably president, few will actually become so. The president-elect, however, will very likely have the power of the president in the fullness of time. Similarly, unless some intervening act prevents it, a fetus will, in the ordinary natural course of events, become a baby, and then an adult. Don Marquis (1989: 192) argues that a fetus has a *"future like ours."* This is not merely a *potential* property that it will come to have later, but something it has right now. Possession of *a future like ours* distinguishes a human fetus from other relevantly similar groups of cells. The skin cells left behind when you skin your knee are living human cells like the cells of a conceptus. But they will not develop in the same way, in the normal course of events, and therefore they don't have *a future like ours*.

8.36   Marquis regards the possession of *a future like ours* as a characteristic
that confers moral standing, and perhaps even full personhood, on a newly
conceived fetus. But even if one accepts the view that a new conceptus has
such a future, can a fetus have an interest in fulfilling it? Why should the
possession of a future like ours be thought to confer moral standing on an
individual who can have no such interest, since a new conceptus can have
no conscious interests at all? If a conceptus has no interests at all, can we
protect its interest in having a future like ours?

8.37   But suppose, for the sake of argument, that we accept Marquis's argument and conclude that a conceptus or a fetus does have moral status.
Before deciding what this would imply about the permissibility of abortion,
we would need to consider how the interests (?) of a conceptus compare to
the interests of a woman. In this case we have a conflict of interest between
a woman and the fetus she carries. How can they be compared?

8.38   On one hand, the interest of the fetus (if a fetus has interests) is fundamental and central: the interest in life—in not dying or being killed—is as
central an interest as any. The interests of the woman, however, are the
interests of a full-blown person. In making the comparison, it would be a
mistake to discount either interest as trivial. Having a child at the wrong
time can radically change the course of a person's life. Women who choose
to have abortions may do so because having a child would scuttle their
career plans or their relationships with others, or make it impossible for
them to pursue their life plans and dreams. Perhaps not *all* women who
choose abortions have such weighty interests at stake, but it is unlikely that
women make such a choice for trivial reasons. In considering whether
abortion is permissible, we need to consider the strongest arguments in
favor of the competing interests on both sides of the question.

8.39   If one thinks of abortion in terms of the conflict of interests at play, how
should we weigh these interests against one another? One way would be to
try to think of an analogous situation where one's obligations might be
clear. Here is an example offered by Judith Jarvis Thompson:

> You wake up in the morning and find yourself back to back in bed with an
> unconscious violinist. A famous unconscious violinist. He has been found to
> have a fatal kidney ailment, and the Society of Music Lovers has canvassed all
> the available medical records and found that you alone have the right blood
> type to help. They have therefore kidnapped you, and last night the violinist's
> circulatory system was plugged into yours, so that your kidneys can be used
> to extract poisons from his blood as well as your own. The director of the

hospital now tells you, "Look, we're sorry the Society of Music Lovers did this to you—we would never have permitted it if we had known. But still they did it, and the violinist now is plugged into you. To unplug you would be to kill him. But never mind, it's only for nine months. By then he will have recovered from his ailment, and can safely be unplugged from you." (Thompson, 1971, p. 49)

Thompson asks: "Is it morally incumbent on you to accede to this situation? No doubt it would be very nice of you if you did, a great kindness. But do you *have* to accede to it?" (Thompson 1971, p. 49). Thompson thinks not. Because she believes that the described situation is relevantly similar to the situation of at least some pregnant women whose interests would be better served by aborting than by carrying a child to term, she concludes that abortion is sometimes morally permissible.

But is Thompson's example really analogous to the situation of a pregnant woman? For one thing, pregnancy is often a predictable risk, voluntarily undertaken. The violinist example is most similar to pregnancy due to rape, with added medical complications that make confinement to bed a requirement. If the pregnancy was voluntary, intentional, and normal, would this change your view of her obligation? Would the weight of that obligation change if it were easy for her to find an adoptive family? 8.40

If Thompson's violinist example is inadequate, perhaps you can think of a better analogy to the case of abortion. Should an appropriate example take into account the diminished capabilities of the conceptus or fetus? If a fetus has any moral standing at all, should it be understood to be *diminished* moral standing by comparison to the competing interests of a pregnant woman? 8.41

Hard Case II: Childhood and Disability

Another set of hard cases applies to persons who may not have all the characteristics and capabilities of nondisabled adults. Children, for example, don't have the capacity to reason very well when they are very young. Ordinarily this capacity grows with us as we grow older, but sometimes things don't work that way. People who are mentally disabled may not have all of the capabilities that are typically included among those considered relevant for the possession of moral standing. Should we conclude that children and people with disabilities *matter less* than more developed adults? Babies are remarkable indeed, but, by comparison to an older child 8.42

or an adult, their capabilities are weak. Should we conclude that they matter less—that they have lower standing than adults?

8.43   In one sense, this view accords with standard ways we treat children: children don't have the same rights as adults—children aren't permitted to make autonomous choices about many aspects of their own lives. For example, children don't have a legal right to decide to go to school or not. children can't vote, are not eligible for a driver's license, and are not permitted to hold full-time jobs. Children don't have the right to refuse medical treatment—their parents have the right to make medical decisions on their behalf, and even expressly against their will. We can ask whether there are good reasons—good moral reasons behind these legal restrictions. Certainly the restrictions stand in need of justification. But perhaps they are justified by the fact that children have different characteristics—different abilities and tendencies. Children don't have all the capacities that adults have, and the constraints on their rights reflect this fact.

8.44   In another sense, it seems very odd to say that children and babies matter less than adults, or that they have lower moral standing: in certain circumstances it might be absolutely appropriate to sacrifice the interests of an adult to the interests of a child. If we are distributing scarce food resources or lifesaving medicines, or if we transplant organs, it might be appropriate to make sure that children's needs are satisfied first, before we take care of adults. Perhaps children matter even more than adults, at least in some contexts: older people have had their chance, and if tragic choices need to be made fairness would seem to dictate that children should get the same opportunities that most adults have already had.

8.45   One thought is that children need to be recognized as early-stage persons whose later adult selves need to be protected against the bad choices children might make if they weren't subject to parental guidance. A child might not want to go to school, but the adult the child will become will be glad that parents didn't let her neglect her early education. Childhood is temporary. People grow out of it in time.

8.46   It may not be reasonable, however, to expect people with serious disabilities to grow out of them with time. Does the *constitutive view* imply that people with disabilities have lower moral standing than people who do not have disabilities? If so, this might be a reason to question, revise, or abandon the constitutive view.

8.47   Some people with cognitive disabilities are not able to organize their own lives or to make choices about medical care or about where to live. They need help. Once again, however, it would be repugnant indeed to say that disabilities make disabled people *less valuable*, or that we should discount their interests when we compare them with the interests of others, who are not disabled. Quite the opposite: disabled people require *accommodations* designed to mitigate the effects of their disability, and they may need special help so that they can live as independently as possible.

Advocates of the constitutive view might consider several strategies to respond to the challenge presented by children and people with disability. One strategy would be to focus on what we can know and on the degree to which we are uncertain about others' abilities. People who are disabled often exceed the expectations of their caregivers. Because of our uncertainty about what other people can do or feel, we should avoid making potentially inappropriate assumptions about others' inabilities. We should treat people *as if* they were more fully able, since they might be. But this strategy is vulnerable: it is repugnant to think that we might treat others as having less standing as we gain more confidence in our judgments about their abilities. 8.48

Another strategy would be to assert that we value people as members of our community for reasons that may be independent of their raw moral status. People with disabilities are our friends, colleagues, and family members, or our *selves*. We love and care for them even when we are unable to ground that care in their constitutive capabilities. The care nonetheless provides a reason to treat them well. 8.49

A critic may say that this does not go far enough. Not everyone has similar feelings. Certainly those who mistreat severely disabled people have acted wrongly. If my only protection is the fact that certain people happen to care about me, what if there are other people about whom no one cares? 8.50

A different strategy appeals to prudence: all of us face the likelihood that we will ourselves live with disabilities at some time in the future. This gives us good reasons to ensure that other people get the same care, assistance, and respect that we hope to receive if we ever have similar needs. 8.51

These prudential reasons quickly shade into considerations of justice. Disabilities are not chosen, and in that sense disadvantages associated with disability typically reflect *luck*. Luck egalitarianism (on which see Chapter 3) implies that it is wrong if people are disadvantaged because of circumstances beyond their control. If we had to choose rules of justice not knowing whether we would be disabled, we would choose to recognize rights for people with different challenges and abilities. We may not always be able to understandfully others' circumstances, or imagine ourselves in their places. But we may gain some insight into others' rights and needs when we 8.52

imagine what it would be like to face similar challenges ourselves. In the case of disabilities, this imaginative effort may be easier to make, since we all face the possibility of becoming disabled. In this case, by protecting the rights of others, we also protect ourselves.

8.53   Perhaps each of these strategies gets something right. But if we accept them, have we left behind the constitutive view? If the moral standing of others has to do with their membership in our community, if our treatment of others is based on an understanding that their fate may at some time be our own fate, then our judgments about others' moral status no longer seem to be simply a function of these others' abilities and isolated characteristics. Should we conclude that the constitutive view is too simplistic to accommodate the way we value other people? If so, does the view need to be supplemented, or should it simply be abandoned?

Hard Case III: Distant Peoples and Future Generations

8.54 Children and people with disabilities are members of our families and communities. But there are other people who are more distant from us and are not, or cannot be, immediate members of our community. Some members of the world community live far from us and we do not see their lives. Distant people are, of course, moral *persons*, but it is difficult for us to regard their plight as an immediate problem. Our ability to communicate almost instantly with people all over the world might make many distant people members, or potential members, of our community. Certainly our choices can change the lives of people we may never encounter, so perhaps members of the world community can be considered members of our community as well.

8.55   While some people are distant in space, others are distant in time. Distant future generations, whose lives will not overlap our own, cannot be friends or fellow travelers. They do not presently possess any of the characteristics people associate with moral standing, but they will possess them. If they are potential people, should we conclude that they have only potential moral standing? Our decisions may affect future generations in decisive ways: we could blight their lives by using up the resources they will need, by destroying the environmental systems on which they would depend, or by neglecting or destroying the human institutions that will sustain their lives. But surely it would be wrong to do this. Wrongs and injustices perpetrated against people we will never meet are still unjust.

Hard Case IV: Posthumans?

Is it possible that some individuals might have a moral status *higher* than 8.56
persons? For some people, the answer may be obvious: some theists believe
in a God whose moral status is far beyond that of a human being. But others
hold that persons have *full* moral status and that all individuals who have
such status should be regarded as moral equals.

While genetic engineering has been applied to animal and plant species, 8.57
it has not yet (?) been used to alter or "improve" the human genome. Already,
however, genetic selection is used to prevent the conception of people who
would have a damaging genetic disease or disability. The same techniques
that are used to select *against* such damaging conditions could be used to
select *for* characteristics that are desired. For example, if scientists were to
find genes or gene sets associated with unusual intelligence or agility or
musical talent, it might become possible to use these tools to make it more
likely that our children will have these characteristics. As our knowledge
and technology improve, it might become possible to ensure that our children will be faster, smarter, and stronger than they would otherwise be.

Many people have moral reservations about whether we should use such 8.58
technologies in this way. Perhaps we would put our children at risk of unan-
ticipated side effects; perhaps people would come to view their children as
consumer items with properties selected from a list, the way we purchase
cars; perhaps people would be less tolerant of their children's weaknesses
and challenges if they had paid for a technological fix designed to make
these children "better." But set these reservations aside for a moment.

On the *constitutive view*, is it possible that enhanced human beings would 8.59
have a moral status *higher* than the status of normal, unenhanced people? Or
should we consider full personhood to be the *highest* level of moral standing,
not to be exceeded even when some individuals have extraordinary capacities?
Instead of regarding moral standing as a variable standard that increases with
increasing capacities and abilities, perhaps we should regard every individual
whose capacities pass some *threshold* as having full and equal moral standing.

Hard Case V: Ecosystems and the Natural World

Many advocates of the *constitutive view* hold that conscious experience and 8.60
interests are necessary for moral standing. Joel Feinberg suggests that we
cannot act "for the sake of" something that has no conscious experiences,

cannot feel pain or pleasure, and has no interests. But what about ecosystems and the natural world? When we pass laws to protect the environment, one good reason to do so is to protect people from the consequences of environmental destruction. But many people urge that we should also be more directly motivated to protect and preserve the environment itself.

8.61   American naturalist and philosopher Aldo Leopold argued that it is a mistake to think that ethics and morality should be bounded by a narrow concern for human beings, or even by what he would have regarded as a narrow concern for *conscious* beings. Careless or rapacious treatment of the natural environment, he argued, is wrong not because of the harm it causes to human beings, but because of the harm to the environment itself.

8.62   According to Leopold, the history of morality has been a history of *progress*, whereby we have gradually come to extend the boundaries of direct moral care and concern. In ancient Greece, he noted, slaves were considered to be chattel, with no moral significance of their own. "The ethical structure of that day covered wives," he writes, "but had not yet been extended to human chattels. During the three thousand years which have since elapsed, ethical criteria have been extended to many fields of conduct, with corresponding shrinkages in those judged by expediency only" (Leopold, 1966, p. 237).

8.63   The narrowest ethical views—those with the smallest "guano ring"— would be tribal views like those of ancient Greece. The Greeks are reported to have regarded non-Greek peoples as outside the boundary of direct moral concern. As we extend our ethical focus to other peoples, to all peoples, perhaps to animals as well, how far should we go? Leopold recommended what he called the *land ethic* as a guide to our treatment of the natural world:

> LEOPOLD'S LAND ETHIC: A thing is right when it tends to preserve the integrity, stability, and beauty of the biotic community. It is wrong when it tends otherwise. (Leopold, 1966, p. 262)

If we followed it, this principle would not only imply dramatic changes in the way we make private moral decisions, it would also change the way we organize public and political institutions. Because of human activities, the earth's biological systems have changed dramatically in recent years: great forests have been cut to make room for cattle or for the extraction of oil; many fish species have been driven to the point of extinction by increasingly effective technologies, which can capture virtually every living thing in their path. Rising levels of CO_2 in the earth's atmosphere threaten to change the stable weather patterns on which our lives and welfare critically depend. Our treatment of the natural world is character-ized by rampant destruction, perpetrated in the name of "development" of resources. Would we do better if we followed an ethic like the one Leopold recommends?

Perhaps our "crimes against nature" are wrong in a more conventional 8.64 sense as well: environmental damage, especially *global* environmental dam-age, is likely to lead to human unhappiness as well. Perhaps we don't *need* a new land ethic to explain why these actions are wrong and reprehensible.

Can we act "for the sake" of the environment, or of smaller ecosystem 8.65 biomes? At least one Supreme Court justice has argued that we can. Justice Douglas, dissenting in the 1972 case ***Sierra Club v. Morton***, urged that people should be able to bring a legal cause of action on behalf of natural areas. In effect Douglas argued that people should be able to stand in court for the *interests of the biotic community*:

> Those who hike the Appalachian Trail into Sunfish Pond, New Jersey, and camp or sleep there, or run the Allagash in Maine, or climb the Guadalupes in West Texas, or who canoe and portage the Quetico Superior in Minnesota, certainly should have standing to defend those natural wonders before courts or agencies, though they live 3,000 miles away. Those who merely are caught up in environmental news or propaganda and flock to defend these waters or areas may be treated differently. That is why these environmental issues should be tendered by the inanimate object itself. Then there will be assurances that all of the forms of life which it represents will stand before the court—the pile-ated woodpecker as well as the coyote and bear, the lemmings as well as the trout in the streams. Those inarticulate members of the ecological group can-not speak. But those people who have so frequented the place as to know its values and wonders will be able to speak for the entire ecological community. Ecology reflects the land ethic; and Aldo Leopold wrote in A Sand Country Almanac 204 (1949), "The land ethic simply enlarges the boundaries of the community to include soils, waters, plants, and animals, or collectively: the land." That, as I see it, is the issue of "standing" in the present case and contro-versy. (Justice J. Douglas's dissenting opinion in *Sierra Club v. Morton*, 405 US 727 [1972]; see http://caselaw.findlaw.com/us-supreme-court/405/727.html)

Douglas's view did not gain a majority in the US Supreme Court, but it is interesting to ponder whether it should have persuaded the other justices, and what US environmental law would look like now if the court had taken a different path in 1972. Philosophically, it is interesting to consider the extent to which Douglas's opinion is a practical instantiation of Leopold's view. To say that natural systems should have *legal* standing is different from saying that they have *moral* standing. Ships and corporations have standing in courts, but few people think they have moral standing independent of the people involved with them.

8.66   Still, the analogy with legal standing is interesting and potentially useful. It is clear that Leopold's *land ethic* would take us far beyond the *constitutive view* of moral standing, considered in earlier sections. If we cannot have both, which one of them should we abandon?

Upshot

8.67 The *constitutive view* holds that the moral standing of an individual depends on its possession of morally significant characteristics. The view also holds that moral standing comes in *degrees*, so that some things have more significance than others. The view is plausible, and constitutes a good starting point to think about moral standing—about "who counts" from the moral point of view. Many people accept this view as it is. But others have argued that this view is *incomplete*. A fuller account of the moral significance of others, they argue, would need to incorporate additional considerations. Some critics have argued that a better view might be less individualistic, or that future abilities and capacities should be taken into account. Others urge that group membership itself is morally significant in a way that the constitutive view does not properly recognize.

References and Further Reading

Bentham, Jeremy. 1988 [1789]. *An Introduction to the Principles of Morals and Legislation*. New York: Prometheus Books. Jeremy Bentham was a British utilitarian philosopher who famously argued that the capacity for pain or pleasure is sufficient for moral standing.

Dworkin, Ronald. 1993. *Life's Dominion*. New York: Knopf. Dworkin tries to articulate a prochoice position that acknowledges some of the force of the prolife position in an accessible way.

Feinberg, Joel. 1992. "Abortion." In Joel Feinberg, *Freedom and Fulfillment: Philosophical Essays*. Princeton, NJ: Princeton University Press, pp. 37–75.

Feinberg's essay is a comprehensive and widely read treatment of the problem of abortion. After more than 20 years, it is still a classic.

George, Robert P. and Christopher Tollefsen. 2008. *Embryo: A Defense of Human Life*. New York: Doubleday. A prolife defense of the status of the fetus.

Gould, Stephen Jay. 1994. *Hen's Teeth and Horse's Toes*. New York: Norton. Gould's essay "The Guano Ring" is the source of the metaphor used to introduce this chapter.

Leopold, Aldo. 1966. *A Sand County Almanac*. New York: Oxford University Press. Aldo Leopold argues that we have moral obligations to promote the "integrity, stability, and beauty" of the biotic environment. He is often interpreted to advocate the view that nonhuman nature has independent moral standing.

Marquis, Don. 1989. "Why Abortion Is Immoral." *Journal of Philosophy*, 86: 183–202. A criticism of abortion from a secular perspective that focuses on the wrong of depriving the fetus of its future life.

Nozick, Robert. 1974. *Anarchy, State, and Utopia*. New York: Basic Books. The source of the pumpkin/kitten example contains a much larger discussion of the idea of rights as constraints on action.

Schoenwolf, Gary C., Steven B. Bleyl, Philip R. Brauer, and Philippa H. Francis-West. 2014. *Larsen's Human Embryology*. Philadelphia, PA: Saunders/Elsevier. Among other things, this work provides empirical background on human embryonic development.

Thompson, Judith J. 1971. "A Defense of Abortion." *Philosophy and Public Affairs*, 1(1): 47–66. One of the most famous articles on abortion, it contains many interesting hypothetical scenarios to test the view that, if we grant that the fetus is a person, it follows that abortion is wrong.

Warren, Mary Anne. 1973. "On the Moral and Legal Status of Abortion." *The Monist*, 57(1): 43–61. A good introduction to the debates about the status of the fetus; it argues that the fetus is not a person.

Online Resources

1 http://www.nytimes.com/2012/02/27/opinion/thinking-about-pigs-before-theyre-food.html?_r=0
2 http://www.cnn.com/2013/10/21/us/seaworld-blackfish-qa/index.html
3 http://www.peta.org/blog/chicago-pet-stores-ban/
4 http://www.projetogap.org.br/
5 http://www.sciencemag.org/news/2010/02/dolphin-person
6 http://www.ncbi.nlm.nih.gov/pubmed/23896571
7 https://www.youtube.com/watch?v=nTgeLEWr614
8 http://caselaw.findlaw.com/us-supreme-court/405/727.html

9

RELIGION AND POLITICS

SOPHIE   I need to quit reading the news. It just makes me angry.

JUSTIN   What's wrong Soph?

SOPHIE   The debates over gay marriage. I really dislike people claiming
they don't have to obey the same laws as everyone else because
of their religious beliefs. Religion should be a personal thing,
not a political thing.

JUSTIN   Some people use their religious beliefs to justify gay marriage
rather than to criticize it. Does that make you angry too?

SOPHIE   Actually, yes. Not as much because they are agreeing with me,
but I still think that there are plenty of nonreligious arguments
supporting gay marriage and that people should stick to those
when deciding what the law should be and that you shouldn't
be able to opt out because you have a religious disagreement.

JUSTIN   I am surprised to hear you say that.

SOPHIE   Why?

JUSTIN   Because you are such a big proponent of freedom of speech.
It seems to me that people who make religious arguments
opposing gay marriage are just exercising their First
Amendment rights. Given that gay marriage is now legal,
they really are just asking for the right to express their dissent
and to not act in ways that violate their conscience. Many of
the proponents of civil rights legislation in the 1950s and
1960s had religious motivations. Sometimes religious people are right, sometimes they are wrong, just like secular

This Is Political Philosophy: An Introduction, First Edition. Alex Tuckness and Clark Wolf.
© 2017 John Wiley & Sons, Inc. Published 2017 by John Wiley & Sons, Inc.

people. I don't think we should treat the arguments of religious people differently.

SOPHIE   I think religious people have a legal right to say whatever they want, but I still think that imposing your religious beliefs on others is morally wrong. If an employer refuses to fund contraceptives for the company health plan for religious reasons, that is imposing one's beliefs on others. I also think that if the opponents of gay marriage had the power to do so, they would try to outlaw it again.

JUSTIN   Is the issue that they hold beliefs you disagree with or that they try to legislate on the basis of religion?

SOPHIE   It is not just that I disagree with their conclusions. I think it is fine to be religious as long as you keep it within your church and don't try to impose your beliefs on other people. If you are going to impose your views on other people you should do so on the basis of reason, not on the basis of faith. Public policy should be based on arguments that can be rationally defended. If you ask someone about their political views and they just say "God says so," it's a conversation stopper. They haven't given a reason that's a reason for me.

JUSTIN   What do you mean by "reason"? Do you just mean the rules of logic?

SOPHIE   I mean the rules of logic, but also the practices of science. The rules of logic tell you how to make valid inferences from your starting premises, but they don't tell you whether the starting premise is right. We need science to make sure the premises are right.

JUSTIN   So if someone says that we should prevent a certain species from going extinct, we would use science to determine the feasibility of saving it, how much it would cost to save it, and how much benefit we would get from saving it?

SOPHIE   Yes, something like that. Those are all questions that can have objective answers.

JUSTIN   I don't think they are as objective as you think. Scientific-style reasoning might help with the first two questions, but I don't think it can measure benefit.

SOPHIE   Why not? We can investigate the likelihood that species extinction would disrupt the ecosystem or the chances that a species might help us develop a new medicine.

JUSTIN   The whole line of argument you are using about benefits assumes a kind of utilitarian framework, and a human-centered framework at that. Scientific methods can't prove that utilitarianism is right or tell us which forms of happiness count, or how to add them up, or whose happiness to include. All of those are value judgments. It seems to me that public policy is always about value judgments and always involves people imposing their values on other people at some level.

SOPHIE   There is still a difference between religious and nonreligious political arguments. Some value judgments are widely held, but religious judgments are not. In a religiously diverse society, if you legislate on the basis of religion you will be imposing values on many people who do not accept them.

JUSTIN   Kantians and utilitarians often disagree on public policy issues. Whichever side wins will be implementing a policy on the basis of values that their opponents reject.

SOPHIE   But Kantians and utilitarians give philosophical arguments for their positions, they don't just invoke God's will.

JUSTIN   Religious believers don't always invoke God overtly either. Often their religious beliefs explain why their deepest values are the way that they are, but they can express their argument in nontheological terms, unless they are relentlessly pressed with the question "why?"

SOPHIE   That is true. A person may start by talking about how we should preserve animal species, and it might take a lot of questioning and arguing to get them to admit that the reason why they think animal species should be preserved is a religious reason. But, if the ultimate reason is "God wills that we preserve animal species," this is still not a position you can argue with.

JUSTIN   But if you go through a similar series of arguments and someone says "only humans have rights," or "only human happiness should count in our calculations," at some point they are also making a basic moral claim that either you disagree or you agree with.

SOPHIE   So you would say that religious and secular arguments are both equally valid in politics? I'm surprised, because I don't think of you as being religious either.

JUSTIN   My views about religion are complicated, even to myself. But part of the reason why I hold this position is that I think freedom of conscience is important for everyone, not just for religious believers. This is one of my reasons for treating appeals to religion and philosophy the same in politics.

SOPHIE   I didn't follow that. What do you mean?

JUSTIN   Take the example of the military draft. There is a tradition of allowing people from some religious groups to avoid military combat and serve in some other way, so that their conscience is not violated. I think that a person who is a pacifist on nonreligious grounds should have the same protections. Religious believers should have just as much right to make political arguments, and nonreligious people should have just as much right to make claims of conscience.

SOPHIE   I will have to think about that. I am not sure the two cases have to go together. We might give everyone the right to conscientious objection simply because we value autonomy while still thinking that religious arguments in politics don't respect the autonomy of other people.

Religion and Politics

Throughout history and still today, debates over religion and politics promote fierce disputes. Here are some contemporary examples from around the world: 9.1

Many Muslims believe that Islam gives them legal principles applicable to matters like the division of property, divorce, and child custody. Following certain procedures (and not others) is an important expression of their faith. Some Muslims in the UK and in other countries around the world have claimed that they should be able to use Islamic law—Sharia—to settle disputes in such matters. That would mean setting aside some of the normal legal rules that would apply in those situations. **Many non-Muslims believe that using Sharia will be detrimental to women**, but many Muslim women are advocates for it. Should religious communities receive exemptions from the normal laws that apply to other groups, so that they may live according to their religious beliefs? 9.2

In France, many citizens put a high value on keeping the state secular. **There are ongoing disputes about whether people should be allowed to** 9.3

express their faith publicly. In French public schools, students are forbidden to wear clothing that proclaims their religion in an "ostentatious" way. This would forbid the wearing of Muslim head coverings just as much as the wearing of a "large" cross or Star of David. It would also ban some of the t-shirts popular among American evangelicals.

9.4   The first dispute is about religious exemptions. If freedom of religion is an important right, should religious believers receive special accommodation and dispensation from the normal rules, so that they may honor their religious convictions? This will be our first topic. It forces us to ask the question: "Is religion special?" The second dispute is about whether we need to require the public square to be secular. At issue here are the use of religious symbols in public spaces (nativity scenes in the city hall, for example) and the use of religious arguments in political debates. This will be our other major topic in this chapter: the place of religion in the public square.

Is Religion Special?

9.5 One of the most familiar political disputes in America is over religious exemptions, cases where a person or a group claims that it should be exempt from a law or regulation because that law or regulation conflicts with its religious beliefs. Here are a few famous examples with links to related court cases:

> *Sicurella v. United States* (1955; see http://caselaw.findlaw.com/us-supreme-court/348/385.html): Religious groups claimed that they should be exempt from the military draft. Many religions place restrictions on when, if ever, it is morally permissible to kill. Governments often claim the right to require citizens to serve in the military, where they may be asked to kill. The *Sicurella* case was about a request for *exemption from the draft*.

> *Oregon Employment Division v. Smith* (1990; see http://caselaw.findlaw.com/us-supreme-court/494/872.html): Two Native Americans lost their jobs when they tested positive for the use of peyote, a banned substance. They claimed the right to use peyote as part of religious ceremonies, so long as they would not come to work under the influence. They requested *exemption from drug laws*.

> *Wisconsin v. Yoder* (1972; see http://caselaw.findlaw.com/us-supreme-court/406/205.html): Amish communities claimed that their children

should be able to quit school after eighth grade. These parents asked for *exemption from public school attendance.*

Church of the Lukumi Babalu Aye, v. City of Hialeah (1993; see http://caselaw.findlaw.com/us-supreme-court/508/520.html): A community banned animal sacrifice after a religious group started practicing it. The group in question claimed *exemption from a rule that it claimed was targeted directly at its religious practices.*

Burwell v. Hobby Lobby (2014; see http://caselaw.findlaw.com/us-supreme-court/13-354.html): Owners of a major US company had religious objections to certain forms of birth control, but their employees will have access to these forms of birth control through government-mandated health insurance. The company owners sued the government for the right not to provide birth control for their employees. This was a request for *exemption from the requirement to provide medical services to employees.*

Newman v. Piggie Park (1966; see http://www.leagle.com/decision/19661197256FSupp941_11032.xml/NEWMAN%20v.%20PIGGIE%20PARK%20ENTERPRISES,%20INC): The owner of a private restaurant had a religious objection to serving black and white patrons together, arguing that his religious beliefs "compel him to oppose any integration of the races whatever." The restaurant did allow black patrons to come to the restaurant for take-out service. The owner asked for an *exemption that would allow him to deny service to black patrons.*

Ingersoll v. Arlene's Flowers (2015; see http://documents.latimes.com/arlenes-flowers-judgment): Because of her religious convictions, a flower-shop owner objected to gay and lesbian unions. She objects to providing flowers for the marriage of gay couples. **State law requires that public businesses provide services equally to all customers.** She asked for an *exemption that would allow her to deny service to gay patrons.*

In each of these examples religious believers argued that the law violates their religious convictions. They claimed that they should not have to obey rules that require them to do what is contrary to their deepest beliefs. In a society where religious views find expression in public, conflicts similar to those due to religions convictions can arise for people without religious convictions, or for people whose convictions are different from those of the majority. Here are two examples:

Engel v. Vitale (1962; see https://www.oyez.org/cases/1961/468): The New York State Regents authorized a short Judeo-Christian prayer at the opening of the school day. The prayer was voluntary. Parents of children at the school argued that this prayer violated the establishment clause of the constitution. They argued that recitation of the prayer, in which their children could not conscientiously participate, put their children in the position of outsiders in their own school. They asked that the policy to begin the day with a prayer should cease.

Newdow v. Carey (2005–2010; see http://undergod.procon.org/view. resource.php?resourceID=003656): Classes at Rio Linda Schools begin the day with a recitation of the Pledge of Allegiance. A kindergartener in this district was raised in a secular household. This child could not assert that we are "one nation under God" without lying. Her parents argued that the daily practice of saying the pledge resulted in their child being singled out, since she was the only member of the class who could not conscientiously participate. They asked that the policy to begin the day with the pledge should cease.

In each of these cases, courts had to consider the significance of religious practice for those who wish to engage in it, but also people's right not to be forced to participate in *other people*'s religious practice. In the United States as in many other countries, courts have gradually tried to clarify what exemptions are permitted and what accommodations for religious practice are required by law. But the cases continue to be controversial and the boundaries have changed over time.

9.6   What can people do when public laws require activity that is contrary to their deepest convictions? Perhaps they should simply break the law. In doing so they would avoid acting against their beliefs, but would subject themselves to legal consequences. Those who argue for religious exemptions or for freedom not to participate in others' religious practices argue that individual persons should not be put in this position. They should not be punished for living with integrity, according to their deepest convictions.

The limits of toleration

9.7 Religious claims don't always trump the law; in consequence, the law is enforced. While the Supreme Court upheld the right of the church to engage in animal sacrifice, it would have been different if the group had wanted to sacrifice children. Most (though not all!) agree that religious freedom does not give you the right to physically harm other people. The hard cases tend to arise when there is no direct harm to others but either some additional public expense is involved or protecting some people's religious convictions imposes burdens on other people. It takes resources to provide children with alternative textbooks or to make religious accommodations for prisoners, particularly if their religion is uncommon and makes unusual demands. Sometimes requests for exemption have been honored: for example, some prisons have built **sweat lodges** to accommodate the religious prac- tices of inmates. In other cases they have not: Piggie Park restaurant was not permitted to deny service to black patrons, nor was Arlene's Flowers per- mitted to deny service to gay patrons.

Some have argued that religious convictions do not merit special 9.8 protections at all, while others urge that the central place of religious beliefs makes it appropriate to accommodate them when this can be done without unreasonable cost. How should we decide when the burden is too great? There are two main approaches used to answer this question. The first approach proceeds through a *balancing test*. This test simply asks us to weigh the importance of religious freedom and to compare it to the costs to society if accommodation is made. One way to compare costs is utilitarian: just ask whether the benefits of accommodation outweigh the costs. But many proponents think that we should give additional weight to things like freedom of conscience and the significance of religious practice when we make such judgments. Legal rules that require that religious con- victions be overruled "only for a compelling state interest," for example, are simply a way to approximate how much harm or inconvenience we are willing to tolerate in order to help people practice their religious beliefs. By considering cases where accommodation seems appropriate and cases where it seems excessive, we can assess how important we think religious freedom is.

The balancing test does not necessarily require the government to be 9.9 neutral toward different religions. For example, US courts have granted Quakers, but not Catholics, the right to be conscientious objectors, even though in Catholic thought there is a long tradition of upholding just war theory (a topic we investigated in Chapter 7). Quakers believe that all wars are unjust, and they are exempt from combat. Catholics believe that some wars are unjust, and they are not exempt even if they are con- vinced that they are being asked to fight in an unjust war, which would be a sin.

Why the differential treatment? A major reason is the logic of balancing. 9.10 Pacifists make up a small percentage of the population. Granting them an exemption does not substantially affect the country's ability to defend itself. Catholics, on the other hand, are the largest religious denomination in the United States. Moreover, most Protestant groups subscribe to some version of just war theory as well, and so allowing Catholics to be, selectively, conscientious objectors would mean letting Protestants do the same thing. There are also many nonreligious citizens who strongly believe that they should not fight in unjust wars. If all of these groups were granted the right to opt out of particular wars that they thought unjust, this could have a substantial impact on national security. Thus a balancing test might grant permissions to some groups but not others because the costs of granting an exemption are not the same in all cases.

Neutrality and religion

9.11 The other approach to deciding whether to grant exemptions focuses on neutrality rather than on balancing. One way to enact this approach is to say that the government should avoid policies that advantage some religious groups over others, or religious groups in general over nonreligious groups in general. This view is sometimes called *neutrality of effect*.

9.12 This position is not popular among philosophers or legal scholars, because it is impossible. Any policy will always make it easier on some religious groups and harder on others. Suppose the government gives parents complete authority to teach their children in the areas of morality and politics. This gives advantages to groups that emphasize tradition. Secular worldviews that emphasize the importance of encountering other views would be at a relative disadvantage. Suppose instead that the government requires all children to attend public school in order to expose them to a wide variety of religious beliefs. This advantages those religions that think of religion as a choice and those philosophies that emphasize autonomy. If the school curriculum includes material that affirms or denies a particular religious view, that would obviously create advantages or disadvantages. If, on the other hand, the school removes all references to religion from the curriculum, it encourages people to assume that the study of religion is unrelated to the study of science or history, a view that some religions strongly reject. In other words, there is no way to have a policy that is neutral in terms of its effects on various religions.

9.13 This is not just an issue in education. Some religions, including some forms of Islam and Christianity, have traditionally held that there should be close cooperation between the state and religious authorities. Many countries have had established churches that received direct support from the government, even tax support and attempts to craft laws that fit with the beliefs of the dominant religious group. Obviously a state church is not neutral in a country where people have different religious convictions. But not having a state church isn't neutral either, since such an arrangement serves the interests of some and not those of others. Even **having "In God We Trust"**—the official motto of the United States—stamped **on money is nonneutral between theists and atheists**. When there are religious symbols and slogans that are a part of the public culture, this may be advantageous to the religious groups that value those symbols. But, if we remove all these symbols, we benefit the religions and philosophies that believe that political life should be essentially secular.

In every area of human life and in every branch of knowledge there are $\quad$ 9.14 religions and philosophies that make conflicting claims. Any policy you pick will create a climate more hospitable to some points of view than others. For this reason, many political and legal theorists have abandoned the goal of neutral effect and have focused instead on *neutrality of intent*.

Neutrality of intent

When the government passed laws against using peyote (and many other $\quad$ 9.15 narcotics), it did not do so with the intention of infringing upon the religious practices of Native Americans. The purpose was to regulate a potentially addictive drug that could cause social harm. Nonetheless, even though religious infringement was not the intention of the law, that was its effect. The law made it more difficult for some Native Americans to practice their religion. Proponents of the neutrality of intent standard would argue that a law like this is just. It is impossible to avoid laws that have the effect of helping or hurting different religious groups, but we can avoid laws that have helping or hurting particular groups as a primary purpose.

The philosopher John Locke argued for this position in the seventeenth $\quad$ 9.16 century. In fact his writings directly influenced the US Supreme Court case on animal sacrifice, because he had used a very similar example in his *Letter Concerning Toleration*. Locke argues that a person who owns a calf may lawfully slaughter it at home and may

> burn any part of it that he thinks fit. For no injury is thereby done to any one, no prejudice to another man's goods. And for the same reason he may kill his calf also in a religious meeting. Whether the doing so be well-pleasing to God

or no, it is their part to consider that do it. The part of the magistrate is only to take care that the commonwealth receive no prejudice, and that there be no injury done to any man, either in life or estate. And thus what may be spent on a feast may be spent on a sacrifice. (Locke, 2014 [1689])

On the other hand, argues Locke, the magistrate may legitimately forbid *all* slaughter of healthy animals if there is a good public reason, and if the same rules apply to everyone. In that case, there is no *special* restriction that applies to people who would like to engage in ritual sacrifice, even though they are more burdened than other people by the rules that apply to all.

9.17   According to Locke, the permissibility of such a restriction depends on the motives of the legislators. If people are allowed to kill animals for nonreligious reasons, they should be able to kill them for religious reasons as well. The only reason to stop only religiously motivated animal killing would be a desire to hinder the religion that practices animal killing. On the other hand, if there is a legitimate secular purpose to a law that bans the killing of all animals (say, repopulating a nation's cattle stocks after a terrible plague), the law is legitimate even though it will hinder the religious practices of some groups but not others. In Locke's day, the law was sometimes used to require people to take communion in a particular way. He responded: "If any man may lawfully take bread or wine, either sitting or kneeling in his own house, the law ought not to abridge him of the same liberty in his religious worship" (Locke, 2014 [1689]).

9.18   Locke's position has more promise than the neutrality of effect standard, but many people have still found it problematic. One objection is that it simply doesn't take religious liberty seriously enough. It implies that any secular purpose, no matter how trivial, justly overrides religious liberty no matter how central the latter is to a person's faith. Proponents of the balancing approach would point out that it might be possible to allow Native Americans to use peyote under reasonable regulations (perhaps only with advance notice to law enforcement personnel and with prohibitions on operating vehicles under the influence) without seriously compromising the war on drugs. After all, during prohibition churches were given exemptions to serve wine at communion. This objection assumes that religion is deserving of special protection and that Locke does not go far enough. From the government's perspective, conflicts between secular purposes and religious liberty are decided in favor of the former.

9.19   A second objection to Locke is that he assumes that it is easy to tell the difference between a secular and a religious goal. There are certain types of

purposes governments can pursue (protecting the rights of citizens, for example) that Locke thought were not religious and did not depend on religious
reasons or motives. But some people believe that God is the source of human
rights. If someone argues for the emancipation of slaves because slavery denies
slaves their God-given freedom, is that a religious motive or a secular one?

Exemptions for nonreligious reasons

Religious people are not the only ones who have conscientious convictions   9.20
that can be burdened by laws or public actions. Should requests for exemption be treated differently when they come from religious people and when
they come from nonreligious people? Can it be right, for example, to exempt
religious pacifists from the draft, while not providing the same exemption
for pacifists whose convictions are secular? Both the balancing approach
and the neutrality of intent approach assume that religious freedom deserves
special protection. Not everyone agrees with this view. Does the whole concept of religious freedom treat people who are not religious unfairly?

Consider, for example, the American Pledge of Allegiance, in which it is   9.21
affirmed that Americans are "one nation under God." In some US states
school children recite these words every morning. Some Americans have a
conscientious objection to the pledge not because they are not patriotic but
because they regard it as a prayer. Others object for political reasons,
perhaps because they believe that forced patriotism is always wrong. Still
others object because they do not believe in God, and therefore cannot
honestly affirm that we are "one nation under God." For this last group,
a requirement to say the pledge is a requirement to *lie* in public.

Most democratic governments now provide similar treatment for reli-   9.22
gious and nonreligious conscientious convictions. Americans cannot be
required to say the pledge, for example, and there are legal protections for
"rights of conscience" for all people, whether religious or not. The rights to
freedom of conscience and intellect are sometimes regarded as fundamental rights—rights that cannot be justified by reference to any deeper value at
all. But some political theorists root them in underlying rights to either
autonomy or utility. Those who value autonomy highly see it as an extremely
severe violation of autonomy to legally compel someone to do something
she believes is morally wrong (or to force her to face legal penalties if she
chooses to stick to her conscience). Those who focus on utility will note
that it causes people great unhappiness when laws and policies compel
them to act contrary to their beliefs. Rule utilitarians may point out that a

general policy to avoid laws that violate citizens' freedom of conscience makes people better off in the long run, even if there are some relatively rare occasions when it would not.

9.23   Some people argue that, if we shift the argument to rights of conscience, we can do without a specific right to religious liberty. If such rights are based on an underlying value of autonomy, then their value does not change, no matter whether people's convictions are religious or secular. Many deep convictions have roots in people's cultural traditions and norms. Perhaps freedom of conscience can be protected as a way to respect people's cultural traditions regardless of whether they are religious or not?

Multiculturalism

9.24 One influential school of thought that takes this approach is multiculturalism. The word can mean different things—sometimes people use it descriptively, just to say that a given state is pluralistic. Pluralistic states include many different cultural groups. In this chapter "multiculturalism" refers to a philosophical position according to which governments should make special accommodations for minority cultural groups. Different multicultural theories will permit or require different accommodations, but they all share the underlying view that the preservation of minority cultures is a legitimate and high-priority social goal. Protections for cultural integrity and cultural practices help ensure that these cultural groups can persist and maintain their integrity. A policy directed at the protection of cultural practices is broader than religion; it also encompasses things like language, patterns of family life, patterns of work, patterns of recreation, and much more.

9.25   Culture is important, and cultural groups may face disadvantages similar to those faced by people with religious convictions. In a pluralistic society, minority cultures may be swamped or swallowed up by the cultural traditions of the majority and may sometimes be at risk of disappearing altogether. Some argue that this is the prerogative of the majority; if minority cultures dwindle because their members voluntarily choose not to perpetuate them, we should simply accept that as the consequence of liberty and voluntary choice. Still others argue that cultural *unity* is valuable and that members of minority cultures should abandon their traditions and cultural identities. On this view, members of cultural minorities should embrace full participation in the majority culture. Should we value and protect multicultural pluralism, or should we seek to eliminate it?

Justifications for multiculturalism

Since multiculturalism is broader than just the protection of religious 9.26
freedom, it has to appeal to something broader for its justification. There
are a quite a few different approaches. One is to emphasize the importance
of communities and to critique the individualistic emphasis of law in many
liberal democracies. This approach is *communitarian*. Sometimes we
imagine people standing back from all their commitments, such as religion,
and then choosing which ones to pick. In reality, many people feel more like
their religion picked them, not the other way round. Likewise, family is
extremely important for people, yet people do not choose their parents and
siblings, and in much of human history have not picked their spouses.
Things do not have to be autonomously chosen in order to be important to
a person's life. In fact it is the groups to which we belong (often involuntar-
ily) that help us figure out who we are. If we take social groups rather than
individuals as our starting point, then thinking of how to help and protect
those groups follows naturally.

Cultural communities provide a sense of belonging for their members and 9.27
are, perhaps, the context in which people learn the virtues that make it possible for us to live together in a society where people respect one another's rights.
Multiculturalists often criticize liberalism for its inability to provide certain
kinds of belonging and psychological security for its members. In this spirit,
Steven Macedo, a *defender* of liberal principles, writes that a liberal society

> would probably pay for [its] diversity, tolerance, and experimentation with a
> degree of superficiality, the consequence of a lack of depth or persistence in
> commitments. There might be a certain amount of feigned or affected eccen-
> tricity. And with all the self-critical, self-shaping introspection, perhaps also
> a degree of self-absorption or even narcissism…. Liberalism holds out the
> promise, or the threat, of making all the world like California. By encourag-
> ing tolerance or even sympathy for a wide array of lifestyles and eccentrici-
> ties, liberalism creates a community in which it is possible to decide that next
> week I might quit my career in banking, leave my wife and children, and join
> a Buddhist cult. (Macedo, 1990, p. 278)

Is it reasonable to think that, by protecting the integrity of varied cultural
communities within our pluralistic society, perhaps we can avoid such root-
less anomie?

A second approach is *liberal egalitarianism*. If we value autonomy, we 9.28
should want people to be able to pursue a course of life that they choose.

If we value equality, we should want people to have roughly equal ability to do so. It is unfair that members of minority groups have a much harder time preserving their culture, when culture is so central to a person's life and sense of identity.

9.29   A third approach is *historical*; it focuses on the history of injustices against particular minority groups and justifies multiculturalism as appropriate restitution. This view requires some criteria for how different cultural groups should treat each other in order to know when in the past groups have done wrong. It also requires an account of how past injustices should affect contemporary policies.

9.30   A fourth and final argument for multiculturalism focuses on the *value of pluralism*. Advocates of this position urge that pluralistic societies are better for their members, or better in other respects, than societies that are unified around a single cultural tradition. One of the most articulate defenders of pluralism is John Stuart Mill. In *On Liberty*, Mill argues that freedom is valuable because it enables people to experiment by pursuing different ways of living, whether they are traditional or innovative. In a similar mode, the more cultural pluralism a society contains, the more likely it is that people will find a way of life that suits them.

Which policies would multiculturalism recommend?

9.31 If cultural pluralism is valuable, and if, as multiculturalists propose, cultural minorities should be protected, what measures can appropriately be taken to protect them? Here are some examples of policies that might make it easier for minority cultures to survive and thrive:

1. The history curriculum in public schools could be adjusted so that children spend more time on the experiences and achievements of people from minority cultures.
2. Children could be required to learn more than one language in public schools.
3. Employers could be required to grant reasonable accommodations, so that employees may observe religious holidays and times of prayer.
4. Government publications, ballots, and websites could be made available in more than one language.
5. Traditional groups could be allowed to turn to their traditional practices and shape family law on questions such as divorce, inheritance, and child custody.

6. Traditional groups could be allowed complete discretion to develop and manage a legal system, including criminal punishment, that conforms to their cultural tradition.

Some of these proposals would be easy—and perhaps relatively uncontroversial—to implement. Others are quite radical. As in the case of religious liberty, the question is: where do we draw the line? Which measures aimed at the protection of cultural diversity are appropriate and just, and which ones would permit or support injustices? Some of the proposals might facilitate religious practice even though they are not specifically religious. For example, knowledge of Arabic is important to Islam, so efforts to facilitate the children's learning of Arabic may benefit minority Muslim communities. Religious traditions may in turn influence views on a wide variety of different cultural practices.

The least controversial forms of multiculturalism require only minimal 9.32 accommodations, which are designed to preserve the integrity of cultural communities. The more controversial forms would require radical restructuring of basic institutions. As in the case of religious liberties, the question is where to draw the line. At what point would it become inappropriate to provide special protections for cultural diversity on the grounds that such protections would put other central values at risk?

Criticisms of multiculturalism

Multicultural views are controversial. This chapter considers objections to 9.33 multiculturalism as it relates to religion.

One criticism asserts that cultural groups are and should be fluid, and 9.34 that they have vague boundaries. Most people are associated with multiple, overlapping cultural groups. In many ways people who work in international finance have a "culture" and may have more in common with people in other countries with similar jobs than with people in their own country who have the same language and religion. Globalization has rapidly accelerated the blurring of cultural identities. If measures designed to protect cultural groups are appropriate, which groups merit such protection?

This problem is complicated by the fact that people do not live in neat, 9.35 self-contained cultural areas. In Northern Ireland, Protestants have historically outnumbered Catholics. On the island of Ireland as a whole (including the North), Catholics outnumber Protestants. If Northern Ireland is part of Great Britain or independent, Catholics will be the minority. If it joins with

Ireland, Protestants will be the minority. No matter which system you pick, some religious group will be the minority. The powers given to protect members of one group may seem oppressive to others who live among them.

9.36   When we try to create special rights for groups, someone has to decide which groups "count" and are worthy of protection. In the case of religion, over time, new religions come into existence and some older religions cease to exist. At what point in history should Baptists, or Quakers, or Mormons have received group rights? All of them were new at one point. What criteria should be used to decide which groups get special rights? Once the rights are granted, it is often very difficult to change things as circumstances change. If policies intended to protect these groups make it more difficult for people to *leave* the groups, such policies may conflict with fundamental liberties.

9.37   This leads to a second objection: granting special rights to groups may put minorities within the minority at risk. Allowing minority communities to use traditional cultural norms to handle divorce, for example, might put women in these communities at risk. Laws that make it easier for a cultural group to survive might accomplish this by making it harder for people to leave the group, thereby diminishing their autonomy. Greater rights for groups may mean restricting individuals' right to freedom of association. When minority groups ask for exemptions so that they can live out their own culture, there are potential harms to other groups and to dissenting members of their own group.

9.38   Defenders of multiculturalism respond in a variety of ways. Liberal multiculturalists emphasize that there are core individual rights that the state must protect even if this interferes with minority culture and minority religion. Others emphasize ways to make the democratic process fairer, so that minority groups have more influence and voice. Can an appropriate multicultural theory respond to and incorporate the points of critics?

Freedom of religion, freedom of conscience, or freedom of culture?

9.39 We have reviewed three different ways of making the case for various forms of religious exemptions and accommodations. The first approach is the narrowest. It simply takes religious freedom to be valuable and worthy of special protection. The second approach takes a broader approach by focusing on freedom of conscience, so that any individual, whether religious or not, is entitled to similar levels of accommodation based on deeply held convictions. The third approach is broader still, protecting whole cultures.

The last two approaches have been more popular among philosophers over the past several decades because it seems unfair to many people to protect only deep convictions that are religious, or only those parts of a culture that are religious.

This raises a problem of consistency. Is it consistent to say: "When it 9.40 comes to demanding exemptions from the law, religious claims deserve no more weight than other claims. But when it comes to passing laws, those with religious justifications are suspect"? This was one of the key issues in the dialogue at the beginning of the chapter. Should religious and nonreligious claims for exemption be treated the same? Should religious and nonreligious arguments for public policies be treated the same? Can we consistently answer one question yes and the other no? In the next section we will explore this question by looking at arguments about the use of religious justifications.

Is Religion Suspect in Politics?

Most religions (perhaps all of them) have moral positions that relate to 9.41 politics. When, if ever, is war justifiable? Are fetuses and babies entitled to similar protections? Are the poor full members of society, or are they second- or third-class citizens, or even less? How should human beings treat animals? Should people work every day of the week? Should there be public holidays, feasts, or festivals that have religious purposes? Should politicians refer to their religious beliefs when speaking in public? What sorts of entertainment should be legal? What sorts of art should receive public subsidies?

Some people assume that religious reasons are also politically conserva- 9.42 tive, but this is not always so. While it is true that there are countries where secularism and left-wing political views are correlated, even in those countries many people justify liberal policies through appeal to religious reasons. Historically many reform movements, including slavery abolition and the civil rights movement, drew heavily on religious arguments.

Why might someone claim that religious arguments should not be used 9.43 to justify laws and public policies? Perhaps the concern is that policies motivated by religious reasons create conflict and strife. But many actual policies have religious motivations and are widely accepted. Getting rid of them would create far more conflict than keeping them. Let's consider a hypothetical example of religiously based justifications, to see whether there are better reasons for the claim that religious arguments should not be used in politics.

Four sample views on the environment

9.44 Consider the following four perspectives on policies for environmental protection:

> PETER thinks that the government should protect the environment because the book of Genesis states that human beings were put on earth with a job to do: caring for God's creation. When humans destroy the environment God created, they sin against God. They should instead care for creation, so that plants, animals, and humans can all flourish.

> QUINCY doesn't believe in God and doesn't think that nature is God's creation. But he also favors environmental protection, because be believes that, when we behold nature, we are filled with awe and wonder. One might even call it a kind of spiritual experience. To harm nature is to fail to show nature respect.

> ROSALINDA thinks that we should adopt whatever environmental policies will most benefit human beings. If the extinction of certain species threatens human goods, then we should try to stop species extinction. Species have been going extinct for millennia and the normal pattern is that each species looks out for itself. Human beings should do the same.

> SARAH is a utilitarian. She thinks that we should minimize the pain of both human beings and other sentient animals. She believes that plants have only instrumental value, since they cannot feel pleasure or pain. In her view, policies should promote the happiness of all sentient beings, but it is an open question whether trying to stop species extinction would actually improve overall levels of happiness.

Here we have four different views about the environment. Each of these people will vote for political candidates and laws on the basis of his or her views. Those laws will impact people who disagree with the rationale for the law. Suppose that the majority of voters agree with one of the four. Would it be wrong to pass a law justified by one or more of these views? Does it matter if one of the four is the majority view?

Reasons everyone can accept

Here is one common argument for why it would be a bad thing if a majority 9.45
of the citizens followed Peter and appealed to the Bible to support policies:
many people do not accept the Bible as an authority. If Peter's justification
for the law is "the Bible says so," then many citizens will feel that *other peo-*
ple's reasons and beliefs are being used to justify laws that apply to *them.*
When politicians speak from their religious beliefs, nonadherents are often
left with the sense that their representative is not speaking to them at all,
but only addressing her fellow believers. If politicians explain or justify
their views as based on their religious beliefs, they are offering reasons that
are not really reasons at all in the eyes of those who do not share those
beliefs. These people have not been given a reason that *justifies* the policy *to*
them. The underlying argument is that, for government action to be legitimate, the government must offer citizens justifications that all citizens can
reasonably accept.

So what can we reasonably expect people to accept? John Rawls argued 9.46
that, in modern societies characterized by freedom of speech and freedom
of religion, there is no one way of viewing the world that has anything like
unanimous support. This is the *fact of pluralism*: there are many different
religions and philosophies that citizens hold, and these conflict with one
another. According to Rawls, pluralism is the predictable result when
people are free to reason for themselves. Pluralism creates disagreement:
even if we limit ourselves to *reasonable* pluralism (by excluding the views of
those who are patently unreasonable), reasonable people will disagree about
fundamental matters of religion and philosophy. There are many different
reasons for this. The evidence we need for our judgments is complex. When
faced with conflicting values, it is hard to know how to weigh them against
each other. Rawls thinks we should all admit that there are many religious
and philosophical positions that are reasonable even if we believe that our
particular religion or philosophy is the right one.

Rawls also thinks that political power must be exercised such that those 9.47
subject to it can accept it under fair terms. In his view, we can reasonably
object if someone tries to force a policy on us that is justified by reasons we
don't share. If we had to choose rules on this matter without knowing
whether our religion would be in the majority or the minority, we would
want rules that protect the minority from religious imposition.

This creates a dilemma. It seems that there is no way to justify any policy. 9.48
Since there is a plurality of reasonable views, any attempt to justify a policy

by appeal to one of them will draw objections from the people who hold the others. If Peter has a majority, the other will object, but if Sarah has a majority, the others will still object. Rawls does not differentiate between the two cases. He thinks that people can reasonably reject Christianity or Judaism, and he also thinks people can reasonably reject utilitarianism or Kantianism.

Overlapping consensus

9.49 The solution Rawls proposed is that we take out all appeals to religion and basic philosophies for our most important political debates. In their place, we should look for an *overlapping consensus*. An overlapping consensus is one where there is a political principle that all of the reasonable viewpoints can endorse, even if they don't endorse it for the same reason. If we propose the principle "gratuitous cruelty to animals is wrong," all four people described in the sample above would endorse it. They would each have different reasons, which rest on each one's different point of view, but they would all accept it. Similarly, the principle "we should respect freedom of religion" might be accepted from all reasonable points of view, even though people would disagree about the justification they offer for the principle. Some would appeal to their religion, others to the value of autonomy, and still others to the greatest human happiness principle.

9.50 This solution is not without difficulties. What happens if we start trying to get more specific? Suppose there is a particular plant species at risk in a forest, but there is little evidence that the quality of human life will be affected by its absence. Peter and Quincy think we have important moral reasons to protect plant life for its own sake, but Rosalinda and Sarah do not. As the debate rages, they find themselves in a dilemma. If they appeal to their underlying religious and philosophical beliefs, the others will object that it is wrong to legislate on that basis, since not all reasonable people have the same religious and philosophical beliefs. But if they do not appeal to their religious and philosophical beliefs, how can they explain their views on the matter at hand?

Should religion and philosophy be treated the same?

9.51 In Rawls's view, appeals to Kant or Bentham can be just as suspicious as appeals to Jesus or Buddha. Since there is reasonable disagreement about philosophy as well as about religion, it is just as wrong to legislate on the basis of your particular philosophy as it is to legislate on the basis of your particular religion. Not everyone agrees with this. In the dialogue, Sophie thinks that religious arguments should be treated differently because they don't appeal to reason in the same way philosophy does. Let's look at the four arguments and see how this holds up.

Peter's argument is religious in the most common sense. He appeals to a 9.52 religious text as authoritative. Peter might argue, as some defenders of Christianity do, that there are rational arguments for believing in the Bible, the possibility of miracles, and so on. Some people are persuaded by these arguments, but some are not. What is clear is that many people reject the Bible as a proper source of political justifications.

Quincy's argument is less obviously religious, but one could argue that his 9.53 attitude toward "nature" is quasi-religious. Let's use "Nature" with a capital N to identify the people who think of nature in this way. Nature is not, for him, a value-neutral word for talking about the planet earth. Human economic development is interfering with Nature's plan, which is presumably the normal pattern of species extinction in the absence of significant human intervention. He thinks that humans are treating Nature with disrespect. Some environmentalists openly ascribe a spiritual significance to Nature, while others do so implicitly, and still others entirely reject this way of thinking. But some attitudes, like those of Quincy, amount to replacing "the Bible says so" with "Nature says so."

Rosalinda rejects any appeals to religion or to spiritual values, but her 9.54 position is still based on a controversial social Darwinism. In this context "Darwinism" does not refer to the belief in evolution as a scientific theory; rather "Darwinist" refers to those who turn a scientific theory into a moral and political philosophy. The statements "species compete with each other to survive" and "members of a species compete with other members of their species to survive" are attempts to describe how organisms act. The statements "a species is morally justified in harming other species for its own benefit" and "the strong members of a species are morally justified in taking resources from the weak members of the species" make moral and political claims that go beyond science.

Social Darwinism was a philosophical position that opposed the idea of 9.55 helping the weakest members of society, because its promoters believed that the species would improve if the strong were to survive and the weak were not. On this view, helping the weak interferes with nature's course. Like Quincy's, Rosalinda's worldview ascribes moral force to nature's plan. But Rosalinda and Quincy come to opposite conclusions about nature's plan.

This leaves us with Sarah's position, which is based on a widely known 9.56 philosophical theory: utilitarianism. Sarah's position rests on the claim that what matters from a moral point of view is pleasure and pain. Organisms that can feel pleasure and pain count, while those that cannot feel pleasure and pain do not count. Objections to utilitarianism are dealt with in Chapters 1–4 and animal rights are discussed in Chapter 8, so we will not rehearse here the various reasons someone might invoke to explain why it is reasonable to object to utilitarianism.

9.57   Should positions that appeal to a particular philosophy be treated differently from positions that appeal to a quasi-religious worldview? Should appeals to philosophy be treated differently from appeals to a specific religious tradition? Is the statement "pleasure and pain are the things that count morally" that different from the statement "all plant and animal species have intrinsic value" as an underlying philosophy?

9.58   One answer is that, even if there are controversial metaphysical claims in all four positions, we still show more respect for our fellow citizens when we minimize obvious appeals to fundamental religious doctrines that others reject. If Peter simply says "the Bible says so" in public debate, that shows disrespect for those who do not accept the Bible as an authority. On the other hand, if Peter argues for the same positions without being quite so explicit—say, if he simply claims that human beings have a duty to help plants and animals flourish, without saying where he derives his view from—then his view becomes more like those of Quincy and Rosalinda.

Arguing fairly

9.59 Some people view traditional world religions with suspicion. They regard arguments based on religious ideas as false or harmful or both. It is understandable that a person might prefer to minimize false or harmful beliefs in politics, but we normally don't create rules restricting the kinds of arguments people may introduce.

9.60   Historically, religious arguments have sometimes justified oppressive laws and policies. While it is true that religious arguments also helped abolitionism and the Civil Rights Act, there were other religious believers arguing against those same things. Some people think that, on balance, appeals to religious arguments are more likely than other arguments to lead to oppressive laws. It is easy to see why people who believe this would wish to restrict the use of religious reasons. But is this view fair? Nonreligious ideologies have been used to justify some of the most oppressive regimes the world has ever known.

It would be unfair to exclude religious arguments from the public square   9.61
because they are not accepted by everyone, unless other views that are not
accepted by everyone were also excluded. It is a virtue of John Rawls's view
that he recognizes this and treats contentious philosophical and religious
views in the same way. Rawls would ask that people justify public policies
on the basis of reasons that others can accept, but this is not a matter of
exclusion. It reflects an underlying view about what it is to justify policies *to
others*. When policies apply to everyone, we should endeavor to justify
them on the basis of reasons that are neither parochially religious nor parochially philosophical. We should work to justify them on the basis of shared
values that others can reasonably accept, even if they do not share the same
underlying religious or philosophical views.

Conclusion

It is common for people to make arguments for treating religion in a special   9.62
way. Sometimes the argument is that religious freedom entitles people to
exemptions from the standard laws, rules, and procedures or to other forms
of special accommodation. At other times religion is singled out as something
that needs to be kept out of politics, so that policies justified by religious reasons are illegitimate while policies justified by appeal to other values are not.
Is there a satisfying way to consistently answer both of these objections?

References and Further Reading

Audi, Robert. 2000. *Religious Commitment and Secular Reason*. Cambridge:
    Cambridge University Press. A powerful defense of the secular view, written
    by a philosopher with deep religious convictions.
Eberle, Chris and Terence Cueno. 2015 [2008]. "Religion and Political Theory." In
    Stanford Encyclopedia of Philosophy. http://plato.stanford.edu/entries/religion-
    politics (accessed February 12, 2016). An excellent overview of the arguments
    about whether religious arguments have a place in politics.
Eberle, Christopher. 2002. *Religious Conviction in Liberal Politics*. Cambridge:
    Cambridge University Press. Eberle defends the position that liberals should
    permit religious argumentation in politics.
Kukathas, Chandran. 1992. "Are There Any Cultural Rights?" *Political Theory*, 20:
    105–139. Kukathas is skeptical of claims that cultures have rights and thinks
    that the rights of individuals can provide sufficient protection for members of
    minority groups.

Kymlicka, Will. 1995 *Multicultural Citizenship*. Oxford: Oxford University Press. Kymlicka argues that we should accommodate religious groups on the basis of liberal principles.

Leiter, Brian. 2013. *Why Tolerate Religion?* Oxford: Oxford University Press. Leiter gives powerful and provocative arguments *against* making special exemptions for religious beliefs and practice.

Locke, John. 2014 [1689]. *A Letter Concerning Toleration*, translated by William Popple. http://www.constitution.org/jl/tolerati.htm (accessed February 12, 2016). Locke's letter is probably the most famous philosophical work on the subject of toleration and is interesting today both for what it tolerates and what it does not.

Macedo, Stephen. 1990. *Liberal Virtues*. Oxford: Oxford University Press. Macedo considers the qualities of character that make liberal society possible and the circumstances in which people acquire these virtues. He considers, in particular, whether political liberalism supports the virtues that it requires for survival, or whether liberal theories need to do more to accommodate the significance of culture.

Rawls, John. 1993. *Political Liberalism*. New York: Columbia University Press. Rawls developed his views about religion and politics in this book, but made adjustments and clarifications on the legitimate place of religion in the public square in later works. (See next entry.)

Rawls, John. 1997. "The Idea of Public Reason Revisited." *University of Chicago Law Review*, 64: 765–807. Clarifies Rawls's position in *Political Liberalism*.

Song, Sarah. 2010. "Multiculturalism." In *Stanford Encyclopedia of Philosophy*. http://plato.stanford.edu/entries/multiculturalism/#Com (accessed February 12, 2016). This article presents an overview of debates about religious accommodation as part of a larger debate about multiculturalism.

Online Resources

1   http://www.telegraph.co.uk/news/uknews/law-and-order/9975937/Inside-Britains-Sharia-courts.html

2   http://www.bbc.com/news/world-europe-21997089

3   http://caselaw.findlaw.com/us-supreme-court/348/385.html

4   http://caselaw.findlaw.com/us-supreme-court/494/872.html

5   http://caselaw.findlaw.com/us-supreme-court/406/205.html

6   http://caselaw.findlaw.com/us-supreme-court/508/520.html

7   http://caselaw.findlaw.com/us-supreme-court/13-354.html

8   http://www.leagle.com/decision/1FSupp941_11032.xml/NEWMAN%20v.%20PIGGIE%20PARK%20ENTERPRISES,%20INC.

9   http://documents.latimes.com/arlenes-flowers-judgment/
10   http://www.latimes.com/nation/nationnow/la-na-nn-florist-same-sex-
     wedding-20150218-story.html
11   https://www.oyez.org/cases/1961/468
12   http://undergod.procon.org/view.resource.php?resourceID=003656
13   http://www.kplu.org/post/idaho-prison-removes-tribal-sweat-lodge
14   http://www.huffingtonpost.com/2013/09/12/atheists-in-god-we-trust_n_
     3916762.html
15   http://www.constitution.org/jl/tolerati.htm
16   http://undergod.procon.org/view.resource.php?resourceID=003656

10

MONEY, LIES, AND POLITICAL CORRUPTION

SOPHIE I think I have thought of a way to really help our political system.

JUSTIN What is your idea?

SOPHIE We make it a criminal offense for politicians to lie about things related to their official duty. If a politician makes false promises to win an election, he should go to jail.

JUSTIN Lying isn't a crime.

SOPHIE Some lying is. If a person lies in court, it is perjury. I think a politician lying to win an election is even worse than a person lying in court. In both cases lying affects the public, but the outcome of an election impacts even more people.

JUSTIN I thought you were a proponent of free speech.

SOPHIE I am, but freedom does not include the freedom to harm others. Corporations can be sued for false advertising because their lie harms consumers. Politicians who lie are guilty of false advertising.

JUSTIN There is a difference between a civil suit and a criminal one. You are talking about throwing people in jail.

SOPHIE I worry that the big interest groups would just pay the fines for the politicians they support if the case is only a civil one; but allowing civil suits would be better than nothing. Suppose we agree that politicians who lie are only subject to paying damages. Would you agree with that?

This Is Political Philosophy: An Introduction, First Edition. Alex Tuckness and Clark Wolf.
© 2017 John Wiley & Sons, Inc. Published 2017 by John Wiley & Sons, Inc.

JUSTIN   No. There is no way for politicians to anticipate what they will have to do once in office. How do we tell the difference between new circumstances and a lie? Besides, a jury with a political vendetta might make life miserable for a candidate.

SOPHIE   We could screen out jurors with strong partisan leanings the same way we screen out people from regular juries who can't be objective about the facts.

JUSTIN   What is true and false in politics is too debatable. Sometimes politicians tell outright lies, but typically they are afraid of getting caught. Much of what they do is tell half-truths, things that are technically true but very misleading. Would you make those against the law too?

SOPHIE   No, in those cases I would say "let the voter beware," just as I would say "let the buyer beware" in the market place. If the statement isn't technically false, it is up to the voter to look at it carefully, to see if it is misleading or vague.

JUSTIN   What about after they are in office? Don't you think there are times when lying might actually be beneficial? Remember Cesare Borgia, who used deception to restore order in Florence—a tumultuous part of Renaissance Italy?

SOPHIE   I've done some reading since our earlier discussion. I think Borgia was out to promote Borgia, not order and peace.

JUSTIN   OK, let me give you a more current example. Suppose the economy is in a very precarious state and the press questions the chairman of the central bank about the health of the economy. If he tells the truth, that will create panic and an almost certain recession. If he tells a lie that boosts consumer confidence, the recession might be avoided. I think in that situation he should lie.

SOPHIE   But once we say that, we no longer have any reason to believe him when he says things are going well. Once we say that politicians and government leaders have permission to lie to us, we never know when to believe them.

JUSTIN   But they already live in a world where people lie. A politician who never lied would be at a huge disadvantage.

SOPHIE   That is why we need a change in the law. Everyone rationalizes lying because everyone else does it. It is like in countries where politicians routinely take bribes and they rationalize it by saying everyone does it. The only way to change things

is to enact a law that creates a new standard people have to
live up to. The law will provide an advantage for the politicians who don't lie.

JUSTIN   It won't work. The reason politicians lie is because we want
them to. We want them to promote our interests, whatever
it takes. We want the politicians we support to win, whatever it takes.

Lying Politicians

10.1 In most countries people associate politics with corruption. Sometimes this
is not fair: there are many people who work for the government yet are
honest and have integrity. But the people most often singled out for scorn are
not government bureaucrats; they are the politicians. There is a widespread
perception that, to make it in politics, you have to be at least a little corrupt
and that, consequently, corruption is rampant in politics. There is a great
variety of forms of corruption. One of the most common criticisms of politicians is that they are liars. In one **poll**, a majority of British voters agreed that
politicians lie "all the time and you can't believe a word they say."

10.2   In fact politicians may not be much different from the rest of the population in their capacity for dishonesty. Psychologist Jarold Jellison, in a book
entitled *I'm Sorry, I Didn't Mean to, and Other Lies We Love to Tell*, reports
a study where he recorded all the statements that 20 people made over a
24-hour period and found that the average person in his study told around
200 lies per day. How did he arrive at such high number? As the title of the
book indicates, he was counting things like saying "I'm sorry to bother you"
as a lie if you were not really sorry to bother the person but merely being
polite. But is it really a lie if you are having a bad day and still say "fine"
when someone asks you how you are doing?

What is a lie?

10.3 There are different ways of defining what a lie is. In a **story** by Jean-Paul
Sartre, a man named Pablo believes that Ramon is in his cousin's house, so
he tells men who want to kill Ramon that he is at the cemetery. He intends
to lie to them. It turns out that Ramon actually did go to the cemetery, and
his enemies find him there. The words Pablo spoke turned out to be true
even though he intended the opposite. Did Pablo lie?

Here we can get some help from Question 110 of Thomas Aquinas's 10.4 (2008 [1920]) *Summa theologica*. To paraphrase **his approach**, we can think about lying in terms of (1) speaking false words, (2) the intention to speak false words, (3) the intention to bring about deception, and (4) the ultimate goal of one's deception. In terms of speaking false words (1), Pablo did not lie. He says that Ramon is at the cemetery, and Ramon is at the cemetery. But in terms of the intention to speak false words (2), Pablo did lie. His lie just backfired when what he said accidentally turned out to be true. Aquinas thought that the second sense was more central to the definition of lying than the first. There was no way for Pablo to know that his intended lie would turn out to be the truth. Conversely (and more frequently in real life), a person may say something sincerely thinking it to be true, and then it may turn out to be untrue. We tend to call that a mistake rather than a lie. So far we have a good argument for defining a lie as speaking with the intention to say what is false (2).

The problem is that one can deliberately say something false but not 10.5 actually intend for anyone to be deceived (3). Consider jokes and sarcasm: **Aquinas thought that many jokes were technically lies, and therefore sins**. If you say: "Three men walked into a bar"—and tell a story that didn't actually happen, you are intentionally saying words that are false. You expect, however, that the person will know the convention and will understand that you are just telling a story or a joke. The words are false but no one is deceived, nor is there any intention to deceive. Similarly, when a person using sarcasm says something literally false but intends this to be recognized by others as sarcasm, there is no intent to deceive. It seems inappropriate to call these lies. Doesn't it?

It can work the other way as well. We can say things that are literally true 10.6 but intended to deceive. Politicians often do this. **When President Bill Clinton denied having "sexual relations" with Monica Lewinsky, he claimed that the denial was not a lie since—so he claimed—he did not consider receiving oral sex to fall under the definition of having sexual relations**. Of course, the way he had formulated the denial gave the impression that there was nothing of a sexual nature going on between them, which was clearly false. Politicians often want to mislead, but not to be branded as liars. They frequently look for ways to say things that are misleading but not literally false. This is a staple of political advertising. In the United States **fact-check organizations** note not only instances where politicians lie, but also cases where they say things that are literally true but also clearly misleading.

Why do people lie?

10.7　While the question "Why do people lie?" could call forth an answer like "evolution" or "original sin," our intention is to ask what purposes people have for lying (Aquinas's fourth aspect of lying). If a liar were to answer honestly the question "Why did you do that?"—what might she say? She might say that she wanted something and lying was the easiest way to get it, or that she wanted to avoid an unpleasant consequence. In other circumstances, though, she might claim that she did it because it was the right thing to do. Is this plausible? It depends on which ethical system you think is correct.

Utility

10.8　For a utilitarian, it is easy to explain why lying might be the right thing for a politician to do in some situations. If telling the truth may lead to a needless war that will cause millions of deaths, lying may well produce more happiness and less pain than telling the truth. **Many critics of America's use of drones believe that President Obama lied about the nature of the US policy**. A defender of the administration might claim that the deceptive policy was necessary for the protection of national security. Likewise, President Obama's promise regarding healthcare reform—the promise that, **"if you like your healthcare plan, you can keep your healthcare plan"**— **didn't actually turn out to be true**, but it helped get the law passed (Jackson, 2013). Perhaps Obama believed that his promise was true when he made it. If so, the fact that it turned out to be false doesn't make it deceptive. On the other hand, if Obama knew (or believed) that his promise was false when he said it, then he was deceptive when he made it. For utilitarians, whether Obama intended to deceive is not the important question. If the law is expected to be very beneficial and if Obama's statement was necessary for its implementation, then utilitarianism implies that the deception was worth it.

10.9　　Rule utilitarians will claim that a general practice of telling the truth may produce more utility than deciding whether to tell a lie on a case-by-case basis, since we may tend to rationalize lies by telling ourselves that they will benefit other people when mainly they are self-serving. Lying may help you get a bill passed, but it undermines people's overall trust in government. Even a rule utilitarian will formulate the rule in such a way that, when the consequences of telling the truth are bad enough, lying is the right thing to do.

Intentions

Others think that intentionally speaking what is false is wrong regardless of 10.10
the consequences. Aquinas, for example, thought that it was always wrong
to intentionally say what is false, but **he didn't think that all lies were**
equally wrong. Telling a lie to save a life is a much less serious wrong than
telling a lie to extricate yourself from a problem of your own making. Telling
a lie with the intention of harming someone is still worse. **Kant is the most**
famous advocate for the claim that lying is always wrong. He argued that
lying is wrong since it treats the other person as a mere means and deprives
others of the opportunity for autonomous rational choice. Even in cases
where a lie does no harm to another person, even in cases where a lie might
be necessary to save the lives of other people, a person acts against her own
rational nature by resorting to a lie.

Hugo Grotius and the rights approach

Hugo Grotius sketched a different approach in **Book 3, chapter 1 ("What** 10.11
Is Lawful in War," sections 11–19) of his book *The Law of War and Peace.*
He focused on the fact that normally a lie prevents the other person from
being able to make rational judgments. When we speak to one another, we
enter into a tacit agreement to speak truthfully, so that we can act as
rational agents. By putting the matter in terms of rights, Grotius came to
different conclusions. First, he concluded that, if I speak false words but
these words do not actually impair the judgment of anyone else, they are
not wrong. Grotius can thus account for why jokes and sarcasm are not in
themselves wrong. He would also say that false words to a baby are not
wrong, since the baby doesn't have the necessary rational capacities.
Grotius also rejects the idea that misleading true statements are OK while
simple lies are not. If we are undermining the other person's right to judgment, it doesn't matter how we do it.

Second, sometimes a person's right to the truth is overridden by an even 10.12
stronger right. Grotius thought that in politics the ruler's duty to protect life
often overrides the duty to tell the truth. A more contemporary statement
of this position is that of the philosopher **W. D. Ross**, who believes that all
people, politicians included, have an obligation to keep their promises—
and speaking involves a kind of tacit promise to be truthful—but that we
also have duties to protect others from harm and to do good to them.
Sometimes these latter duties override the duty to tell the truth.

10.13   Third, Grotius thought that, if I have a right to the truth, I can give up that right. When people sit down to play poker, they do so knowing that the other people at the table will try to be deceptive about the strength of their hands. No one is wronged, however, by a good bluff. Everyone in a sense gave permission to everyone else to be deceptive (within the rules of the game; playing with marked cards is a different story). Many contestants on reality TV shows have used this approach: they reason that deception and promise breaking are just "part of the game" and that everyone who went on the show consented to be there in full knowledge that this is how the game works. In politics, citizens might give their consent to a law that authorizes undercover police officers to lie while undercover. Similarly, citizens might consent to the practice of allowing public officials to lie in order to protect national security.

Virtue

10.14   In addition to the utility, intention, and rights-based approaches, there is a fourth one, based on the idea of virtue. Aristotle thought that it is a mark of excellence to be truthful, in particular that you should not pretend to be either more or less than what you really are. What should we think of the constant self-promotion and spin of politics? Aristotle might say that it is not primarily a problem that campaign commercials deprive people of their rights or cause harm, but instead that there is something shameful about the whole spectacle. A politician who cares more about winning than about being truthful is pandering. **Aristotle thought that a virtuous person would not try to appear better or worse than he really is.**

A license to lie?

10.15   A basic premise of James Bond movies is that certain spies are given permission to kill, a permission they only have because of the position that they hold. Some people hold that politicians have a license to lie, in at least some cases. One interpretation of Machiavelli suggests that he thought politics had a different morality from that of everyday life. In everyday life it is a virtue to be merciful, but **in politics mercy can encourage lawlessness and cause great harm**. In everyday life generosity is a virtue, but **in politics generosity is not a virtue**, because politicians are really being generous with other people's money! **With respect to honesty**, in everyday life it is a virtue but in politics keeping your word will bring great harm to many people, yourself included. Machiavelli advised rulers to try to have a reputation for honesty while being prepared to be dishonest when the situation makes it necessary.

A different explanation of the "license to lie" is utilitarian. In a court- 10.16 room, some countries encourage the attorneys on each side to "spin" the facts in the way that most benefits their side. This means that lawyers will frequently make statements that, while not literally false, are intended to be misleading. At the very least, a defense attorney may give the impression that she is convinced of her client's innocence when in fact she thinks he is guilty. We normally don't think of this as problematic, because we understand that these people are playing roles and doing what the role requires. But why have a role that encourages lawyers to be deceptive? If an assassin tried to justify his action by saying that he was simply trying to live up to the expectations of the job, we would find that an insufficient answer. A utilitarian would say that roles are justified when the net effect of each playing her part is better than the alternatives. If hearing two sides, neither of which is fair and objective, is the best way for the jury to get to the truth, that is all the justification that is needed. The assassin's role, by contrast, does not help society.

Not everyone is convinced by this account. For those who are not utili- 10.17 tarians and do not believe that the ends justify the means, granting public officials permission to do things that in other circumstances would be wrong is very problematic. If we have moral convictions about how we achieve our goals as well as about the goals themselves, then role morality risks compromising the former. Arthur Applbaum asks whether Henri Sanson, an executioner during the French Reign of Terror, can claim that he was just acting according to professional norms. Sanson was, as it turns out, very nonpartisan in his executions. Even as political power changed hands, he kept his job and carried out his orders. There is a utilitarian argument that having a public executioner decreases vigilante violence and that professional executioners kill more humanely, but is that enough to make it justified?

Sneaky ways to win an election

Suppose that a politician believes that the policies the other party would 10.18 enact will have disastrous results and that therefore some kind of deception and manipulation intended to win the election is justified. This might come in the form of an outright lie—say, making false charges against an opponent, making a campaign promise that the politician knows he will not even attempt to follow through later on, or overstating how much he will actually be able to accomplish.

10.19   He could also use true but deceptive comments about the opponent's or his own positions. Suppose a politician wants to win votes from two groups of people who agree on some issues but disagree on others. Group A favors a strict regulation of abortions that allows them only to save the life of the mother. Group B thinks that women should have the right to an abortion. When speaking to Group A, the politician says: "I believe that life begins at conception and that abortion is a terrible evil." When speaking to Group B, he says: "Although I personally think abortion is wrong, I don't think my own personal views should determine the question of whether abortion is legal."

10.20   Neither statement actually contradicts the other. In fact, neither statement actually commits the politician to a particular policy position. With respect to group A, one might believe that something is a terrible evil but also believe that respect for individual rights means we must tolerate that evil. Defenders of the freedom of speech will often defend uses of that freedom that promote evil. Similarly, the politician might explain to Group B after the election that he is not voting to restrict abortion because of his own personal views but because that is what a majority of his constituents think. The statements in the above paragraph give the impression that the politician will vote the way the voter wants without actually committing him to anything.

10.21   A third strategy is distraction and obfuscation. A politician who is about to be on the receiving end of a lot of negative publicity might launch commercials on a topic of minor importance with the specific purpose of distracting attention. Allegations about the private lives of candidates are sometimes used to distract voters from other issues. At other times a politician may use technical language or euphemisms in hopes of confusing voters.

10.22   George Orwell wrote a famous essay, "**Politics and the English Language**," where he described how vague and confusing words are rampant in political speech:

> The word Fascism has now no meaning except in so far as it signifies "something not desirable." The words democracy, socialism, freedom, patriotic, realistic, justice, have each of them several different meanings which cannot be reconciled with one another. In the case of a word like democracy, not only is there no agreed definition, but the attempt to make

one is resisted from all sides. It is almost universally felt that when we call a country democratic we are praising it: consequently the defenders of every kind of regime claim that it is a democracy, and fear that they might have to stop using the word if it were tied down to any one meaning. Words of this kind are often used in a consciously dishonest way. That is, the person who uses them has his own private definition, but allows his hearer to think he means something quite different. (Orwell, 2002 [1946])

While this is not lying according to strict definitions, Orwell thinks it is "consciously dishonest."

When is lying justified?

Under what conditions is a politician justified in lying to win an election? There are several possible answers. The first is an appeal to consequences. If the good you can do in office outweighs the harm of the lie, a utilitarian would claim that lying is justified. The reason why politicians lie and deceive, they might argue, is that it works. It is naïve to think that politicians who scrupulously tell the truth will win elections in the long run. If we insist on such a standard, all the honest people will be out of politics, because they will all lose. 10.23

A second approach is more rights-based. Some rights are alienable, others are not. While Kant thought that telling a lie was always wrong, an alternative view is that lying is permissible in response to your opponent's having lied first. Imagine that you are playing a game with someone and the other person keeps cheating. There is no way for you to stop her from cheating, but you can start cheating yourself. We might think that the opponent, by lying, gives you a right to lie. Lying in a campaign where the other side lies is analogous to using violence in self-defense. While both lying and violence are presumptively wrong, it is not wrong to protect yourself by retaliating. 10.24

Both justifications have their problems. Politicians presumably think that their policies are better than their opponents', so both sides will always think that getting themselves elected will benefit the people and that they are justified in lying. Consider an analogy with war: in a typical war both sides think they have justice on their side. For this reason we require prisoners of war to be treated well by both sides, since we don't think in practice the just side and the unjust side can reliably identify themselves. Similarly, we might require both sides to tell the truth, since otherwise both sides will lie. 10.25

10.26   The self-defense justification is also problematic. The biggest problem is that in self-defense you are normally intending to harm the very person who is attacking you. The attacker has given up some of his rights by choosing to attack. In politics, however, politicians are not primarily speaking to each other. They are speaking to voters. Even if the other politician has lied, does that mean that the first politician is entitled to lie to the voters? Even if the other politician has given up her right to the truth, have the voters? The first politician might claim that voters consent to the current system with its practice of lying and manipulation. Do all of them? Critics will think that this sort of logic just perpetuates the cycle of dishonesty and cynicism about politics.

Dirty hands

10.27 People sometimes say of politics that those who want to get involved have to be willing to get their **hands dirty**. They need to be willing to be deceptive, to break promises, to take money from unsavory characters, and so on. In earlier chapters we have already encountered other versions of this same problem. Suppose the only way to avert a terrible disaster involves violating the rights of some citizens. What if protecting your own citizens means harming citizens of other countries? Is it true that politicians have to get their hands dirty?

10.28   Not everyone agrees. Utilitarians might well deny it. They would say that our mistake is in thinking that, just because a person violates a rule of common morality, such a person is guilty of wrongdoing. For the utilitarian, maximizing human happiness is the ultimate moral standard. If a politician lies and the net result is an increase in human happiness (because the lie saved many lives), then the politician has not done anything wrong. There is no guilt.

10.29   But won't politicians who think this way help themselves to the "right to act unethically" too often? Won't they rationalize lies and other forms of immoral behavior, being driven by a desire to pursue their own interests, not those of the common good? Here a rule utilitarian will note that we can adopt rules that put fairly strict limitations on when lying is permissible; such rules would balance the worries about misuse with the need to authorize lying in some cases. For example, we might require that the politician reasonably think that there is clear and convincing evidence that lying is the only way to avoid a substantial harm to the community. When a politician's lie is found out, we would evaluate the politician not on the actual outcome of the lie but on whether, on the basis of the information available at the time, the politician reasonably believed that there was clear and convincing evidence that the lie was necessary to avert a substantial harm.

Kantians would object to the "dirty hands" characterization from the other direction. They would say that it is always wrong to get your hands dirty and that, if staying clean means losing an election, it is better to lose the election. Right and wrong are not about consequences. Instead of affirming a right to do wrong, the Kantian simply states that what's wrong is always wrong. Period. **10.30**

Against these two positions is a third. It claims that in "dirty hands" situations we confront a moral paradox. For the politician, the thing that must be done is something morally wrong. No matter what the politician does, there will be guilt. If the only way to save lives is to lie, the politician will either be guilty of lying or guilty of allowing people to die. **10.31**

If we accept the idea of dirty hands, is it only the politicians whose hands are dirty? If we elect people into office knowing that their jobs will require them to act in ways that are morally wrong in order to benefit us, don't we share in the guilt as well? If a mob boss hires an assassin, doesn't the mob boss share in the guilt of what the assassin does? If we put people in office expecting them do evil on our behalf, are we innocent? **10.32**

Bribery and Corruption

Money is a powerful force in politics. It takes money to run a successful campaign. The 2012 elections in the United States cost more than $6 billion, and nearly $1 billion went to President Obama's successful reelection bid alone. Even in countries that utilize a more public financing of campaigns, money is still a powerful influence. These countries still typically allow for individual contributions that the rich and the middle class are better positioned to make than the poor. Does the power of money in politics mean that politics is corrupt? If a politician accepts a bribe, we normally label that corruption, but is a campaign contribution really that different from a bribe? In both cases people give money to a politician in order to influence governmental action. **The US Senate has rules in place to specify what sorts of gifts senators may receive.** **10.33**

A typical bribe is a case where someone secretly gives a public official something of value in return for that official's using her power in a way that benefits the person who gave her the bribe. A person might secretly give the **10.34** mayor $50,000 in return for the mayor's pledge to award a lucrative city contract to the briber's company. A first ethical problem is one of fairness. The bribe will skew the judgment in such a way that the most deserving company does not get the contract. Let's call this a problem of *unfair outcomes.*

Now suppose a person comes to a judge and offers him $50,000, asking him to rule in her favor in a case. The judge, already familiar with the case, had been planning to decide the case in favor of the briber anyway. The judge thus decides that the money would not change his decision and that accepting it is ethically permissible. Assuming the briber would (and should) have won anyway, the bribe doesn't change how political power is used. This is not a case of unfair treatment, but something is still wrong. Why?

There is more than one way to explain what is wrong here. First, we have a politician using a public office as a means to private gain. If a public official uses government funds for family vacations, she is also using the powers of public office for private benefit. Let's call this type of corruption *misuse of office.* In the case of the judge, even if it doesn't change the judge's decision, it is still wrong to use a public office for private gain.

10.35   When South Carolina Governor Mark Sanford left the country in order to have an affair with a woman in Argentina, most of the headlines were about the lie used to cover up his absence: "hiking the Appalachian Trail." **Less well known is the charge that he used government planes to go for a haircut and rode first class when state law required him to take the least expensive ticket**. One could say that in doing so he was misusing the powers of his office.

10.36   Second, the other side might claim that, even if the outcome didn't change, the process did. While it is true that in theory a politician could accept bribes without being influenced by them, we might still object to such a process. Let's call this *unfair process.* Critics of the US Supreme Court's decision in the **Citizens United v. Federal Election Commission** (558 US 310 [2010]) say that it made it even it even easier for the very wealthy to have a disproportionate impact on elections. The decision held that corporations had a right to free speech and that restrictions on their political advocacy violated that right. We will return to the issue of campaign finance later in the chapter.

10.37   Third, even if it is true that accepting the bribe didn't change the judge's decision, this acceptance still gives the appearance of impropriety. There is no way for the rest of us to know for sure what the judge would have done. Let's call this problem *appearance of impropriety*.

A real-world case of violating the appearance of impropriety standard is that of the **Keating Five**. There were five senators who jointly pressured regulators to help Charles Keating, a savings and loan owner who was himself under pressure from federal regulators. All of them received from Keating campaign contributions (or related contributions made to political action committees associated with them). Senator Alan Cranston received the harshest verdict, a "reprimand," after repeatedly calling the bank regulator on Keating's behalf. Many of these calls came shortly after large donations from Keating. Although there were lots of pieces of circumstantial evidence, the Senate Ethics Committee admitted: "No evidence was presented to the Committee that Senator Cranston ever agreed to help Mr. Keating in return for a contribution." Even though there was no smoking gun, the close connection created a very strong appearance of impropriety. Two of the other senators received a lesser condemnation and were specifically accused of conduct that "gave the appearance of being improper." The last two were less involved, but still criticized for poor judgment. One of them, John McCain, said: **"The appearance of it was wrong. It's a wrong appearance when a group of senators appear in a meeting with a group of regulators, because it conveys the impression of undue and improper influence. And it was the wrong thing to do"** (Nowicki and Muller, 2007).

The appearance of impropriety consideration is important and complex. It is important because it is often difficult to prove that a bribe has taken place. When **Rod Blagojevich** said, of a US Senate seat he had the power to appoint, "it's a [expletive] valuable thing, you just don't give it away for nothing" (Davey, 2011), what was most unusual was how upfront he was. More commonly, politicians either make sure that their statements are not recorded or choose their words more carefully, so that there is more vagueness. It is much more likely that we know two facts: (1) Smith gave $20,000 to Jones; and (2) Jones made a decision that benefited Smith. What we lack is any direct proof that the $20,000 was the reason for the decision. Since most corruption is very difficult to prove, laws often require politicians to avoid actions that give the appearance of impropriety, which is much easier to enforce. The request also acknowledges that the mere appearance of impropriety is enough to cause damage to people's confidence in the democratic process. **This is important when levels of trust in government are already low.**

Is Blagojevich that different?

10.40 When a politician is charged with corrupt behavior, the most common response (other than outright denial) is probably "everyone does it." Blagojevich was charged with considering a variety of different "offers" in exchange for appointment to the vacant US Senate seat. Some of them involved his own appointment to a cabinet position or ambassadorship. Others involved granting him or his wife lucrative positions on corporate or union boards. Is there a difference between the two types of requests? The first sort of gain is political (holding an office) while the second is private (money for his family).

10.41 This distinction is important, because bargaining for political gain is very common in politics. Suppose that Hillary Clinton had promised not to contest Barack Obama's nomination at the Democratic Party National Convention in return for an appointment as secretary of state if he won the election. She would also be trading a political decision for a future office. When politicians are deciding whom to endorse in a presidential race in the United States, it is not uncommon for them to do so with the implicit or explicit understanding that an early endorsement will lead to a future presidential appointment. In legislatures, vote trading between individuals and parties is routine. How do we identify corruption?

Individual versus institutional corruption

10.42 Dennis Thompson has argued that our focus on cases like bribery keeps us from seeing other forms of corruption, that may be even more important. Often when we think of corruption we think of individuals breaking some law, say, by taking a bribe. We assume that lawful conduct is also ethical conduct. If we then ask what the laws are supposed to prevent, that thing tends to be some combination of the wrongs we discussed earlier: rules designed to reduce unfair outcomes, perceptions of unfair procedure, and the use of public office for private gain. This paradigm, which identifies corruption with the choices of individual people, is what Thompson calls *individual corruption.*

10.43 There is another form of corruption, which he calls *institutional corruption.* Here the rules and practices in place permit and encourage behavior contrary to the purposes of the institution. If a politician is in the habit of enacting policies that favor those who contribute lavishly to his campaign, this may not fall under the definition of bribery and may not mean that he is corrupt as an individual, but we might say that the system as a whole is corrupt. The excessive influence of money distorts decision making and encourages politicians to spend an inordinate amount of time raising funds rather than attending to their actual duties.

Campaign finance

One of the most important and controversial ethical issues in politics is 10.44 campaign finance reform. Here we see converging many of the philosophical ideas we have studied in this book: happiness, freedom, equality, justice, and democracy. The rules of campaign finance vary widely from country to country. Although the stories of how these rules emerged are complex and contain plenty of political maneuvering and bargaining, the defenders of all of these systems offer philosophical arguments on their behalf.

In the United States it is possible for individuals, unions, corporations, 10.45 interest groups, and political action committees to give money directly to candidates, elected officials, and political parties. The campaign finance rules that exist are often easily circumvented by running ads that fall short of specifically mentioning the candidate by name or ads that are run by groups sympathetic to the campaign rather than by the campaign itself. In other words, even if there are limits on how much the Smith campaign can take from various sources, other groups can spend money to help Smith or to hurt her opponents, and this sort of expenditure is difficult to regulate. The United States does have some public funding available, but in the 2012 elections both candidates turned it down because it came with restrictions and they could raise even more on their own without the restrictions.

The best defense of the US system of campaign finance is one that 10.46 emphasizes individual liberty. If we begin from the assumption that political speech deserves protection and add to that an assumption that it is permissible to use one's wealth for political purposes, then campaign restrictions are a restriction on both freedom of speech and property rights. There is also a common good argument insofar as defenders of this system worry that giving the government control over election spending could have disastrous results if the government is corrupt.

The Canadian election system, by contrast, relies heavily on public fund- 10.47 ing and places a much higher value on equality. In the past, each political party that met a certain minimum threshold received a subsidy that was based on the number of votes it receives. This **subsidy ended in 2015**. There are still subsidies for individual donations. If you make a political contribution of $400, you get a 75 percent rebate. After that the percentage of rebate starts to drop. If you make $1,275 in contributions in one calendar year, you would get $650 back and after that would not be eligible for any more subsidies. Lastly, political parties can get 50 percent of their election expenses reimbursed as long as they get at least 2 percent of the vote (see https://en.wikipedia.org/wiki/Federal_political_financing_in_Canada).

10.48   The logic behind the Canadian system is that public funding should increase the equality of influence that people can have on elections. The per vote subsidy was the most egalitarian element, since, regardless of income, each voter can direct resources to her preferred party just by voting for it. The other forms involve subsidies where you have to have money first in order to get more. Still, these subsidies increase the impact of people who make smaller contributions, increasing equity by comparison to a system where anything goes.

Ethics and institutions

10.49 Governments sometimes commit terrible atrocities. How does one allocate responsibility for something like the enormous atrocities committed in Rwanda, where nearly 1 million people were killed over the course of a few months, many by being hacked to death with machetes? No individual can carry out something like that—it takes a group of people working together. Part of what makes governments valuable is their ability to coordinate the actions of many people so that they can accomplish more. When governments use that power for evil, it raises complicated ethical issues.

10.50   One of the things that make political ethics challenging is the problem of responsibility. In cases of individual misconduct, like bribery or misuse of office, we normally hold the particular person responsible. In politics, questions of responsibility are hard because of the nature of institutions. First, there is the problem of authority. If we turn from elected officials to those who work for the government more generally, the latter can often try to justify their actions by explaining that they were just following the rules or the orders of their superiors. Second, when governments act wrongly, how do we allocate responsibility for their actions?

Just following orders

10.51 Most people's immediate reaction to stories of human rights atrocities is that those responsible should be punished. Now consider the following scenario: an 18-year-old is forced to join the army or go to prison. He agrees to join the army. He is assigned to a unit where his commander orders him to commit human rights violations. If he refuses to do so, he faces severe punishment. As everyone else around him begins to fire on an unarmed village, he joins in. How should we think about his level of responsibility in a case like this?

One issue is coercion. Those in positions of power and authority can 10.52 threaten their subordinates with punishment if they fail to comply. Most people would agree that, to the extent that a person is pressured into doing something wrong, he becomes less blameworthy than if he had not been pressured. Being pressured may not completely exonerate him, but surely we would agree that the person in our story is less blameworthy than someone who volunteered and sought out opportunities to do those same things. The degree of pressure matters here. The threat of death is very different from the threat that someone else will get the promotion.

The second issue is related to the concepts of obligation to obey the law. 10.53 A public official may have a moral obligation to comply with the law even if that law is unjust. In Chapter 6 we used the idea of a *prima facie* obligation to capture the idea that, while the obligation to obey the law may be real, it is not absolute. In cases of grave atrocities the *prima facie* obligation is overridden by other considerations. There are, however, many other kinds of ethical dilemmas that public officials face where it is more ambiguous whether the action is sufficiently wrong to override the normal obligation the official has to obey they law.

Who is responsible?

In the 1960s a boxer named Davey Moore was killed in the ring. Bob Dillon 10.54 wrote a song "Who Killed Davey Moore?" that nicely captures the problem of collective responsibility. Davey Moore was killed in the ring, but everyone had an explanation for why he was not at fault. The referee was under pressure from the fans not to stop the fight. The fans say they were there just to enjoy some boxing; they didn't kill anyone. The manager said he thought Davey was in good health. The gambler says his money was on Davey to win. The boxer whose blows caused Davey's death says he was simply doing his job. Yet Davey is dead. Who is responsible?

Something similar can happen in political systems. In Nazi Germany 10.55 there were accountants who meticulously transferred the funds between different governmental agencies to fund the transport of Jews to death camps. How much of the blame do the accountants have? What about the people who provided the soldiers at the death camp with food and drink?

10.56   There are several possibilities of thinking philosophically about how to allocate responsibility. One is to say that, unless my actions are *sufficient* to bring about the effect, I am not responsible. There are not many situations in politics where the actions of one person are alone sufficient to make something happen. A different answer is that I am responsible if my actions are *necessary* to bring about the effect. This standard would restrict responsibility to a very small number of people whose decisions or actions were actually necessary for bringing about a certain effect. In many cases, however, we think about responsibility differently. Suppose that a gang of five men kills a sixth man. None of the five could have killed the sixth man alone, but any three of them could have accomplished it. No one person was either necessary or sufficient to bring about the murder. Does that mean that none of them is responsible? We could instead say that all five are *equally responsible*, but what does that mean? If each person contributed equally to the murder, should each of the five receive 20 percent of a life sentence? Normally we would say that each person who willingly contributed to the outcome is culpable for the whole outcome and each person would face a full murder charge. This standard would lead to a much wider number of people being held responsible if we used it to evaluate governmental action.

Compromise

10.57   Issues of collective responsibility are also at work when there is a need for compromise. Sometimes a difficult compromise requires each side to enact a policy that it thinks is (at least in part) morally wrong. If a pro-environment politician votes for a policy that will authorize greater pollution in rivers but will also decrease CO_2 emissions, does the politician bear responsibility for the parts of the policy that he agreed to despite his opposition? He agreed to it, presumably, because he thought that the benefits of the policy as a whole were greater than those of other available alternatives. Yet if he visits a river that is dying from pollution and thinks that his legislation contributed to the pollution, should he feel responsible? Or could he rightly say that the people who forced him to accept that compromise are responsible?

Conclusion

10.58   What unites all of these different ethical questions is the following basic dilemma. Public officials are put in a position where they are expected to act for the welfare of others and where their decisions have potentially massive consequences. They are frequently in a competitive environment where other people are willing to lie, accept bribes, or take money to further their cause. In everyday life, we normally think that deceiving people and manipulating people is wrong. The influence of money does cast a shadow on the legitimacy of democratic government. What, then, is the role of a public official? Does the role that a politician occupies make it permissible to act in ways that in other contexts would seem corrupt? Or should we say that there are binding moral rules about honesty and equity and that two wrongs don't make a right?

This is what makes cases like Cesare Borgia's complex. We normally think 10.59 of mercy, generosity, and honesty as praiseworthy qualities and we recoil at the idea of someone who seems quick to engage in cruelty and deception. Yet at the same time the circumstances of politics create a unique environment. A character in Shakespeare's *Measure for Measure* argues that a ruler is most cruel when he is most lenient, since leniency will only increase crime. Machiavelli pointed out that we think differently about generosity in a prince because political leaders are typically generous with other people's money. This leads us to explore how to apply wisely the moral principles we hold in everyday life to this very different context, or to formulate a new set of moral principles destined to guide political behavior.

References and Further Reading

Applbaum, Arthur. 1995. "Professional Detachment: The Executioner of Paris." *Harvard Law Review*, 109(2): 458–486. A very readable exploration of the impact roles have on what is morally permissible.

Applbaum, Arthur. 2000. *Ethics for Adversaries: The Morality of Roles in Public and Professional Life*. Princeton, NJ: Princeton University Press. Applebaum provocatively explores the legitimacy of role morality. He opens with a chapter that compares lawyers to public executioners, to ask whether the role justifies the action.

Aquinas, Thomas. 2008 [1920]. *Summa theologica*, 2nd edn., edited by Kevin Knight, translated by Fathers of the English Dominican Province. New Advent. http://www.newadvent.org/summa/index.html (accessed February 12, 2016). Aquinas's greatest work contains an interesting account of the ethics of lying and influenced later theorists in terms of what makes something a lie and whether lying is ever permissible.

Bok, Sissela. 1999. *Lying: Moral Choice in Public and Private Life*. New York: Vintage. As the title would suggest, Bok's book examines the moral status of public and private lies.

Davey, Monica. 2011. "Blagojevich Sentenced to 14 Years in Prison." *New York Times*, December 7. http://www.nytimes.com/2011/12/08/us/blagojevich-expresses-remorse-in-courtroom-speech.html (accessed February 12, 2016). This article from the *New York Times* describes Illinois Governor Rod Blagojevich's conviction and sentence. Blagojevich is sometimes regarded as a person whose actions present a clear case of public misconduct by an elected official.

Dobel, Patrick. 2001. *Public Integrity*. Baltimore, MD: Johns Hopkins University Press. Dobel explores ethical issues related to public officials and deals extensively with ethics for unelected holders of public office.

Grotius, Hugo. 2016 [1901]. *The Law of War and Peace*, translated by A. C. Campbell, with introduction by David J. Hill. New York: M. Walter Dunne. Online Library of Liberty. http://oll.libertyfund.org/titles/553 (accessed February 12, 2016). Grotius formulated a rights-based approach to the question of permissible deception in the context of a larger work about ethics in war.

Jackson, Brooks. 2013. "Reality Confronts Obama's False Promise." FactCheck.org, October 29. http://www.factcheck.org/2013/10/reality-confronts-obamas-false-promise (accessed February 12, 2016). A discussion of whether President Obama lied when he promised that people could keep their existing insurance after the Affordable Care Act went into effect.

Nowicki, Dan and Bill Muller. 2007. "McCain Profile: The Keating Five." AzCentral.com, March 1. http://www.azcentral.com/news/election/mccain/articles/2007/03/01/20070301mccainbio-chapter7.html (accessed February 12, 2016). The Keating Five case raises questions about when it is legitimate for elected officials to use their influence on behalf of campaign contributors.

Orwell, George. 2002 [1946]. "Politics and the English Language." http://gutenberg.net.au/ebooks02/0200151.txt (accessed February 12, 2016). Orwell argues that the sloppiness and vagueness of political language is intentional. According to Orwell, politicians use sloppy vague language to confuse and mislead other people and to conceal their own motives.

Thompson, Dennis. 1987. *Political Ethics and Public Office*. Cambridge, MA: Harvard University Press. Thompson explores a variety of issues related to dirty hands, the nature of corruption and political responsibility in an accessible way.

Thompson, Dennis. 2002. *Just Elections: Creating a Fair Electoral Process in the United States*. Chicago, IL: University of Chicago Press. An accessible examination of ethical issues related to how we hold elections.

Walzer, Michael. 1973. "Political Action: The Problem of Dirty Hands." *Philosophy and Public Affairs*, 2: 160–180. Walzer's article is one of the most famous accounts of the problem of dirty hands. He argues that politicians face a moral paradox where they would be morally wrong if they failed to perform acts that nonetheless leave them morally blameworthy.

Online Resources

1   http://www.independent.co.uk/news/uk/politics/politicians-lie-all-the-time-says-poll-7536473.html

2   http://faculty.risd.edu/dkeefer/pod/wall.pdf

3   http://www.newadvent.org/summa/3110.htm

4   http://www.newadvent.org/summa/3110.htm#article2

5   https://en.wikipedia.org/wiki/Lewinsky_scandal

6   http://www.factcheck.org/

7   http://www.theguardian.com/commentisfree/2013/apr/11/three-lessons-obama-|drone-lies

8   http://www.factcheck.org/2013/10/reality-confronts-obamas-false-promise/

9   http://www.newadvent.org/summa/3110.htm#article4

10 http://www.mesacc.edu/~davpy35701/text/kant-sup-right-to-lie.pdf

11 http://www.constitution.org/gro/djbp_301.htm

12 http://plato.stanford.edu/entries/william-david-ross/

13 http://oll.libertyfund.org/titles/903/70700

14 http://www.constitution.org/mac/prince17.htm

15 http://www.constitution.org/mac/prince16.htm

16 http://www.constitution.org/mac/prince18.htm

17 http://gutenberg.net.au/ebooks02/0200151.txt

18 http://plato.stanford.edu/entries/dirty-hands/

19 http://www.ethics.senate.gov/public/index.cfm/gifts

20 http://www.economist.com/node/14367217

21 http://www.nytimes.com/2010/01/22/us/politics/22scotus.html?pagewanted=all&_r=1

22 https://en.wikipedia.org/wiki/Keating_Five

23 http://www.azcentral.com/news/election/mccain/articles/2007/03/01/200703 01mccainbio-chapter7.html

24 http://www.nytimes.com/2011/12/08/us/blagojevich-expresses-remorse-in-courtroom-speech.html?_r=0

25 http://www.gallup.com/poll/164393/fewer-americans-ever-trust-gov-handle-problems.aspx

26 http://www.macleans.ca/politics/federal-parties-in-year-end-fundraising-frenzy-as-per-vote-subsidy-nears-end/

27 https://en.wikipedia.org/wiki/Federal_political_financing_in_Canada

INDEX

abortion xi, 187–8, 197, 198, 200–1, 244
absolute (categorical) obligations, definition 139–40, 253
absolute monarchies 39–40, 107, 120
Adams, Douglas 197
Adams, John 108–9
addictions, freedom 35–7, 219, 220–1
affirmative action policies xiii, 55, 65, 75–8
  definition 76–7
  Regents of the University of California v. Bakke (1978) 76–7
African National Congress (ANC) 157–62
age factors, wealth inequalities 70–1
Al-Qaida 172
'all men are created equal' 55–6, 60, 137
Americans with Disabilities Act 66
anarchists 87–8, 134, 137–8, 145, 149
Anarchy, State, and Utopia (Nozick) 14–15
animal rights xi, 185–98, 207–8, 212–13, 230–2
  see also moral standing
animal sacrifices, religion 215, 216–17, 219–20
anthropomorphism 188–9

apartheid, South Africa 157–62
Applbaum, Arthur 243
Aquinas, Thomas 239–41
Ariely, Dan 69–71
aristocracies 107
Aristotle 16–17, 61–2, 242
atrocities, governments 75, 165, 252–5
authority xi, 1–101, 165–8
  see also law
  freedom 34–5, 41–2
autonomy 18, 63, 87–91, 114–15, 119–20, 137–8, 148–9, 202, 213, 221–2, 223–4
  see also libertarianism

balancing tests, religion 217–18, 220–1
baseline setting, equality 61–2, 76–7
Benn, Stanley 199
Bentham, Jeremy 7, 8–10, 15, 17, 22, 24, 25, 176–8, 194, 230–1
Berlin, Isaiah 41
bias 68–9, 75–6, 77–8, 84–5, 189
  see also discrimination
the Bible 135, 228–9, 231–2
  see also religion
biotic communities 207
  see also environmental ethics

This Is Political Philosophy: An Introduction, First Edition. Alex Tuckness and Clark Wolf.
© 2017 John Wiley & Sons, Inc. Published 2017 by John Wiley & Sons, Inc.

birth control 211, 215
Blagojevich, Rod 249–50
Borgia, Cesare 3–4, 237, 255
Brave New World (Huxley) 4–5, 24
breaking the law 120–1, 132–47, 153,
    157–64, 210–11, 216
  see also law
  civil disobedience 134, 135–6,
      139–41, 143–6, 157–8, 162–4,
      210–11, 216
  concepts 135–7, 140–7, 153, 157–64
  Henry David Thoreau 140–1
  'how to' guide 140–7
  ideal/nonideal agents and
      principles 144–7
  Mahatma Gandhi 134, 144–5, 163–4
  Malcolm X 142
  methods 136–7, 140–7, 159–64
  motives 135–6, 139–47, 161–2
  Nelson Mandela 158–62, 164
  principles 135–6, 144–7
  proportionality requirements
      143–4, 146–7, 153
  reasons 135–6, 145–7, 161–2
  reciprocity considerations 143–4,
      147, 153
  revolutions 120–1, 134, 136–7,
      142–3, 144, 146–7, 159,
      161–2, 179
  strength of obligations 139–40, 144
  unjust laws 135–8, 139–47, 152–3,
      157–9
  violence 134, 141–3, 146–7, 148
bribery 237–8, 247–55
  see also corruption
  definitions 247–9
The Brothers Karamazov
    (Dostoyevsky) 14
Buckley v. Valeo (1974) 128
Burke, Edmund 122
Burwell v. Hobby Lobby (2014) 215
Bush, George W. 168, 171

campaign finance 248, 251–2
Canada 107, 251–2
capabilities, personhood characteristics
    196–7, 201–4
capabilities approach 18–22, 27–8, 60
  see also equality; utilitarianism
  Amartya Sen 18–19
  choice aspects 21–2
  concepts 18–22, 60
  critique 21–2
  Nussbaum's list of
      capabilities 19–22, 27–8
  thresholds 20–1
capitalism 37, 38, 99, 105–7
  see also corporations; free markets
  subjective freedom concepts 37, 38
Cast Away (film) 41
caste societies 74
  see also social class
Catholics 217–18, 225–6
character
  see also virtue
  concepts 15–17, 22, 83
childcare, gender issues 75–6
children
  see also parents
  consent 149
  freedom concepts 34–5, 42–3
  gender issues 75, 108
  rights 114, 187–8, 196–7, 201–4
  torture 175
  wealth inequalities 67–8
  who-counts debates 114, 187–8,
      196–7, 201–4
chimpanzees 192, 196–7
choice 7, 8–12, 16–17, 20–2, 24–5,
    31–2, 35–52, 58–9, 87–91, 124–5,
    137, 148–9, 223–4, 229–33
  see also autonomy; economic
      theories; freedom; utilitarianism
  capabilities approach 21–2
  equality 58–9, 223–4

choice (*cont'd*)
    maximum utility theory 24–5
    uncertainties 9, 10
choice theories of rights 114–15
Christianity 214, 216, 217–20, 225–6,
    228–9, 230–1
Church of the Lukumi Babalu Aye. v.
    Hialeah (1993) 215
Citizens United v. Federal corporations
    (2012) 128, 248–9
citizenship 27, 40–1, 73, 118–19, 123,
    126–7, 148–51, 152, 242
civic republicanism 118–19
    see also democracies
civil disobedience 134, 135–6, 139–41,
    143–6, 147, 153, 157–8, 162–4,
    210–11, 216
    see also breaking the law
    definition 141
    Mahatma Gandhi 134, 144–5,
    163–4
    reciprocity considerations 143–4,
    147, 153
    religion 210–11, 216
Civil Rights Act 232
civil rights protests 134, 135–6, 140–1,
    145–6, 210–11, 232
Civil War, USA 109, 133, 135
claim rights 113–14
    see also rights
climate change 10, 26, 204–7, 254
    see also CO_2 emissions;
    environmental ethics
    discounting 10
Clinton, Bill 239
Clinton, Hilary 250
CO_2 emissions 26, 207, 254
    see also climate change
cognitive disabilities 201–4
collective responsibilities, atrocities
    252–5
colonialism 75

communicative theories, punishments
    178–9
communism 37, 74
communitarian critique, justice 96–7,
    223–4
comparisons, moral standing 195–7
compassion 13, 83, 190, 193–4
    see also empathy; sympathy; virtue
compensation for present disadvantages,
    affirmative action policies 78, 98–9
    complex equality 73–4
    see also equality
Condorcet 123
conscientious objectors 213, 217, 221–2
    see also pacifism; wars
consent
    A. John Simmons 149
    children 149
    freedom 38–9, 45–6, 120, 142–3,
    147–9
    law 142–3, 147–9, 253
    obligations 142–3, 147–9, 253
    slavery 39
    voluntary considerations 148
    voting rights 149
consequentialism
    See also utilitarianism, capabilities
    approach
    do the ends justify the means? 14
    utilitarian critique of Rawls 91–93
    consequentialist theories of
    punishments 176–8
Constant, Benjamin 40–1
Constitution formation
    slavery 137
    USA 45, 55–6, 110–11, 125, 127,
    137, 145, 210
constitutional democracy
    concepts 110–15, 166
    see also democracies; rights
constitutive view, moral standing
    195–6, 197–8, 201–4, 205, 208

constraints
  freedom 5, 19, 31–4, 35–6, 37–8,
    41–2, 50–2, 89–91, 139–40, 221–2
  law 139–40, 221–2
contraceptives 211, 215
contractual principles, justice 83–5,
  87–91, 142–3
copyright laws 132–5, 136, 138
core values in political philosophy
  103–82
corporations
  see also capitalism
  democracies 105–7, 128–9
  freedom of speech 105–7, 128–9
corruption 128–9, 236–8, 247–55
  see also bribery; lies; money
  individual/institutional contrasts
    250–2
  types 248–9, 250–1
cosmopolitan critique, justice 97–8
Cranston, Alan 249
creativity 18, 19–22
crimes 7, 8–9, 23–4, 114, 132–6,
  140–3, 148, 156–7, 175–6,
  236–55
  see also arrests; bribery; corruption;
  law; murder; prisons;
  punishments; robbery; theft;
  violence
Crito (Plato) 147
Crow, Jim 128
Cudd, Ann 95
cultural issues 74–6, 94–5, 97, 152,
  170, 210–33
  see also ethnicity; religion
  equality 74–6, 94–5, 223–4
  justice 94–5, 97
  multiculturalism 96, 222–7
  obligations 152
  oppression 94–5, 223–4
  sense of belonging 223–4
  wars 170

Darwin, Charles 231
death sentence 176, 177, 179, 243
Declaration of Independence, USA
  55–6, 112, 137, 142, 147, 159
decline and fall of democracies 128–9
deliberative democracy 109–10, 125
democracies 52, 74, 91, 105–31, 136,
  140, 226–7, 244–5, 251–5
  see also voting
  benefits 115–17, 118–19
  Buckley v. Valeo (1974) 128
  campaign finance 248, 251–2
  Citizens United v. Federal
    corporations (2012) 128, 248–9
  civic republicanism theory 118–19
  concepts 73, 74, 91, 105–29, 136,
    140, 244–5, 251–5
  constitutional democracy
    concepts 110–15, 166
  critique 128–9, 247–55
  decline and fall 128–9
  definitions 106–8, 117–18, 125,
    126–7, 244–5
  deliberative democracy 109–10, 125
  distortions 126–8
  Edmund Burke 122
  electoral inequalities 126–8
  epistemology 116
  equality 109–10, 126–8
  happiness 117–19
  historical background 107, 108–10,
    120–1, 127
  intrinsic values 117, 118–19
  Iraq 119–20
  Jean Jacques Rousseau 118–19, 123
  John Stuart Mill 118, 126–7, 224
  justice 91, 136–7, 140
  law 136, 140–7
  legitimacy 121–2
  minorities 126–8, 222–8
  money 105–7, 128–9, 247–55
  paradoxes 123–5

democracies (*cont'd*)
  Plato 129
  Plutarch 128
  political advertising 74, 105–7,
    128–9, 247–8
  political self-governance 107, 118–29
  representative democracies 117–19,
    122–3
  respect 128–9
  rights 110–15, 142–3
  'rule of the people' concepts 108
  self-reliance benefits 118–19
  Thomas Jefferson 118, 142
  'tyranny of the majority' concerns
    110–11
  USA 105–10, 123–4, 127
  wealth inequalities 73, 74, 128–9,
    247–55
Democratic Republic of Congo 165
Democrats 40, 69, 106–7, 250
deprivation 71–3, 82, 90–1
  see also poverty
desegregation 123–4, 135, 145
desire satisfaction 5, 12–13, 14–15,
    17–18, 35–6, 63–4
  see also happiness; hedonism;
    pleasure
  concepts 12–13, 14–15, 17–18
  Nozick's experience machine
    14–15, 28
dictatorships 115–17, 120, 129, 142
difference principle, definition 85–7,
    91, 94, 98
Dillon, Bob 253
direct/indirect harm concepts 46–8
dirty hands, lies 246–7
disabled/handicapped people 21, 62–3,
    65–6, 188, 198, 201–4
  empathy 203–4
  equality 62–3, 65–6, 188, 201–4
  justice 203–4
  prudent self-interests 203–4

rights 21, 62–3, 65–6, 188, 198,
    201–4
who-counts debates 21, 62–3, 65–6,
    188, 198, 201–4
discrimination xiii, 20, 49, 54–5, 58,
    59–61, 65, 66, 68–9, 73–8, 84,
    93–5, 108–10, 123–4, 127, 134–6,
    142, 145–6, 157–9, 168–70, 189,
    215, 217
  see also affirmative action policies;
    bias; equality; ethnicity; prejudice;
    racism
  Birmingham Alabama 135–6, 145
  caste societies 74
  concepts xiii, 54–5, 58, 59–61, 65,
    68–9, 73–8, 84, 93–5, 108, 189
  critique 60–1, 68–9, 76–8, 93–5, 189
  elimination efforts 68–9
  gender issues 69, 75–6, 77–8, 93–5,
    108, 127, 226–7
  historical background 54–5, 59–60,
    76, 224
  justice 93–5
  law 66, 73, 74, 93–5, 110–11, 133, 135
  literacy tests 59–60, 73
  Montgomery Alabama in 1955
    59–60
  relevant differences 60–2
  USA 59–60, 66, 68–9, 73, 76–7, 95,
    108–10, 123–4, 127, 134–6, 142,
    145–6, 215, 217
discrimination requirement, *see just
    war theory*
distant peoples and future generations,
    who-counts debates 204–8
The Doctrine of the Sword
    (Gandhi) 163
dolphins 190, 191–2, 196, 197
dominant good, complex equality 74
Dostoyevsky, Fyodor 14
Douglas, Justice J. 207
drones, wars 240

drugs 5, 23, 35–7, 42–4, 138, 177, 202,
        214, 219–21
    legalization debates 44, 177
    rehabilitation programs 42–3
duties 34–5, 82–99, 151–2
    see also obligations
    parents 34–5, 152
Dworkin, Ronald 127–8
dystopias 129

economic theories
    see also choice; wealth…
    utilitarianism 7, 8, 16–17, 24–7
education 19, 21–2, 23, 34, 38, 54–5,
        58, 59–68, 70–1, 75–7, 82, 86–7,
        88, 93, 126–7, 129, 202–3, 214–15,
        216, 218–19
    equality 59–68, 75–7, 86–7
    multiculturalism 224–5
    religion 214–15, 216, 218–19
egalitarian ideals 57–9, 62–4, 72, 179,
        203–4, 223–4, 251–2
    see also equality
    luck egalitarianism 62–4, 65, 90–1,
        203–4
    resource egalitarianism 62–4, 65–7,
        72, 86–7, 91–9
    welfare egalitarianism 64, 65
elections 74, 105–7, 128–9, 243–6,
        247–8, 251–2
    see also governments
    campaign finance 248, 251–2
    Canada 251–2
    costs 247–8
    equality 251–2
    lies 243–6
    political advertising 74, 105–7,
        128–9, 247–8
Electoral College, USA 127
electoral inequalities 126–8
emotions element of Nussbaum's list of
        capabilities 19–22

empathy 7–8, 13, 190, 193–4, 203–4
    see also compassion; sympathy
employment 17, 19, 20–2, 23, 37, 38,
        40, 68–9, 70–1, 75–6, 77–8, 93–5
    gender issues 75–6, 77–8, 93–5
    implicit bias 68–9, 75–6, 77–8, 95
ends-justifying-the-means debates,
        utilitarianism 14, 246–7
Engel v. Vitale (1962) 216
enhanced interrogation
        techniques 156, 173–5
environmental ethics xi, 10, 20, 25,
        26, 27, 197, 204–8, 211–12,
        228–33, 254
    see also animal rights; climate
        change; ethics
    Aldo Leopold 206–8
    discounting 10
    religion 228–33
    Sierra Club v. Morton (1972) 207–8
    who-counts debates 197, 204–8
epistemology, definition 116
equality xi, xiii, xiv, 4, 20–2, 52, 54–80,
        82, 84–7, 90–1, 109–10, 126–8,
        201–4, 223–4
    see also capabilities approach;
        discrimination; political
        philosophy; rights
    affirmative action policies xiii, 55,
        65, 75–8
    'all men are created equal' 55–6,
        60, 137
    Anatole France 58
    Aristotle 61–2
    Birmingham, Alabama 135–6, 145
    choice 58–9, 223–4
    complex equality 73–4
    concepts xiii, 20–2, 52, 54–78, 82,
        84–7, 90–1, 109–10, 126–8, 201–4,
        223–4
    cultural issues 74–6, 94–5, 223–4
    definitions 55–6

equality (*cont'd*)
democracies 109–10, 126–8
disabled/handicapped people 62–3,
65–6, 188, 198, 201–4
education 59–68, 75–7, 86–7
elections 251–2
enforced equality problems 57–8
ethnicity 54–5, 59–61, 65, 68–9,
75–6, 95, 109–11
expensive tastes 63–4
freedom conflicts 52, 58
gender issues 69, 75–6, 77–8, 93–5,
108, 127
government roles xiii, 55, 65, 67–8,
75–8
happiness conflicts 22–3, 28
implicit bias 68–9, 75–6, 77–8, 84, 95
Jean Jacques Rousseau 71–2, 118–19
justice 67, 73, 74, 76–8, 84–7, 137
law 57–9, 66, 71–2, 73, 74, 93–5,
110–11
leveling-down/up debates 66–7,
72–3, 91–3
luck egalitarianism 62–4, 65, 90–1,
203–4
Montgomery Alabama in 1955
59–60
opportunity 64–8, 72–3, 76–7, 82,
85–7, 90–1, 92–3, 97
parents 67–8
perceptions 56–7, 69–70, 73–4
Plato 60–1
principle of equality 61–2
principle of proportional
equality 61–2
Procrustes 57–9, 66–7
real-world inequalities 56–7, 68–71,
86–7, 145
*Regents of the University of California
v. Bakke* (1978) 76–7
resource egalitarianism 62–4, 65–7,
72, 86–7, 91–9

slavery of the talented 63, 67, 89–90
social class 74, 76–7
Socrates 60–1
stereotypes 75–6, 95, 188
sufficientarianism 72–3, 92–3, 98
Thomas Jefferson 55–6, 112, 118, 142
USA 54–78, 95, 108–10, 123–4, 127
wealth inequalities 23, 27, 37,
56–78, 82, 83–4, 86–99, 128–9,
247–55
welfare egalitarianism 64, 65
ethics xi, 19–20, 144–7, 204–8, 236–55
see also bribery; environmental…;
lies; moralism; political…; virtue
Aldo Leopold 206–8
definitions 206–7
ancient Greece 206
historical background 206
'just following orders'
justifications 252–5
prima facie obligations 139–40,
147–8, 150, 152, 253
responsibilities 252–5
ethnic cleansing 169
ethnicity 20, 49, 54–5, 59–61, 65, 68–9,
73, 75–8, 84, 93, 95, 109–11, 134,
135–6, 142, 152, 157–60, 189, 215,
217, 219, 220–1
see also cultural issues;
discrimination; race
equality 54–5, 59–61, 65, 68–9,
75–6, 95, 109–11
eudaimonia ('happiness'/'flourishing'),
definition 15–16
evolution 231
exemption debates, religion 213–22
expected utility 9–10
see also utilitarianism
expensive tastes, resource
egalitarianism critique 63–4
exploitation aspect of oppression 94–5
extinct species 211, 212, 228, 230

fair play principles, law 139–40, 150–1
fairness 83–5, 91–3, 139–40, 150–1,
 229–30, 232–3, 248
 justice 83–5, 91–3, 139–40, 229–30,
 232–3, 248
 obligations 150–1
 religious arguments 232–3
families 93–5, 223
 see also children; gender issues;
 parents
fascism 4–5, 244–5
Feinberg, Joel 47–8, 51, 115, 193, 195,
 205–6
feminism 37, 93–5
 see also discrimination; gender issues
fetuses 187–8, 198–201
Fields, W.C. 58
first-order desires, definition 35–6
Fletcher, Joseph 193
flourishing 16–17, 18, 21–2, 23
 see also virtue
 concepts 16–17, 18, 21–2, 23
 definition 16
 equality 23
 pleasure byproduct 16
Food and Drug Administration
 (FDA) 43–4
France 121, 152, 213–14, 243
France, Anatole 58
fraud 22, 176
 see also money
free markets 27, 87, 88–91, 107
 see also capitalism; corporations
free movement rights 41
free riding concepts 25–7
freedom 4–5, 6, 18, 19–22, 28, 31–53,
 58, 81–2, 84–91, 93–5, 109,
 111–12, 133–5, 139, 142–3, 206,
 210–33, 244–5, 251–2
 see also harm principle; liberty
 addictions 35–7, 219, 220–1
 authority 34–5, 41–2

Benjamin Constant 40–1
capitalism 37, 38
concepts 4–5, 19, 22, 28, 31–52, 58,
 84–91, 93–5, 142–3, 210–33
consent 38–9, 45–6, 120, 142–3,
 147–9
constraints 5, 19, 31–4, 35–6,
 37–8, 41–2, 50–2, 89–91, 139–40,
 221–2
definitions 32–7, 41–2, 51–2,
 90, 142
drugs 35–7, 42–4, 138, 214, 219–21
equality conflicts 52, 58
first/second-order desires 35–6
fundamental question 34–5
Goethe 36–7
happiness conflicts 4–5, 22, 28,
 33–4, 50
Isaiah Berlin 41
Joel Feinberg 47–8, 51, 115
John Stuart Mill 44, 45, 118, 224
law 22, 31–5, 42–8, 51–2, 93–5,
 133–5, 139–40, 210–11, 227
moralism 48–52
multiculturalism debates 226–7
negative/positive liberty
 concepts 41–2, 90
North Korea 37–8
paternalism 42–8
plural values principle 49–50, 57,
 126, 222–3, 224, 229–30, 233
private/public freedom
 concepts 40–1, 93–5
public good conflicts 22, 31–2
religion 38, 45, 51, 110, 114, 125,
 210–33
republican liberty 39–40
See also civic republicanism
Robert Nozick 87–91, 95–6
slavery 6, 36–7, 39, 40, 89, 109,
 111–12, 133, 135, 139, 142, 206,
 221, 227, 232

freedom (*cont'd*)
  subjective/objective freedom
    concepts 36–7
  Thomas Jefferson 45, 112, 118, 142
  threats of violence 38, 46, 48, 94–5,
    112–14, 136–7, 148
  'true selves' 35–6
freedom of association rights 41
freedom of conscience 213, 221–2,
  226–7
freedom of speech 18, 19, 22, 41, 45,
    51, 105–7, 115, 128–9, 210–11,
    229–30, 236–7, 244–5, 251–2
  corporations 105–7, 128–9
  critique 18, 22, 51, 115
  law 22, 210–11
  money 128–9
friendships 12–13, 17
Fugitive Slave Act, USA 133, 135, 142
future potential, moral standing
    197–201, 202–3

Galapagos Islands 188–9
Gandhi, Mahatma 134, 144–5, 163–4
gay marriage 210–11, 215, 217
gender issues 20–1, 37, 48, 54–5, 60,
    69, 75–6, 77–8, 93–5, 108, 127,
    213, 226–7
  see also discrimination; feminism
  childcare 75–6
  children 75, 108
  discrimination 69, 75–6, 77–8,
    93–5, 108, 127, 226–7
  employment 75–6, 77–8, 93–5
  equality 69, 75–6, 93–5, 108, 127
  housework 75–6, 93–4, 108
  Islam 213
  pregnant women 21, 244
  religion 213, 226–7
  voting rights 108–9, 127
genetic modifications 4–5, 205
Geneva Conventions 172, 173

genocide 120, 169
Georgia 127–8
Germany 111, 152, 163–4, 170, 253–4
global justice demands 97–9, 120–1
globalization effects
  multiculturalism 225–6
  wars 170
God's will 147, 211–13, 216, 219, 221,
    228–9, 232
  see also religion
Goethe 36–7
Gould, Stephen Jay 188
governments 4–6, 22, 23–6, 27, 28,
    41–50, 51, 67–8, 74, 75–8, 81–2,
    87–91, 105–29, 134, 136–7, 142,
    155–82, 222–33, 236–48, 252–5
  see also democracies; law; political
    violence; politics; taxes
  affirmative action policies xiii, 55,
    65, 75–8
  atrocities 75, 165, 252–5
  campaign finance 248, 251–2
  equality xiii, 55, 65, 67–8, 75–8
  functions 4–6, 22, 23–6, 28, 41–2,
    49–51, 67–8, 73, 75–6, 81–2,
    87–91, 112–15, 150, 179, 236–47,
    251–5
  happiness 5–6, 22, 23–6, 117–19
  'market failures' 27
  money 105–7, 118–19, 128–9,
    247–55
  natural (moral) rights 112, 142
  nazi Germany 170, 253–4
  overthrow/abolition 142, 146–7, 179
  political advertising 74, 105–7,
    128–9, 247–8
  public good 25–7, 115–16, 122–3
  revolutions 120–1, 134, 136–7,
    142–3, 144, 146–7, 159, 161–2, 179
  types 107, 115–16, 129
gratitude, obligations 150
great apes 192, 196–7

Great Apes Project (GAP) 192
ancient Greece 15–17, 57–9, 60–1,
    108–9, 117, 128, 206
    see also Aristotle; Plato; Procrustes;
    Socrates
    ethics 206
    slavery 206
Grotius, Hugh 241–2
the 'guano ring' 188–9, 206
guerrilla warfare 159, 161–2

happiness 3–30, 50–1, 91–3, 117–19,
    176–7, 207–8, 212, 228, 232, 240,
    246–7, 251–2
    see also capabilities approach; desire
    satisfaction; future…; pleasure;
    utilitarianism; virtue; welfare;
    well-being
    Aristotle 16–17
    concepts 4–28, 50–1, 91–3,
        117–19, 176–7, 207–8, 212,
        228, 232, 240, 246
    definitions 5–6, 8–9, 15–16, 18,
        27–8
    democracies 117–19
    diseases 6
    ends-justifying-the-means
        debates 14, 246–7
    equality conflicts 22–3, 28
    freedom conflicts 4–5, 22, 28,
        33–4, 50
    governments 5–6, 22, 23–6, 117–19
    Jeremy Bentham 7, 8–10, 15, 17, 22,
        24, 25, 176–8
    John Stuart Mill 17–18, 118
    liberty conflicts 4–5, 22, 28, 33–4
    measures 5–6, 8–10, 12–13, 17–18,
        22–3, 27–8, 91–3
    Nozick's experience machine
        14–15, 28
    Nussbaum's list of
        capabilities 19–22, 27–8

objective views 6, 16
political institutions 27–8, 88–91,
    117–19
psychological egoism 7–8, 24, 25–6
public good 24–6, 246
the pursuit of happiness 6–14
Socrates 17, 18
subjective views 6
harm principle 43, 44–8, 50–2, 160
    see also freedom
    definitions 44–5, 47–8, 50
    direct/indirect harm concepts 46–8
    intentional/unintentional harm
        concepts 46–7, 160
    moralism 50
    offensiveness 45, 50–1
    rights 45, 46, 47–8, 50–1
    subjective/objective
        understandings 45–6, 47–8, 50–1
Harrison Bergeron (Vonnegut) 56
Hart, H.L.A. 139–40, 178
health inequalities 67–8, 93, 98
health insurance 31–4, 41–4, 47, 81–2
healthcare 17, 19–22, 23, 31–4, 41–4,
    47, 67–8, 81–2, 86–7, 93, 113–14,
    202, 240
    liberty rights 113–14
hedonism 8, 12–13, 25–6, 58–9
    see also desire satisfaction; pleasure
Hitchhiker's Guide to the Galaxy
    (Adams) 197
Hobbes, Thomas 113–14
Holmes, Oliver Wendell, Jr 22
Homelessness 58
housework, gender issues 75–6,
    93–4, 108
'how to' guide for breaking the
    law 140–7
Human Development Index 18–19
human rights 41, 112–13, 173, 186–7,
    198, 221–2, 252–3
Human Rights Watch 173

humanitarian catastrophes 165–6
humiliation 4, 12, 20, 44–5, 59–60, 68
Hutu of Rwanda 75
Huxley, Aldous 4–5, 24
hybrid theories, punishments 179
hyperindividualism 186–7

ideal political theories, definition
     179–80
ideal/nonideal agents and principles,
     breaking the law 144–7
identity 186–7, 223–4
  see also personhood characteristics
immigration, republican liberty 40
implicit bias 68–9, 75–6, 77–8, 84–5, 95
  see also discrimination
income factors, wealth
     inequalities 70–1
India 97, 144
individualism 96–7, 186–7, 208,
     223–4
inequalities 23, 27, 37, 54–78, 85–7,
     90–1, 97–8, 108–10, 126–8
  see also discrimination; equality;
     health…; wealth…
  deprivation 71–3, 82, 90–1
  electoral inequalities 126–8
  Jean Jacques Rousseau 71–2
  perceptions 56–7, 69–70, 73–4
  real-world inequalities 56–7, 68–71,
     86–7, 145
  social construction 75–6
  statistics 56–7, 68–71, 97–8
  USA 54–78, 95, 108–10, 123–4, 127
infant mortality rates 19
Ingersoll v. Arlene Flowers (2015)
     215, 217
institutional rights 111–15
  see also rights
instrumental values, definition 6–7,
     8, 116
intentional/unintentional harm
     concepts 46–7, 160

inter-racial marriage prohibitions,
     USA 49, 110–11
interest theories of rights 114–15
International Criminal Court in the
     Hague 168, 170
intrinsic values
  definition 6–7, 8, 116, 118
  democracies 117, 118–19
Iraq 119–20, 168, 171–2
Ireland 225–6
irrational decisions 24–5
Islam 213–14, 218–19, 225
Italy, the Renaissance 3–4, 237
ius ad bellum ('right to wage war')
     164–8, 169–70
  see also just war theory
ius in bello ('right during war') 165,
     168–70, 172, 174, 245
  see also just war theory
ius post bello ('right after war') 165
  see also just war theory
iustitia ('justice')
  see also justice
  definition xiv

Japan 155, 170
Jefferson, Thomas 45, 55–6, 112,
     118, 142
Jellison, Jarold 238
Jesus 135, 230
  see also religion
jokes, lies 239, 241
Judaism 214, 216, 230
judgments, second-order desires 35–6
'just war' theory 164–72, 217–18,
     227, 245
  manipulability problems 167–8
  preemptive war 166, 168, 171–2
  requirements 165–72, 217
  testing 166–8
  vagueness problems 167
just-cause aspects of just war theory
     165–8

justice xi, xiii, xiv, 13, 20–2, 23–4,
31–2, 67, 73, 74, 76–8, 81–101,
133–7, 142–7, 151–2, 178,
187–208, 229–33, 244–5, 251–2
see also law; political philosophy;
rights
communitarian critique 96–7,
223–4
concepts 67, 73, 74, 76–8, 81–99,
133–7, 142–7, 151–2, 178,
187–208, 229–33
contractual principles 83–5, 87–91,
142–3
cosmopolitan critique 97–8
definition 82–4, 137, 142
democracies 91, 136–7, 140
difference principle 85–7, 91, 94, 98
disabled/handicapped people 203–4
discrimination 93–5
equality 67, 73, 74, 76–8, 84–7, 137
fairness 83–5, 91–3, 139–40,
229–30, 232–3, 248
feminism 93–5
global justice demands 97–9, 120–1
individualism critique 96–7
libertarianism 84–97
Michael Walzer 97
power 94–5, 229–30, 253
principles 83–7, 90, 93–5, 137,
144–7, 178
Rawls's theory of justice 83–99,
139–40, 141, 229–33
Robert Nozick 87–91, 95–6,
189–90
Robert Paul Wolff 137–8, 139
Thomas Pogge 98–9
unjust laws 135–8, 139–47, 152–3,
157–9
utilitarianism 91–3
veil of ignorance 84–5, 97
who-counts debates xi, 59–60,
108–10, 185–209
Will Kymlicka 96–7

Kant, Immanuel 27, 193–5, 212, 230,
241, 245, 247
Keating Five 249
King, Martin Luther, Jr 134, 135–6,
145, 164
kittens 189–91, 194
Kymlicka, Will 96–7

land ethic concepts 207–8
see also environmental ethics
languages, multiculturalism 224–5
last-resort aspects of just war
theory 165–8, 171
law xi, 4, 17, 22, 23–4, 31–5, 42–50,
51–2, 57–9, 66, 71–3, 74, 90–1,
93–5, 110–15, 132–54, 210–11,
213–33, 243
see also authority; breaking the law;
crimes; governments; justice;
obligations; rights
absolute (categorical)
obligations 139–40, 253
civil disobedience 134, 135–6,
139–41, 143–6, 157–8, 162–4,
210–11, 216
concepts 71–3, 111–15, 132–53,
227–33, 243, 253
consent 142–3, 147–9, 253
definitions 135–40
democracies 136, 140–7
discrimination 66, 73, 74, 93–5,
110–11, 133, 135
drugs 44, 138, 177, 214, 219–21
duties 138–53
equality 57–9, 66, 71–2, 73, 74,
93–5, 110–11
fair play principles 139–40,
150–1
freedom 22, 31–5, 42–8, 51–2, 93–5,
133–5, 139–40, 210–11, 227
freedom of speech 22, 210–11
Henry David Thoreau 140–1
H.L.A. Hart 139–40, 178

law (*cont'd*)
  'how to' guide for breaking the law
    140–7
  Islam 213–14
  John Locke 137, 142, 219–21
  moralism 51, 133–4, 136–8, 140–7
  natural law 71–3, 111–15, 132–7,
    140–7
  Plato 147–52
  prima facie obligations 139–40,
    147–8, 150, 152, 253
  Rawls's theory of justice 139–40,
    141, 229–33
  religion 147, 213–22, 227–33
  Robert Paul Wolff 137–8, 139
  slavery 133, 135, 139, 142, 227, 232
  strength of obligations 139–40, 144,
    147–52
  unjust laws 135–8, 139–47, 152–3,
    157–9
The Law of War and Peace
  (Grotius) 241–2
lawyers, lies 243
'left libertarianism', definition 91
legal justice, definition 137
legal rights 84–5, 111–15, 157
  see also rights
legal standing contrasts, moral
  standing 207–8
legalization debates, drugs 44, 177
legitimacy, democracies 121–2
legitimate-authority aspects of just war
  theory 165–8
Leopold, Aldo 206–8
leveling-down/up debates,
  equality 66–7, 72–3, 91–3
libel 22, 51
liberal egalitarianism, definition 223–4
liberalism 43, 51, 78, 93–7, 223–4
  communitarian critique 96–7, 223–4
  definition 43, 93, 223
  Steven Macedo 223

libertarianism 43, 78, 84–97
  definition 43, 78, 91
  justice 84–97
  'left libertarianism' 91
  Robert Nozick 87–91, 95–6
liberty xi, 4–5, 17, 19–22, 28, 31–53,
    58, 84–91, 93–7, 113–14, 119–20,
    139–40, 220–1, 223–4, 251–2
  see also freedom
  concepts 4–5, 19, 22, 28, 31–52, 58,
    84–91, 93–7, 119–20, 139–40,
    220–1, 223–4
  definitions 32–5, 41–2, 90
  happiness conflicts 4–5, 22, 28, 33–4
  negative/positive liberty
    concepts 41–2, 90
  political institutions 28, 41, 88–91
  republican liberty 39–40
'liberty of the ancients' 40–1
liberty rights 113–14
  see also rights
lies 3, 8, 236–57
  see also corruption; money
  Aristotle 242
  Bill Clinton's interpretation of sexual
    relations 239
  concepts 236–47, 255
  definition 238–9
  dirty hands 246–7
  elections 243–6
  George Orwell 244–5
  Hugh Grotius 241–2
  Immanuel Kant 241, 245, 247
  Jean-Paul Sartre 238–9
  justifications 245–7
  'license to lie' debates 242–3
  Machiavelli 242–3
  politicians 236–47
  reasons 240–5
  rights 241–2, 245–6
  Thomas Aquinas 239–41
  utilitarianism 240–1, 243, 245–6

virtue 242
W.D. Ross 241
Locke, John 112, 137, 142, 219–21
Louisiana 59–60, 73
Loving v. Virginia (1967) 110–11
Luban, David 174
luck egalitarianism 62–4, 65, 90–1,
   203–4
  see also equality

McCain, John 249
Macedo, Steven 223
Machiavelli, Niccolò 3–4, 242–3, 255
Malcolm X 142
Mandela, Nelson 158–62, 164
manipulability problems, 'just war'
   theory 167–8
marginal utility 91–2
marginalization aspect of oppression
   94–5
'market failures', government
   interventions 27
Marquis, Don 199
Marxism 37, 95
'maximin' decisions 86–7
maximum utility theory 7–9, 11–12,
   14, 15, 20–1, 24–5, 91–3, 212, 246
  see also utilitarianism
  concepts 24–5
Measure for Measure (Shakespeare) 255
meat-eating debates 185–6, 196
metaphysics 232
Mill, James 17
Mill, John Stuart 17–18, 44, 45, 118,
   126–7, 224
minimizing pains 11–12, 14, 19, 25–6,
   196, 228, 230, 232, 240, 246
  see also happiness; negative
   utilitarians; pains
minorities 54–5, 76–8, 84, 126–8, 222–8
  see also ethnicity; multiculturalism
  democracies 126–8, 222–8

mobility factors, wealth
   inequalities 70–1
monarchies 39–40, 107, 120
Mondale, Walter 122–3
money 105–7, 118–19, 128–9, 237–8,
   247–55
  see also bribery; corruption; fraud;
   lies; wealth…
  campaign finance 248, 251–2
  corporations 105–7, 128–9, 251–2
  freedom of speech 128–9
  governments 105–7, 118–19, 128–9,
   247–55
Montgomery Alabama in 1955,
   discrimination 59–60
Moore, Davey 253
moral justice, definition 137
moral personhood 191–201, 205,
   208, 228
  see also personhood characteristics
  definition 191–5
moral standing 191–206, 208
  see also personhood characteristics;
   who-counts debates
  comparisons 195–7
  concepts 191–206, 208
  constitutive view 195–6, 197–8,
   201–4, 205, 208
  definition 191–2, 195, 208
  degrees 195
  fetuses 198–201
  future potential 197–201, 202–3
  group characteristics 198, 204, 223
  intelligence levels 197–8
  legal standing contrasts 207–8
  threshold levels 198, 205
moralism 48–52, 83, 111–12, 115,
   133–4, 136–8, 140–7, 162, 189–206,
   212–13, 227–33, 242–3, 252–5
  see also ethics; natural (moral) rights
  critique 49, 189–98, 206–7
  definition 48–9

moralism (*cont'd*)
  freedom 48–52
  harm principle 50
  law 51, 133–4, 136–8, 140–7
  'parochial' moral values 49–50, 233
  plural values principle 49–50, 57,
    126, 222–3, 224, 229–30, 233
  pornography 48
  sex 48–9
  utilitarianism 7, 12
Mormons 226
multiculturalism 96, 222–7
  see also cultural issues
  criticisms 225–7
  definition 222–3
  education 224–5
  freedom debates 226–7
  justifications 222–4
  languages 224–5
  policy recommendations 224–5
  religion 222–7

national defenses 26, 81, 88, 119,
    120, 150
National Science Foundation 81
native Americans 170, 214, 219, 220–1
natural law 71–3, 111–15, 132–7,
    140–7
natural (moral) rights 71–3, 111–15,
    132–7, 140–7
  see also rights
Nature 228–9, 231
nazi Germany 170, 253–4
negative liberty concepts 41–2, 90
  negative utilitarians 11–12
  see also minimizing pains
neutrality debates, religion 218–21
New Orleans, levees 25–6, 27
New York 77, 216
New York City
  sodas 17, 47
  World Trade Center Towers 171

Newdow v. Carey (2005–2010) 216
Newman v. Piggie Park (1966) 215, 217
Nineteenth Amendment 127
nonideal political theories,
    definition 179–80
noninstitutional rights 111–15
  see also rights
normative theories, definition 7–8
North Korea, freedom concepts 37–8
Northern Ireland 225–6
Norton, Michael 69–71
Nozick, Robert 14–15, 28, 87–91, 95,
    189–90
Nozick's experience machine 14–15, 28
Nuremberg Tribunal 170
Nussbaum's list of capabilities 19–22,
    27–8

Obama, Barack 240, 247, 250
obesity 17, 47
objective freedom concepts 36–7
objective views of happiness 6, 16
objective views of harm 45–6, 47–8,
    50–1
obligations 82–99, 132–54, 253
  see also duties; justice; law; rights
  A. John Simmons 149
  absolute (categorical)
    obligations 139–40, 253
  citizenship considerations 148–51, 152
  consent justification 142–3,
    147–9, 253
  cultural issues 152
  duty justification 151–2
  fairness consideration 150–1
  gratitude justification 150
  H.L.A. Hart 139–40
  membership justification 152
  Plato 147–52
  prima facie obligations 139–40,
    147–8, 150, 152, 253
  Rawls's theory of justice 139–40, 141

Robert Paul Wolff 137–8, 139
strength of obligations 139–40, 144,
147–52
offensiveness, harm principle 45, 50–1
Okin, Susan Moller 93–5
On Liberty (Mill) 44
opportunities, equality of
opportunity 64–8, 72–3, 76–7, 82,
85–7, 90–1, 92–3, 97
oppression 21–2, 94–5, 111–12, 120–1,
137, 161–2, 223–4, 232–3
Oregon Employment Division v. Smith
(1990) 214
original position, Rawls's theory of
justice 84–5, 96–7, 98
Orwell, George 244–5
other-species element of Nussbaum's
list of capabilities 20–2
ova 198–201
overlapping consensus, politics 230–1

pacifism 143, 162–4, 213, 214, 217–18,
221–2
see also civil disobedience; wars
Bertrand Russell 163–4
justifications 164, 213, 217–18, 221–2
Mahatma Gandhi 134, 144–5, 163–4
nonreligious reasons 221–2
religion 213, 214, 217–18, 221–2
pains 9–11, 13, 19, 24, 194–7, 198–9,
228, 230, 232, 240, 246
see also happiness; pleasure
future events 10–11
measures 9
minimizing pains 11–12, 14, 19,
25–6, 196, 228, 230, 232, 240, 246
parents 15, 21, 67–8, 75–6, 93–5, 149,
152, 223–4
see also children
duties 34–5, 152
equality 67–8
freedom concepts 34–5

Nozick's experience machine 15
rights 34–5
Parks, Rosa 135
'parochial' moral values 49–50, 233
paternalism 42–8
see also freedom; parents
personhood characteristics 192–201,
205, 208, 228
see also communication…;
consciousness…; reasoning…;
self…
capabilities 196–7, 201–4
concepts 192–201, 205
future potential 197–201, 202–3
group characteristics 198, 204, 223
threshold levels 198, 205
philosophical anarchism, definition
137–8
philosophy
see also political philosophy; wisdom
definition xiii, xiv, 116
religion 228–33
physical exercise, future happiness
10–11, 34
physiological needs 16, 21, 82
pirates, copyright laws 132–5, 136, 138
Plato 60–1, 129, 147–52
pleasure 5, 8–13, 14–15, 16, 17–18,
19–22, 24–5, 58–9, 194, 196–7,
228, 232, 246–7
see also desire satisfaction;
happiness; hedonism; pains
concepts 5, 8–13, 14–15, 16, 17–18,
19, 24–5, 194, 196–7, 228, 232
flourishing byproduct 16
future events 10–11
measures 8–9, 12–13, 16, 17–18
minimizing pains 11–12, 25–6,
228, 232
Nozick's experience machine
14–15, 28
quality/quantity contrasts 17–18

Pledge of Allegiance, USA 149, 216,
    221–2
plural values principle 49–50, 57, 126,
    222–3, 224, 229–30, 233
Plutarch 128
plutocracies, definition 106–7
Pogge, Thomas 98–9
police 150, 172
political advertising 74, 105–7, 128–9,
    247–8
political arguments xiii
    see also bad...; good...
political ethics xi, 236–55
    see also ethics
political institutions 27–8, 41,
    88–91, 110–29, 137–53,
    179–80, 236–55
    happiness 27–8, 88–91, 117–19
    liberty 28, 41, 88–91
    political violence 179–80
    responsibilities 252–5
political philosophy xi, xiii, xiv, 4–5, 6,
    18, 78
    see also equality; justice; philosophy;
        public good; wisdom
    core values 103–82
    definition xi, xiii, xiv, 4–5
    John Stuart Mill 18, 44, 45, 118,
        126–7, 224
political self-governance,
    democracies 107, 118–29
political violence xi, 3, 19, 23, 26,
    81, 88, 94–5, 119–21, 134–5,
    136–7, 138, 142–3, 144, 146–7,
    155–82, 213
    see also punishments; torture;
        violence; wars
    concepts 155–80, 213
    definitions 159–60
    enhanced interrogation
        techniques 156, 173–5

'just war' justifications 164–72,
    217–18, 227
justification debates 158–60,
    161–72, 217–18, 227
    political institutions 179–80
    relative pacifism 163–4
    revolutions 120–1, 134, 136–7,
        142–3, 144, 146–7, 159, 161, 179
    terrorists 22, 155–9, 161–2, 171–2,
        174–6
    waterboarding 155–6, 173–5
politicians
    see also governments
    dirty hands 246–7
    elections 243–6, 247–8
    lies 236–47, 255
political liberalism (John Rawls)
    229–233
politics xi, xiii, 3, 5–6, 8, 16–17,
    20–2, 73, 105–29, 170, 210–35,
    236–55
    see also capitalism; communism;
        governments; Marxism
    campaign finance 248, 251–2
    definition xiii, 107
    'just following orders'
        justifications 252–5
    lies 3, 8, 236–47, 255
    nazi Germany 170, 253–4
    overlapping consensus 230–1
    religion 210–33
    wealth inequalities 73, 74, 105–7,
        128–9, 247–55
'Politics and the English Language'
    (Orwell) 244–5
pollution 254
Popper, Karl 11–12
pornography 46, 47–8
positive liberty concepts 41–2, 90
positive utilitarians 11–12, 15
    see also maximum utility...; pleasure

posthumans, who-counts debates 205
poverty 19–22, 41–2, 56–7, 66–7,
    68–73, 81–2, 90–1, 97–8, 160
  see also deprivation; wealth
    inequalities
  rich/poor countries 98–9
  statistics 56–7, 68–71, 97–8
Powell, Adam Clayton 123–4
power
  electoral inequalities 126–8
  feminist critique 94–5
  justice 94–5, 229–30, 253
  violence definition 160
preemptive war 166, 168, 171–2
pregnant women 21, 244
prejudice 189, 220
  see also discrimination
presidents of the USA 122, 168, 171,
    199, 239, 240, 247, 250
preventive wars 166
prima facie obligations, law 139–40,
    147–8, 150, 152, 253
The Prince (Machiavelli) 3–4,
    242–3, 255
principles
  breaking the law motives 135–6,
    144–7
  of equality 61–2
  of justice 83–7, 90, 93–5, 137,
    144–7, 178
  of proportional equality 61–2
"prisoner's dilemma" scenario 24
prisoners of war, ius in bello ('right
    during war') 169–70, 172, 173, 245
prisons 141–2, 156, 161–2, 177–9,
    217, 252
probabilities, expected utility 9–10
Procrustes 57–9, 66–7
progressive taxes 86–7, 89, 99
prohibited weapons, ius in bello ('right
    during war') 169–70

property rights 20–2, 87, 88–91, 132–5
proportional representation 123–4
proportionality requirements
  breaking the law 143–4, 146–7, 153
  ius in bello ('right during war')
    168–70
  just war theory 165–70
Protestants 218, 225–6
prudent self-interests, disabled/
    handicapped people 203–4
psychological egoism 7–8, 24, 25–6
  see also happiness
  definition 7–8, 25
  motivation theory 7, 8, 25, 27
public freedom concepts 40–1, 93–5
public good xi, 4, 14, 22, 24–8, 31–2,
    115–16, 122–3, 246–7
  see also political philosophy; welfare
  definition 24, 26–7
  ends-justifying-the-means
    debates 14, 246–7
  freedom conflicts 22, 31–2
  governments 25–7, 115–16, 122–3
  happiness 24–6
punishments 134–5, 138, 155, 163,
    175–80
  see also crimes; political violence
  'an eye for an eye' debates 163, 179
  communicative theories 178–9
  concepts 175–80
  consequentialist theories 176–8
  death sentence 176, 177, 179, 243
  hybrid theories 179
  political contexts 179–80
  retributivist theories 177–9
  Skinner v. Oklahoma (1942) 176
the pursuit of happiness 6–14

Quakers 217, 226
quality/quantity contrasts,
    pleasure 17–18

race 20, 49, 54–5, 59–61, 65, 68–9, 73,
    75–8, 93, 95, 109–11, 134, 135–6,
    142, 157–60, 189, 215, 217, 219,
    220–1
  see also; discrimination, equality;
    ethnicity
  Birmingham Alabama 59–60,
    135–6, 145
  implicit bias 68–9, 75–6, 77–8, 84, 95
  inter-racial marriage
    prohibitions 49, 110–11
  Malcolm X 142
  Martin Luther King, Jr 134, 135–6,
    145, 164
  Montgomery Alabama in 1955
    59–60
  Nelson Mandela 158–62, 164
  South Africa 157–62
  voting 59–60, 73, 109–10
  weapons 68–9
racism 49, 54–5, 59–61, 65, 68–9,
    75–8, 84, 93, 95, 109, 110–11,
    157–60, 215
rape 169, 201
rational decisions 24–5, 27, 124, 237–8
Rawls's theory of justice 83–99,
    139–40, 141, 229–33
  see also justice, political liberalism
Reagan, Ronald 122
reasonableness debates, religion 210–
    13, 229–33
reciprocity considerations, breaking the
    law 143–4, 147, 153
redistribution considerations, wealth
    inequalities 57, 64, 65, 69–70, 74,
    86–99
*Regents of the University of California v.
    Bakke* (1978) 76–7
relative pacifism, Bertrand
    Russell 163–4
relevant differences, discrimination
    60–2

religion xi, 3, 19, 20, 38, 45, 51, 74, 84,
    110, 114, 125, 147, 210–35
  see also Baptists; Buddhism;
    Catholics; Christianity;
    evangelicals; Islam; Judaism;
    Mormons; Protestants; Quakers
  animal sacrifices 215, 216–17,
    219–20
  arguing fairly 232–3
  balancing tests 217–18, 220–1
  Burwell v. Hobby Lobby (2014) 215
  *Church of the Lukumi Babalu Aye,
    Inc. v. Hialeah* (1993) 215
  civil disobedience 210–11, 216
  concepts 38, 45, 51, 110, 114, 125,
    147, 210–33
  conservative politics 227–8
  education 214–15, 216, 218–19
  Engel v. Vitale (1962) 216
  environmental ethics 228–33
  exemption debates 213–22
  freedom 38, 45, 51, 110, 114, 125,
    210–33
  gay marriage 210–11, 215, 217
  gender issues 213, 226–7
  Ingersoll v. Arlene Flowers
    (2015) 215, 217
  law 147, 213–22, 227–33
  multiculturalism 222–7
  neutrality debates 218–21
  Newdow v. Carey (2005–2010) 216
  Newman v. Piggie Park (1966)
    215, 217
  oppression debates 232–3
  *Oregon Employment Division v.
    Smith* (1990) 214
  overlapping consensus 230–1
  philosophy 228–33
  politics 210–33
  public policies 227–33
  reasonableness debates 210–13,
    229–33

secular debates 210–14, 220–1,
  227–8, 232–3
Sicurella v. United States (1955) 214
state churches 218–19
toleration limits 216–18, 219–20
USA 214–33
Wisconsin v. Yoder (1972) 214–15
the Renaissance 3–4, 237
representative democracies 117–19,
  122–3
see also democracies
definition 117
reproductive health
  see also sex
capabilities approach 19, 21
republican liberty, definition 39–40
Republicans 40, 69, 106–7, 122–3
resource egalitarianism 62–4, 65–7, 72,
  86–7, 91–9
  see also equality; wealth…
definition 62–4
disabled/handicapped people 62–3,
  65–6
expensive tastes 63–4
slavery of the talented 63, 67
respect 19–22, 73, 128–9, 141
capabilities approach 19–22, 73
concepts 73, 128–9
democracies 128–9
responsibilities, ethics 252–5
retributivist theories,
  punishments 177–9
Revolution, USA 120–1, 142, 162
revolutions 120–1, 134, 136–7, 142–3,
  144, 146–7, 159, 161–2, 179
right-intentions aspects of just war
  theory 165–8
rights 4, 12, 19–22, 28, 34–5, 40–1,
  45–8, 50–1, 57, 59–60, 82–3,
  87–99, 110–15, 142–3, 164–8,
  179–80, 185–208, 213, 221–2,
  232–3, 241–2, 245–6, 252–3

see also claim…; equality; human…;
  justice; legal…; liberty…;
  natural…
abortion xi, 187–8, 197, 198,
  200–1, 244
animal rights xi, 185–98, 207–8,
  212–13, 230–2
children 114, 187–8, 196–7, 201–4
choice theories 114–15
concepts 41, 51, 88–9, 110–15,
  142–3, 164–8, 185–208, 213,
  221–2, 232–3, 241–2, 245–6,
  252–3
constitutional democracy
  concepts 110–15, 166
definition 111–15
democracies 110–15, 142–3
disabled/handicapped people 21,
  62–3, 65–6, 188, 201–4
fetuses 187–8, 198–201
harm principle 45, 46, 47–8, 50–1
interest theories 114–15
John Locke 112, 142, 219–21
parents 34–5
self-defense rights 113–14, 142, 163,
  165–6, 245–6
slavery 111–12, 120, 137, 142, 221,
  227, 232
sources 111–13
Thomas Hobbes 113–14
Thomas Jefferson 55–6, 112,
  118, 142
types 41, 51, 88–9, 110–15, 213,
  221–2
utilitarianism 12, 28, 221–2
voting rights 40–1, 59–60, 68, 73,
  95, 106–7, 108–10
Ross, W.D. 241
Rousseau, Jean Jacques 71–2,
  118–19, 123
'rule of the people' concepts 108
  see also democracies

run-off problems, voting 123–4
Russell, Bertrand 163–4
Rwanda 75, 165, 252

sabotage 159, 161–2
Sample, Ruth 95
Sandel, Michael 96
Sanford, Mark 248
Sanson, Henry 243
Sartre, Jean-Paul 238–9
satisfaction 5, 12–13
   see also happiness
science 81, 211–12, 231
seatbelts 43, 44
second-order desires, definition 35–6
secular debates, religion 210–14,
   220–1, 227–8, 232–3
self-awareness characteristics of
   personhood 193
self-concepts, characteristics of
   personhood 193
self-defense rights 113–14, 142, 163,
   165–6, 245–6
self-motivated activities, characteristics
   of personhood 192–3
self-reliance benefits,
   democracies 118–19
Sen, Amartya 18–19
Senate, USA 127, 247–8
sense of belonging, cultural
   issues 223–4
sex 11, 19, 20, 46, 47–9, 169, 189,
   198–9, 210–11, 239
   see also reproductive health
   capabilities approach 19
   moralism 48–9
   pornography 46, 47–8
sexual orientation 20, 49, 189, 210–11,
   215, 217
   gay marriage 210–11, 215, 217
   moralism 49, 210–11
sexually transmitted diseases (STDs) 11

Shakespeare, William 255
Sharpeville Massacre 157–9
Shklar, Judith 11–12
Sicurella v. United States (1955) 214
Sierra Club v. Morton (1972) 207–8
Simmons, A. John 149
Skinner v. Oklahoma (1942) 176
slander 22, 51
slavery 6, 36–7, 39, 40, 63, 89, 109,
   111–12, 120, 133, 135, 137, 139,
   142, 206, 221, 227, 232
   see also freedom
   consent view 39
   Constitution formation 137
   Fugitive Slave Act 133, 135, 142
   ancient Greece 206
   law 133, 135, 139, 142, 227, 232
   religion 221, 227, 232
   rights 111–12, 120, 137, 142,
   221, 227
   voting rights 109, 111–12
slavery of the talented 63, 67, 89–90
   see also equality
social class 74, 76–7, 223
   see also caste societies
social construction of
   inequalities 75–6
Social Contract (Rousseau) 118–19
social Darwinism 231
social inequalities 60–1
social policy 18–19, 20–6, 55, 65–6,
   75–8, 81–2, 86–91, 116–18, 212,
   224–5, 227–33
social pressures, freedom
   constraints 38
Socrates 17, 18, 60–1, 135
Sophie/Justin's debates
   democracies 105–7
   equality 54–5
   freedom 31–4, 37, 41–2
   happiness 3–4
   justice 81–2

law 132–5, 136, 138
lies 236–8
political violence 155–7
religion and politics 210–13, 230–1
who-counts debates 185–7, 196
South Africa 157–62
South America 188–9
Stalin, Joseph 126
starting-out positions, equality 58–9, 62–7, 73–4, 91
state churches 218–19
stereotypes, equality 75–6, 95, 188
subjective freedom concepts 36–7
subjective views of happiness 6
subjective views of harm 45–6, 47–8, 50–1
suffering
    ends-justifying-the-means debates 14, 246–7
    minimizing pains 11–12, 14, 196, 228, 230, 232, 240, 246
    personhood characteristics 194
sufficientarianism 72–3, 92–3, 98
    see also equality
    definition 72, 92
Summa theologica (Aquinas) 239
Surowiecki, James 116
sympathy 7–8, 13
    see also compassion; empathy

taxes 23, 25–6, 34, 81–2, 86–7, 89, 120–1
    see also governments
    earmarked contributions 81–2
    progressive taxes 86–7, 89, 99
terrorists 22, 155–9, 161–2, 171–2, 174–6
theft 7, 8–9, 24, 132–6, 176, 179
third-party democracies 120–1
Thompson, Dennis 250–1
Thompson, Judith Jarvis 200–1
Thoreau, Henry David 140–1

threats
    see also violence
    freedom constraints 38, 46, 48, 94–5, 112–14, 136–7, 148
threshold levels, moral standing 198, 205
ticking bombs 173–5
tolerance 50, 52, 216–18, 219–20
torture 22, 111, 155–7, 172, 173–5, 179–80
    see also political violence; waterboarding
    concepts 173–5, 179–80
    justification debates 173–4
    political context 179–80
torturers 174–5
totalitarianism 4–5
traffic laws 136, 138
transport facilities 19, 23, 26, 31, 88, 150
'true selves', freedom 35–6
Tutsis of Rwanda 75
Twain, Mark 115
'tyranny of the majority' concerns, democracies 110–11

UK 171, 213, 225–6, 238
Umkhonto we Sizwe ('Spear of the Nation') 157–62
uncertainties, choice 9, 10
unfair outcomes, definition 248, 250
unfair process, definition 248–9, 250
universalism, justice 97
unjust laws 135–8, 139–47, 152–3, 157–9
    see also law
utilitarianism 6–9, 10–11, 13, 15, 18–19, 24–5, 27–8, 78, 91–3, 176–7, 212, 217–18, 221–2, 228, 230–2, 240–1, 243, 245–6
    see also expected…; happiness; maximum…; pain; pleasure

utilitarianism (*cont'd*)
  capabilities approach 18–22
  definition 6–8, 13, 28, 91–2,
    231–2, 246
  ends-justifying-the-means
    debates 14, 246–7
  justice 91–3
  lies 240–1, 243, 245–6
  morality 7, 12
  positive/negative utilitarians 11–12
  rights 12, 28, 221–2
  wealth inequalities 91–3

values 4–5, 6–7, 49–50, 51–2, 116–17,
    118–19, 174–5, 212–33
  see also democracies; equality;
    freedom
  governments 4–5, 118–19
  plural values principle 49–50, 57,
    126, 222–3, 224, 229–30, 233
veil of ignorance, Rawls's theory of
    justice 84–5, 97
vice 118–19
violence xi, 3, 19, 23, 33–4, 38, 46, 48,
    94–5, 112–14, 134, 136–7, 141–3,
    146–7, 148, 155–82
  see also political violence
  'an eye for an eye' debates 163, 179
  breaking the law 134, 141–3,
    146–7, 148
  definitions 159–60
  'just war' justifications 164–72,
    217–18, 227
  justification debates 158–60, 161–2,
    217–18, 227
  revolutions 120–1, 134, 136–7,
    142–3, 144, 146–7, 159,
    161–2, 179
  self-defense rights 113–14, 142, 163,
    165–6, 245–6
  unjust laws 141–3, 146–7, 157–9

virtue 13, 15–17, 18, 21–2, 27,
    50–2, 67, 82, 119, 144–7, 190,
    242–3, 255
  see also capabilities approach;
    charity; compassion; courage;
    ethics; flourishing; justice;
    tolerance
  Aristotle 16–17, 242
  definition 13, 16, 242
  lies 242
Vonnegut, Kurt 56
voting 40–1, 59–60, 68, 73, 95, 106–10,
    115–18, 122–5, 149, 202, 228,
    236–8, 243–5
  see also democracies
  consent 149
  gender issues 108–9, 127
  historical background 108–9
  literacy tests 59–60, 73
  nonvoting stakeholders 124
  paradoxes 123–5
  procedures 117–18, 124
  slavery 109, 111–12

Walzer, Michael 74, 97
war crimes 112–13, 170
'war on terror' 155, 171
Warren, Mary Anne 192–3, 195, 199
wars 26, 81, 88, 119–20, 155–7,
    163–72, 179–80, 213, 217–18, 227,
    240, 245, 252–3
  see also 'just war' theory; political
    violence
  Al-Qaida 172
  concepts 5, 163–72, 179–80,
    240, 245
  drones 240
  Geneva Conventions 172, 173
  globalization effects 170
  International Criminal Court in the
    Hague 168, 170

ius ad bellum ('right to wage war')
  164–8, 169–70
ius in bello ('right during war') 165,
  168–70, 172, 174, 245
ius post bello ('right after war') 165
pacifism 143, 162–4, 213, 214,
  217–18, 221–2
preemptive war 166, 168, 171–2
prisoners of war 169–70, 172,
  173, 245
rights 164–8, 245
waterboarding 155–6, 173–5
see also torture
wealth inequalities 23, 27, 37, 56–78,
  82, 83–4, 86–99, 105–7, 128–9,
  247–55
see also equality; money; resource
  egalitarianism
age factors 70–1
children 67–8
critique 70–1, 87–93, 128–9, 247–55
democracies 73, 74, 128–9, 247–55
income factors 70–1
Jean Jacques Rousseau 71–2
mobility factors 70–1
politics 73, 74, 105–7, 128–9, 247–55
Rawls's theory of justice 83–99
redistribution considerations 57, 64,
  65, 69–70, 74, 86–99
Robert Nozick 87–91
statistics 56–7, 68–71, 97–8
USA 56–7, 69–71, 97–8, 105–7,
  128–9, 247–55
utilitarianism 91–3
weapons 68–9, 148, 157–8, 169–70, 171
ius in bello ('right during war')
  169–70
of mass destruction 171
prohibited weapons 169–70, 171
robbery 148

Weber, Max 95
welfare 5–6, 14, 64, 65
  see also happiness; public good
welfare egalitarianism 64, 65
  see also equality; wealth…
well-being 5–28, 64
  see also happiness
well-off people
  equal opportunities 66–7
  maximizing happiness 11
who counts debates xi, 21, 59–60,
  62–3, 65–6, 108–10, 114, 185–209
  see also moral…; personhood
  characteristics
abortion xi, 187–8, 197, 198,
  200–1, 244
animal rights xi, 185–98, 207–8
children 114, 187–8, 196–7, 201–4
disabled/handicapped people 21,
  62–3, 65–6, 188, 198, 201–4
distant peoples and future
  generations 204–8
environmental ethics 197, 204–8
fetuses 187–8, 198–201
moral standing 191–201
posthumans 205
Wisconsin v. Yoder (1972) 214–15
The Wisdom of Crowds
  (Surowiecki) 116
Wolff, Robert Paul 137–8, 139
World Health Organization
  (WHO) 160
World Trade Center Towers in New
  York City 171
World War II 155, 163–4, 170, 173

Yoo, John 173
Young, Iris 93–5

Zondo, Andrew 161–2